THE ORIGIN AND DEVELOPMENT
OF
THE STATE CULT OF CONFUCIUS

BL 1851
S 5
1966

THE
ORIGIN AND DEVELOPMENT
OF THE
STATE CULT OF CONFUCIUS

An Introductory Study

BY

JOHN K. SHRYOCK, Ph.D.

UNIVERSITY OF PENNSYLVANIA

PARAGON BOOK REPRINT CORP.
New York
1966

To

DR. BERTHOLD LAUFER

FOREWORD

As the title implies, this study is concerned primarily with the state cult of Confucius, and while such subjects as the life and work of Confucius, the doctrines and development of Confucianism as a school of thought, and the worship of Confucius by the K'ung family are mentioned at times, no attempt has been made to treat these subjects thoroughly, or to do more than sketch them sufficiently to make the state cult understandable. Still less does this book attempt to deal with Confucianism as a religion, if there is any such thing. The more one learns about China, the less he cares to speak of the Confucian religion, because it is doubtful whether the adjective *Confucian* should be applied to the ancient nature worship of the Chinese, about which Confucius was skeptical, or the worship of ancestors, which is not peculiar to Confucians, or the state religion of later dynasties, which Confucius would have thoroughly disapproved, and least of all to the popular cults of modern times. Confucius himself seems to have believed in the worship of his ancestors and in Heaven as approximately a monotheistic deity, but he was in no sense a religious leader, and these doctrines were not peculiar to him. Confucianism is a school of thought based on certain books which have come to be called the canon, and its doctrines are primarily ethical, political and philosophic, rather than religious.

The excuse for this study is the collection of references to the state cult of Confucius contained in the dynastic histories, and in similar sources, such as the government gazette of the republic. These references, the majority of which are imperial edicts, do not seem to have been collected and arranged with any thoroughness even by the Chinese. An adequate study of the cult has not been made, and while there are numerous references to it in western books, the authors have been interested in it only in a secondary way, and have based their statements at times on defective authorities. One would expect the Chinese scholars to have made exhaustive studies of the cult, and there is a vast amount of material available; but whether it was because of the sacredness of the subject to Confucian scholars, or because the Chinese have no concept which corresponds to our idea of religion, or because the doctrines of Confucianism rather than the cult of Confucius have interested the literati, the fact remains that whereas such problems as the text of the canon have been examined with the greatest care and critical insight, the origin and development of the cult of Confucius have usually been allowed to rest upon uncritical tradition and fragmentary statements. It is hoped that this study may make a contribution toward our knowledge of the subject.

In order to place the edicts and other material concerning the cult in their proper setting, it has been necessary to outline the development of the situation in which the cult begin; and, in connection with each period of history, to outline the general historic situation, the position of the schools and the scholar class, and, as far as possible, the intellectual currents of the time. In working up this background, secondary authorities have been used without checking them, because the labor of verifying every minor statement would have been the work of a lifetime. In regard to the actual cult, every statement has been checked with the best available Chinese sources.

The study does not pretend to exhaust the material, as a glance at the bibliography will show. Among the chief omissions are the materials contained in the various gazetteers, especially those of Ch'ueh-li and Ch'ü-fu, such archeological evidence as the inscriptions in Confucian temples, the praise odes and eulogies addressed to Confucius at various times, collections of material such as is found in the Ta Ch'ing Hui Tien, and a comparative study of the various temple plans and records. There is no adequate study of such features of the cult as the pantomime and the music. The *Ch'ing shih kao,* or dynastic history of the Manchu period, has not been used, because it did not seem wise to quote as an authority a work which the present Chinese government considers so objectionable that it has been suppressed, but reference has been made to the places in the history where material concerning the cult is available. The Chinese bibliography given at the end of the book is therefore wider than that actually used in the preparation of the text.

In spite of these limitations, the study is probably the most comprehensive account of the cult of Confucius that has yet been made, at least in a European language. The amount of material in the Chinese language alone which it was necessary to review could not be read by one man, even an expert Chinese scholar, in less than a large number of years. The author wishes to acknowledge his deep indebtedness to a number of Chinese gentlemen, in particular to Messrs. T. C. Ch'en, T. E. Wu, S. S. Ch'in, K. Y. Huang, C. Y. Chang, and E. P. Wang, without whose help this book could not have been written. The translations have been made by them or with their aid, and as far as possible each important passage has been checked by different men working independently. For the English of the translations, except where acknowledgment is made to some one else, for the choice and arrangement of material, and for the generalizations and conclusions, the author must take the responsibility. A number of difficult points have been cleared up in conversations with Dr. Hu Shih and Dr. Chiang K'ang-hu, to whom the author is very grateful. He is glad to have the support of Dr. Chiang on two important points which it is impossible to prove definitely, first, that there was no cult of Confucius, other than that in the K'ung family, prior to the Han dynasty; and second, that the reformation of the cult in 1530 was primarily due to the influence of Chu Hsi. Mr. Hummel, the head of the Chinese section of the Library of Congress, has been very kind, and the author is indebted to him for many favors.

The Japanese have naturally been more interested in Chinese civilization, and more capable of investigating it, than any nation except the Chinese themselves, but the Japanese scholars do not seem to have been properly considered in occidental studies of Confucianism. While the work of only three Japanese writers has been used in preparing this book, the importance of the material available in Japanese should be emphasized, and a much wider bibliography of Japanese works is given than were actually consulted.

The author is also indebted to Professor Duyvendak, of the University of Leiden, for important suggestions concerning the passage in Ssu-ma Ch'ien dealing with the origin of the cult, to Mr. L. Tomkinson, Dr. L. M. Robinson, Professor W. N. Brown, Dr. E. A. Speiser, Dr. C. H. Hamilton, Mr. E. S. Shinozaki, Miss Helen E. Fernald, Mr. W. H. Allen, Mr. C. S. Gardner, Dr. H. G. Creel, and to his wife, Marguerite J. Shryock. He is particularly indebted to Dr. Berthold Laufer and Professor H. F. MacNair for reading the manuscript and making many corrections.

The letters *L* and *R* after references in the notes indicate the left or right side of a Chinese page. The romanization is approximately that of Wade, and the chronology, that found in Mayers' *Chinese Reader's Manual*. The dates of the birth and death of Confucius himself are not certain. While the authority of Chu Hsi has generally been accepted, which would fix the date of the death in 479 B. C., it is not entirely convincing. For a discussion of this point, the reader is referred to Maspero, *La Chine antique,* page 455, note 1. The text of the *Twenty-four Histories* used is that issued in the fourth year of Ch'ien Lung, 1739.

In a study of this kind, covering so long a period and so much material, no amount of care can prevent the occurrence of mistakes. The author will be very glad to have them corrected.

JOHN KNIGHT SHRYOCK.

University of Pennsylvania.

CONTENTS

xi

CONTENTS

THE ORIGIN AND DEVELOPMENT OF THE STATE CULT OF CONFUCIUS

INTRODUCTION

The life of Confucius, or K'ung Fu-tzu, has been told so often in European languages that it is unnecessary to do it again, yet in a study of the cult of the sage it is necessary to begin with the man himself, at least to the extent of finding the reasons why he later came to be worshiped.

Confucius belonged to the upper class of Chinese society, or the nobility. The terms *Superior Man* and *Small Man,* which occur so often in the canon, seem originally to have been used for a dualistic division in society, and while Confucius gave an ethical meaning to the expressions, the Confucian school has always been aristocratic. Confucius himself was descended from a line of minor nobles which traced its origin to the rulers of the Yin dynasty, a fact which the sage never forgot, and his disciples came from noble families. Not only was Confucius associated with the leading men of his own state of Lu, but his position was of sufficient importance for him to be received as an official guest by the rulers of the states which he visited. The effect of this may easily be exaggerated, but the fact should be remembered, particularly because it has always been reflected in the attitude of his followers. It is apparent that he possessed a commanding and lovable personality which was generally recognized by his contemporaries and made an indelible impression upon his followers That he had disciples was not remarkable in itself. Many other men had them also. But the quality of the disciples is itself an estimate of the capacity of the teacher, and the protégés of Confucius included in their number men of considerable ability. That he could impress such men so that they recorded not only what he said, but the most minute details of his habits and appearance, indicates the power of the man. He received extraordinary loyalty from his pupils while he was alive, and after his death they mourned for him as for a father.

Great pupils imply a great teacher, and the records of his conversations as well as his own writings give evidence that he is to be classed with the greatest men. It would be inappropriate to attempt here a eulogy or an estimate of his place as a thinker or as an ethical leader, and it may simply be assumed that whatever reverence and honor were

3

paid him by later generations were not the result of a myth, but had a solid basis in reality, for he was a man worthy of worship.

Yet this does not explain the worship, nor the history of his influence, nor the development of a state cult which centered about him. As a political reformer he failed in his own generation, while his doctrines were not recognized by the state nor were his professed followers appointed to positions of real importance in the government until more than 300 years after his death. Then suddenly the Han emperor, Wu, became a patron of Confucius, and doctrines which had their source in his teaching became the policy of the state. In a general sense this continued for 2,000 years, new dynasties continuing the attitude of their predecessors even in the case of foreign conquerors, during which time there grew up a cult of the sage and of his more important followers which was essentially religious. The cult was always fostered by the state and was never general among the common people, being limited almost entirely to scholars and to the body of officials, past, present, and expectant. The origin and development of this cult are of interest not only to the student of Chinese civilization but also to those interested in the history of religions and of culture. In order to understand the rise of Confucian influence and the eventual position of Confucius himself in the state, it is advisable to consider a few of the features of his work and teaching.

Confucius was admittedly conservative, and loyal to a tradition that was at least as old as the Chou dynasty. This tradition was already ancient by the time of Confucius, and was embodied not only in the mores of the nation but in written records which Confucius mentions by name, the *Book of History,* the *Odes,* and the *Book of Changes.* Not only did Confucius identify himself with this tradition, but he was regarded by later generations as having edited these works into approximately their present form. This is of importance, because later these books became the standards of Chinese education, together with the ritual books which were mainly Han compilations; and when this took place, Confucius had been accepted as the model and authority for all those who studied this material.

The classical tradition recognized a feudal government headed by the Son of Heaven, and an upper class which was governed by an elaborate system of rules of behavior. This social and political organization was reflected in religion. The spirits of the dead, nature divinities, and political deities like the gods of the Land and Grain, were arranged under a supreme god, who by the time of the Chou was called Heaven or the Emperor on High; and just as all important decisions and policies were assumed to originate in the will of the ruler, so in the *Book of History* all the events of history show the will of Heaven.

By the time of Confucius this system, if it had ever been practised, had already fallen into such decay that it was in danger of disappearing. The sage made it his life-long task to renew the system, and when he found that he could not continue in office without forfeiting his self-respect, he tried to accomplish the same result, not only by impressing his ideals upon his disciples, but by writing an historical work, the *Spring and Autumn Annals,* which continued the narrative of the *Book of History* down to his own time in the form of a yearly record of his own state of Lu. Confucius seems to have used the method of the official court historians, and the name was used for other records besides that of the sage, but by means of the careful use of words which implied approval or condemnation, and by occasionally falsifying the account in such a way as to show what ought to have occurred, he produced a work which was in reality a criticism of the period in terms of the classical ideal. He himself considered this as his greatest achievement, and if the judgment of Mencius is accepted, the book had a considerable influence from the first. It eventually took its place beside the older classics, and by the Han period was valued so highly as to insure its author, even though he had no other claim to fame, a prominent place in the history of China. From the Han period onward there is a long list of scholars who made this book the main object of their study.

In defending the classical system Confucius was led into a conception of philosophy which, while based on the older works, owes a good deal to his own genius. He held that ethical values, the structure of society and of the state, the fundamental human relationships, and civilization in general have their origins in the decrees of Heaven, and that the reality of an institution or an object depends upon the degree to which it possesses the qualities decreed for it by Heaven as expressed in its name. In particular, the virtues, such as benevolence and justice, had a constant value given to them by Heaven, while even a common man possessed a moral sense and a will of his own which could not be taken from him.

The *Book of History* contains a corrective theory of punishment, and Confucius went still further in being opposed to killing at all, even that good might come. If the ruler and the nobles set a good example, the commoners would follow. Consequently, while Confucius does not discuss general education, he does emphasize study, particularly the study of the canon, as in his advice to his son. Many of his active years were spent as a teacher, and his life even more than his words shows his belief in the value of education, but it is hardly correct to say that he regarded education as mainly corrective. While he was a great teacher and can be quoted as an advocate of education, it was probably Hsün Tzu who inspired the Han leaders to found schools. Nevertheless, when schools were established, it was natural for them to take Confucius as a model, not only because he was the teacher par excellence, but because of his intimate connection with the ancient canon and his advocacy of the classical ideals. It was correct to attribute to him the desire to substitute education in place of severe punishments in governing the people.

In ethics he was an advocate of virtue, and the Confucians were following their master when they opposed the Taoist teaching which decried virtue. Moreover, he found the origin of virtue in Heaven, and as he accepted the *Book of History* and the *Odes,* Mencius, or Meng Tzu, was a more legitimate follower of Confucius than Hsün Tzu, in declaring that Heaven had implanted virtue in human nature, since both the *History* and the *Odes* contain similar statements.

Politically he upheld the rights of the ruler under the feudal system. It was the only system he knew, but when feudalism was abolished the Confucians continued to support it because it had the stamp of canonical approval. Probably Confucius would have agreed with them, for he loved the ancient ways, but it is unfair to stress his support of feudalism too heavily, since in his day any other system was unthinkable. He defended the authority of the ruler and criticized the feudal lords for usurping the royal prerogatives.

Confucius was insistent that behavior should be regulated by propriety and ritual, while he gave many instances of his love of ceremonies. Consequently it was natural for his followers to consider these things of importance, to lay stress on precedent, and to oppose change. They became authorities on the proper way of doing things, as Confucius had been himself, and here again it was natural that the sage should have come to be the last word in such matters.

This sketch gives the reasons why, when Han Wu Ti changed the policy of his predecessors in some ways, it was obvious that the position of Confucius should be raised and his influence enormously increased, though the question remains as to why Han Wu Ti reversed the position of earlier emperors. Before that can be answered, it is necessary to give a brief account of the fortunes of the Confucian doctrines and those who held them in the time that intervened between Confucius and Wu Ti. And as Confucius appears in the Han period as the patron saint of scholars and of education, the founding and development of schools must also be considered.

CHAPTER I

The Development of the Confucian School from the Death of Confucius to Ch'in Shih Huang, about 479–221 b. c.

Confucius is credited by tradition with having had approximately seventy disciples with whom he came into intimate contact, though he is said to have influenced to some extent a much larger number. Of most of these seventy-odd we know little more than their names, but it may be assumed that when they separated after the death of their master, there was a considerable body of men scattered throughout the older and more conservative feudal states who not only devoted themselves to bringing about the aims of the sage, but perpetuated his memory and strove to increase his reputation. Most of these men were located in the state of Lu, of which Confucius himself and most of his disciples were natives, but their influence extended to other states as well. For instance, Tzu Kung was at various times in the states of Wei, Ch'i, Chin, Wu, and Yüeh [1] in an official capacity.[2] Practically all of these men came from noble families, and many of them were employed by the rulers of feudal states, which must have increased the effect of their influence.

Several of the immediate disciples became themselves the heads of schools. Seven of the names of the pupils of Tseng Tzu are known, and there must have been many more.[3] The disciples of Tzu Hsia are mentioned in the *Analects,* and two of them became famous for their commentaries on the *Spring and Autumn Annals.*[4] Tzu Yu is said to have journeyed as far south as the Yangtze River, and to have been followed by 300 students.[5] Besides these, it is known that the great Confucians of later generations, Tzu Ssu, Mencius, and Hsün Tzu, all had numbers of disciples who considered themselves followers not only of their immediate teacher, but of Confucius as well. Here is the machinery by which the doctrines of the sage were developed and spread throughout the country.

The progress of the doctrines of the school was facilitated by the political conditions of the period. The power of the central ruler had vanished, and the country was divided into feudal states which were

9

continually engaged in a life-and-death struggle, in the course of
which the lords sought to attract into their employment able men
without any consideration of whence these men came. The result was
the creation of a body of peripatetic statesmen and soldiers who
traveled from court to court seeking official employment. Among these
the Confucians took their place, as is shown by the careers of Mencius
and Hsün Tzu.

The courts of the chief feudal princes became centers of intellectual
life in which ideas were debated and developed, and from which they
spread rapidly throughout the country. In the fourth and third centuries B. C. the chief centers were the capitals of the states of Wei
and Ch'i,[6] whose rulers were patrons of philosophy and literature,
attracting to themselves from all sides distinguished scholars and
thinkers whom they entertained and encouraged even when they did
not appoint them to official position.

"To the capital of Liang, in the state of Wei, came all the philosophers.
. . . Seldom had any capital in the world attracted so many profound
original and subtle thinkers as the capital of the state of Wei in the fourth
and third centuries before Christ. . . . The philosophers were treated as
guests of the reigning king, who reserved for them lodging and maintenance, and encouraged all who had any pretense to the pursuit of truth
and wisdom. . . . Here came Mencius and Hsün Tzu." [7]

"The intellectual life . . . was the more animated as it had numerous
contacts with another and still more famous center of scholars. This was
the celebrated academy at the gate of Chi, in the state of Ch'i, in the east.
Here during the second half of the fourth century B. C. and at the beginning of the third century, were assembled several of the leading minds of
the times. . . . All these scholars lived in a kind of academy, which King
Hsüan of Ch'i (319–301), had built for them and where they received rich
subsidies. There were not less than seventy-six of these privileged
scholars, who, as a sign that they belonged to the 'Association of the Hua
Mountain,' as they called it, wore a special cap, flat at both top and bottom.
At some time Mencius himself formed part of this brilliant company. . . .
It is said that several thousands of scholars flocked together, attracted by
the fame of these leading men and by the favorable treatment which they
received at the hands of the king. We know that Hsün Tzu came, probably
as a young man." [8]

It can be seen that there was ample opportunity for the followers of
Confucius to develop and spread the doctrines of their master under
very favorable conditions. Not only was there an easy communication
of ideas, but the Confucians were set in the midst of a group of

thinkers who may be compared on equal terms with those of ancient Athens, and were given the leisure for work through the generosity of cultured nobles.

The Confucians took advantage of this situation not only by attracting students and by debating with representatives of other schools of thought, but by producing a considerable amount of literature. Confucius is credited with having edited the *Book of History,* the *Book of Changes,* the *Odes,* and works on ritual and music which are now lost.[9] He himself wrote the *Spring and Autumn Annals.* To his disciples, both immediate and later, belong the *Analects,* the three great commentaries on the *Spring and Autumn Annals,* the appendices to the *Book of Changes,* the *Book of Filial Piety,* the *Great Learning,* the *Doctrine of the Mean,* and other sections of the present *Book of Rites.* Besides these there are the works of Mencius and Hsün Tzu. Although these are the chief literary results of the Confucian school during this period, the catalogue of the imperial library of the Han dynasty gives a list of works by other Confucians of the time, mentioning nineteen authors whose writings total more than 200 sections.[10] Very little is known about these nineteen, and their work can hardly have been of much importance, but it is a testimony to the activity of the school.

The oral and literary work of the Confucians cannot be called religious propaganda. They were common-sense political and ethical teachers, and were not primarily interested in either metaphysics or natural philosophy. Confucius himself has frequently been regarded as a skeptic on religion. Tseng Tzu, Tzu Ssu, and Mencius say almost nothing about it, and Hsün Tzu takes away all personality from Heaven, which he makes into an impersonal principle of natural law. An examination of the literature of the period shows that while religion of some sort may be assumed, there is no attempt by the Confucians to propagate it, and the books are primarily concerned with other matters.

There is no support for the view of K'ang Yu-wei and his modern school [11] that Confucius was the founder of a new religion. The contention is based mainly on certain apocryphal writings, the *Ch'i Wei,*[12] which first appear in the Han period, and are ignored by Chinese critics. The character of these writings is religious, mystical, and prophetic, and although Confucius and his disciples are claimed as the authors, the spirit of the *Ch'i Wei* is altogether different from

that of the genuine Confucian literature. It seems as if these contemporary scholars had attempted to read into the ancient literature
ideas which they borrowed from Christianity.

On the other hand, skeptical critics like Hu Shih appear to go too
far in the other direction when they deny any religion to Confucius
and his followers. The Confucians were ardent supporters of the
ancient literature, particularly the *History* and the *Odes*. These books
contain the literary evidences of the old Chinese religion, and with the
exception of Hsün Tzu, no prominent Confucian said anything to
lessen the validity of that religion. On the contrary, all may be quoted
in support of it. There is evidence that both Confucius and Mencius
regarded Heaven much as it appears in the *History* and the *Odes,* a
personal supreme deity, and even Hsün Tzu continued to use the
term as his absolute, though he took away its personal qualities. Hu
Shih, like K'ang Yu-wei, appears to be applying western ideas to the
old Chinese sources, though he is partial to science rather than to
religion.[13]

The Confucians were united in their reverence for the canon, and in
their support of religious, ethical, and political views which had
canonical support. Mencius was skeptical of some of the documents
of the *History,* and Hsün Tzu was influenced by Taoist thought, but
the statement is generally true of their position. All of them considered the proper ritual and propriety of great importance, and all
laid stress upon virtue and moral education, which was accomplished
by the study of the canon. While Hsün Tzu and Mencius differed on
the nature of man, the question as to which represented the orthodox
Confucian position was not decided until more than a thousand years
later and did not affect the position of either in the time we are considering. Indeed, Hsün Tzu had greater influence on the Confucianism of the Han period than Mencius. All the Confucians united in
their reverence for their master, all supported the authority of the
ruler in a feudalistic system, and if they differed among themselves,
it was chiefly on questions of ritual and ceremony.

Good evidence for the activity of the Confucians and the increasing
prominence of the sage himself is offered by the criticisms of the
opposing schools of thought. Meh Ti and his followers represented
the older religion of the Chinese, the worship of nature deities, more
truly than the Confucians, who followed the *Book of History* in
emphasizing only the ancestors and Heaven. It is not surprising to
find that Meh Ti refers to those who do not believe in the existence of

spirits in severe condemnation,[14] apparently meaning the Confucians, and Confucius himself is regarded as a political intriguer.[15] No better tribute to the progress of the Confucian school could be found than the fact that both the Micians, or followers of Meh Ti, and the Taoists find it necessary to invent stories to the discredit of Confucius. The Micians relate a scandalous episode which could not have occurred until some time after the death of Confucius.[16]

The Taoists are much more sympathetic to Confucius himself and are enthusiastic over his favorite disciple, Yen Hui. In Lieh Tzu, Confucius is mentioned with respect, and Tzu Kung and Tzu Hsia are favorably noticed.[17] Chuang Tzu and his school are more critical. While Confucius is not attacked, he is made to receive instruction from Lao Tzu which he cannot understand and to marvel at the profundity of the Taoist.[18] Yen Hui is considered to have advanced beyond Confucius. Chuang Tzu is much more severe on the later followers of Confucius, telling a story of the literati robbing a grave and justifying themselves by quoting from the *Odes*.[19] There is probably good ground for this criticism, for Hsün Tzu, himself a Confucian, divides the Confucians into three classes, for the first of which he has nothing but condemnation.[20] It is evidence for the popularity and extent of the school that unworthy men were attracted to it.

The best testimony comes from the bitter opponents of the Confucians, the leaders of the School of Law.

Shang Yang says, "Eminent men all change their occupations, to apply themselves to the study of the *Odes* and the *History,* and to follow improper standards. . . . When the people are given to such teachings, it is certain that such a country will be dismembered." [21]

"Though there may be a bundle of the *Odes* and the *History* in every hamlet yet it is useless for good government." [22]

Han Fei divides the Confucians into eight schools, known by the names of their masters. These were Tzu Chang, Tzu Ssu, Yen, Mencius, Ch'i-tiao, Chung Liang, Hsün Tzu and Yo-cheng. Of these, Tzu Chang and Ch'i-tiao were personal disciples of Confucius, Tzu Ssu and Yo-cheng were pupils of Tseng Tzu, and of Yen and Chung Liang nothing is known.[23] The fact that there were two schools of Confucian thought in the closing days of the Chou period about whch we are entirely ignorant shows both our lack of adequate information and the increasing spread of the Confucian doctrines.

Of these eight schools the one which exerted the greatest influence upon the Confucianism of the Han period was unquestionably that of Hsün Tzu.[24] Three sections of the *Book of Rites,* which was a Han compilation, are identical with passages in Hsün Tzu.[25] Ssu-ma Ch'ien quotes Hsün Tzu extensively.[26] Chang Tsang, a Han authority on the *Spring and Autumn Annals,* was a follower of Hsün Tzu.[27] Shen Kung, the founder of a Han school of Confucian interpretation, studied under a pupil of Hsün Tzu,[28] and Han Ying, one of the leading Confucians of the reign of Wu Ti, quotes from Hsün Tzu.[29] In the year 26 B. C., Hsün Tzu was published, if the word may be used for a time before the development of printing, by Liu Hsiang, the imperial librarian.[30] It will be seen later that Tung Chung-shu, the greatest Confucian of the period of the Western Han, was largely influenced by Hsün Tzu, and it is probable that Hsün Tzu's emphasis on education as the means for correcting the inherently evil nature of man was the inspiration for the development of the schools under Wu Ti and his successors. This is especially important, because it was in the schools that the cult of Confucius developed. A moderate reaction against the influence of Hsün Tzu and Tung Chung-shu commenced about the beginning of the Christian era under Yang Hsiung,[31] but at the time of the Confucian revival under Wu Ti the influence of Hsün Tsu seems to have been predominant.

For the Han period it is hardly accurate to speak of pure Confucians in the sense that the term could be applied to Tseng Tzu, Tzu Ssu, and Mencius. A contemporary Japanese scholar, Miura, says that during the Han period the scholars show the influence of all the preceding schools to such an extent that it is almost impossible to classify them with any one.[32] This difficulty may be illustrated by Huai Nan Tzu, who was a patron of Confucians and of classical researches, yet is usually classed as a Taoist, and also by the emperor Wu, whose behavior makes it difficult to classify him, since he not only patronized, and was largely responsible for, the Confucian revival, but cultivated Taoist magicians and gave himself to the search for the elixir of immortality.

This eclecticism of the Han period may be partly responsible for the popularity of Hsün Tzu, since the latter, more than any other Confucian of the Chou period, adapts his thought to meet the criticism of opposing schools. His elimination of the personal attributes of Heaven appears to be due to Taoist influence, and this may also be true of his shift from the position of Mencius on the nature of man. It was this eclecticism of Hsün Tzu which contributed to his condemnation by the Sung Confucians, who rightly realized that it had caused him to surrender the fundamental assumption for any system of obligatory ethics, the essentially ethical nature of man. Indeed, Chu Hsi accuses Hsün Tzu of being influenced by Shen Pu Hai and Shang Yang, and Su Tung-p'o points out that his teaching could hardly have been pure Confucianism, since it was his scholar Li Ssu who was largely responsible for the burning of the books.[33] But this eclectic spirit was characteristic of the Han period, and probably aided the influence of Hsün Tzu at that time.

This was certainly increased by the emphasis which he placed upon the virtue of *li*.[34] This word is difficult to translate adequately into English, but in Hsün Tzu, it covers correct human behavior of any kind, especially ritual and the rules of society. Indeed, Hsün Tzu considers the virtues to be merely social sanctions, and therefore with him *li* covers the whole of ethics. This led him to exalt a virtue which originally was a narrower concept, often translated as the rules of propriety. With the prosperity and internal peace under Han Wu Ti, an emperor who loved ceremony, the influence of Hsün Tzu was magnified, his writings on *li* becoming the authority for the scholars of the period.

Although the cumulative effect of the evidence for the growth of the Confucian or classical school gives a picture of steadily increasing influence and numbers during the closing centuries of the Chou period, the Confucians were only one of a number of such schools, and in some ways the fight they made was a losing one. They represented the conservative forces of society, and for a time victory lay with the radicals. This struggle was not primarily a religious conflict. Taoism was even less of a religion than Confucianism, and none of the wars which devastated China during the last years of the Chou and Ch'in dynasties can be called religious. It was a battle of differing schools of philosophy, a purely academic struggle of ideas carried on in the centers of intellectual life at the leading courts. But it was more than that. The Confucians were political thinkers, seeking and sometimes obtaining official position in the quarreling feudal states. They were, in politics as in everything, conservative. Unfortunately for them the times had changed, and a newer school had arisen which adapted its views to meet changing conditions instead of appealing to the past, coming into sharp conflict with Confucian political ideas. This group of men were classified during the Han period as the School of Law.

The men who composed this school were not united by loyalty to a master, nor by organization, nor because they were contemporaries, nor did they have the relation of pupil to teacher in the clear-cut way of the Confucians. The list of men included in the group varies, and the classification itself was not made until their epoch had closed, but they were alike in that they were practical and successful statesmen and men of affairs whose political theories resembled each other in important aspects. The Confucians were committed to the classical system of a dualistic division of society into nobles and commoners. The former were governed by *li,* which in ancient China might be compared to the European code of chivalry of a later date. *Li* was the code of behavior of a gentleman. On the other hand, the School of Law was united in its opposition to the nobles and the feudal system which they represented, and stood for a system of universal law to which both the nobles and the people should conform.

The School of Law was strongly influenced by Taoist thought. It naturally neglected the mystical side, but other ideals of Taoism appealed to it, and were applied in ways that would have seemed strange to Lao Tzu. Tao as a universal and unified law was illustrated by it in a system of legal decrees depending for their sanction solely upon the will of the autocratic ruler of the state. They hoped that this system would eventually be perfected to the point where it would work automatically and universally without interference from the heads of the government, and would result in the people living in primitive simplicity without thought or dispute, engaged in farming when they were not serving the state as soldiers. Taoism unquestionably inspired this conception, but it is strange to see its doctrines applied to produce efficiency in war, to which Lao Tzu was opposed. The Taoist influence is also shown in other doctrines of the school. Education in the Confucian sense of a study of the canon of ancient literature was condemned, and Confucian morality was attacked. As all things change continually, customs and methods of government change also, and an immovable form of social and political organization in which precedent would be the principal factor was considered a valueless fiction.[35]

The following quotations from Shang Yang show what the

School of Law thought of the standards and methods of the Confucians.

"Duke Hsiao said, 'I have heard it said, that in poor country districts much is thought strange, and that in village schools there are many debates. What the foolish laugh about, the wise are sad about.' " [36] (This criticism would include other schools beside the Confucian.)

"If the ministers of state and the great officers are not allowed to occupy themselves with extensive learning, brilliant discussions and idle living . . . then the farmers will have no opportunity . . . nor will they become fond of study." [37]

"If in a country, there are the following ten things: odes and history, rites and music, virtue and the cultivation thereof, benevolence and integrity, sophistry and intelligence, then the ruler has no one whom he can employ for defense and warfare. If a country is governed by means of these ten things, it will be dismembered as soon as an enemy approaches, and even if no enemy approaches, it will be poor." [38]

Shang Yang refers to the *Odes,* the *History,* the arts and the virtues, as parasites.[39] The school was especially bitter against the books which were the standard and foundation of the Confucians, the *History* and the *Odes.*

Analysis of the places visited by the prominent Confucians reveals the fact that their influence was much greater in the older and more conservative states which bordered the Yellow River, and which would be included in the modern provinces of Shantung, Chihli, Shansi, Shensi, and Honan. To a certain extent they were welcome in the Yangtse valley. But they could have had little influence in the great northwestern state of Ch'in. Hsün Tzu did go to Ch'in, and was received by the ruler, but the account of the meeting in Ssu-ma Ch'ien shows why the attempt was futile.

"Hsün Ch'ing . . . was received in audience by Chao Wang of Ch'in. Chao Wang at the time enjoyed fighting and killing, but Hsün Tzu argued with him according to the methods of the three kings, so the prime minister of Ch'in, Yin Hou, could not employ him." [40]

It was the central states which welcomed and to some extent employed the Confucians in the government. On the other hand, it was Ch'in which put into practice the principles of the School of Law, and by means of them conquered the entire country. Among the revolutionary changes carried out in Ch'in, and later applied more or less successfully to all China, were the abolition of the feudal system, the application of the common law to the nobility, individual ownership of land, and an attack upon the patriarchal family system. Commerce and the use of money were discouraged, the state was organized for war under a bureaucratic government headed by a ruler with absolute powers; and as the laws were not yet automatic, severe punishments were inflicted for even slight offenses, while failure to report a criminal was punished in the same way as the crime itself. The idea behind this severity was that if misdemeanors were capital offenses, really great crimes would never occur.[41]

The period of the Contending States (475-221 B. C.),which closed the Chou dynasty, saw the gradual advance of the legalistic state of Ch'in as it absorbed the older feudal states one after another until the whole country came under the rule of Ch'in Shih Huang. In spite of the progress made by the Confucian school, the nature of the times made the application of their political theories a complete failure. The Confucian system was shown to be unsatisfactory during a period of protracted warfare; and the later Confucians, like Mencius and Hsün Tzu, found it difficult to secure office.

NOTES

[1] 衞齊晉吳越. Hirth (*Ancient History of China*) gives a map on which these states are located. Two of them are in the Yangtse valley, and the rest in the basin of the Yellow river, to the east of the State of Ch'in. M. Granet (*Chinese Civilization*) attempts to reconstruct this ancient Chinese culture. H. Maspero (*La Chine antique*) gives an excellent account of it.

[2] Forke, *Geschichte der alten chinesischen Philosophie*, p. 143.

[3] *Ibid.*, p. 149.

[4] *Ibid.*, p. 145.

[5] *Ibid.*, p. 147.

[6] 魏齊. The state of Wei mentioned here is not the one mentioned in note 1. It was one of three states which resulted from the division of Ch'in in 403 B. C.

[7] Cranmer-Byng, Introd. to *Yang Chu's Garden of Pleasure*, p. 7. Yang Chu, the egoistic hedonist and opponent of Mencius, refused to accept an appointment, but was patronized by the Duke of Wei in spite of that.

[8] Duyvendak, *Book of Lord Shang*, pp. 73, 74. Many of the soldiers and statesmen of the age were mercenaries, whom the lords sought to attract to their courts by patronage and liberality. The scholars, who were also professional politicians, were questioned by the lords, and if their advice were good, they were appointed to office. Each court tried to rival the brilliance of the others.

[9] Forke, p. 108.

[10] *Ibid.*, pp. 188, 189.

[11] *Ibid.*, p. 108, note. K'ang Yu-wei began his public career as a reformer, the advisor of the unfortunate emperor Kuang Hsü. When the reforms were suppressed by the empress dowager, K'ang Yu-wei escaped. From the founding of the republic until his death he was known, not as a radical, but as a

conservative supporter of the monarchy. Young China moved too quickly for him. A distinguished scholar and author, he urged that Confucianism be made the state religion, and had Yüan Shih-k'ai been successful, his ideas might eventually have been carried out. In support of his contention that Confucius was the founder of a religion, he rediscovered these apocryphal writings of the Han period, which had been proscribed since the Sui dynasty. Although he was always respected, he had little effect on the course of Chinese affairs after the death of Yuan Shih-k'ai. For a discussion of some of his contributions to Chinese scholarship, cf. O. Franke, *Beiträge zum Konfuzianischen Dogma.*

[12] 七緯. The *Tsu yüan,* a Chinese source-book of words and phrases, sect. 子, p. 17. The terms are used (a) for the sun, the moon, and the five planets, and (b) for these writings, which are also called 緯書. *Tsu yüan,* sect. 未, p. 85.

[13] This view of Confucius, found in the *Chung kuo cheh hsioh shih,* sect. 4; pp. 69 f., was supplemented by a conversation which the author had with Dr. Hu in 1927.

[14] Y. P. Mei, *Works of Motse,* pp. 160, 161. Meh Ti does not actually say that these doubters were the Confucians, but the description fits Confucius and his followers very well.

[15] The essay on *Anti-Confucianism,* II, though included in the works of Meh Ti, is certainly not by that master himself, but probably a product of his school. The attacks upon Confucius and his disciples are bitter, unfair, and sometimes unhistorical. Mei, pp. 200-211.

[16] Forke, p. 113.

[17] L. Giles, *Taoist Teachings,* in the Wisdom of the East Series, pp. 27, 51, 73 f. It is now pretty generally held that while the text of Lieh Tzu is very corrupt, it contains a core of old material that probably reflects the views of Lieh Tzu, if such a man really lived. As it stands, the book certainly is Taoist.

[18] *Chuang Tzu,* Bks. 4, 6. These books are generally considered to have been written by Chuang Tzu. Legge, *S. B. E.,* Vol. XXXIX, pp. 203, f., 252, 255 f., etc. In Bks. 22 and 24, which are probably additions by later Taoists, the controversies between the Confucians and the Micians, or followers of Meh Ti, are condemned, and the philosophers are divided into five schools, of which the Confucians, or literati, are one. Legge, *S. B. E.,* Vol. XL, pp. 73, 99.

[19] *Chuang Tzu,* Bk. 26, probably not by Chuang Tzu himself. Legge, *S.B.E.,* Vol. XL, p. 134. The story is invented, and the poetry quoted does not occur in the *Odes.* The passage is pure satire, for robbing a grave would be an unthinkable crime to a Confucian.

[20] Dubs, *Works of Hsüntze,* p. 110. Hsün Tzu accuses these Confucians of being pedants and formalists, who do not understand the principles of the sage, and cannot be called Superior Men.

[21] Duyvendak, *Book of Lord Shang,* p. 185. The question of the text of Shang Yang is also difficult, but the book certainly represents the Legalist point of view.

[22] *Ibid.,* p. 191.

[23] Forke, p. 187. L. Tomkinson (*Early Legalist School*) quotes Han Fei as saying that Confucius was a sage who understood Tao. Han Fei, essay on the "Five Kinds of Maggots." There is a good account of Han Fei in K. C. Wu, *Ancient Chinese Political Theories,* pp. 197-222.

[24] This is the judgment of Forke (p. 218).

[25], [26], [27], [28], [29], Forke, p. 218. The sections in the *Book of Rites* on *Study*, on the *Origin of Ceremonies,* and on *Music,* chaps. I, 19, and 20, are identical with passages in Hsün Tzu. It is difficult to say who did the borrowing, as the text of Hsün Tzu is not above suspicion. Dubs and Forke assume that Hsün Tzu is the original, but Hu Shih (p. 306) says that he is unable to decide the question.

[30] Forke, p. 219.

[31] Yang Hsiung (53 B. C.–A. D. 18), a distinguished scholar and a minister of the usurper Wang Mang, for which latter position he was condemned by Chu Hsi, and his tablet eventually taken from the Confucian temple. His theory of the nature is that it is a mixture, and contains the seeds of both good and evil. He therefore occupies a middle ground between Mencius and Hsün Tzu. He was noted for his refusal to imitate Tung Chung-shu. There is an account of his life and work in Gides, *Chin. Biog. Dict.,* pp. 901, 902.

Mencius was not without influence in the Han period. Ssu-ma Ch'ien wrote an account of his life, and he is quoted by Han Ying and Tung Chung-shu. His works were in the library of the Han emperors, and are mentioned in the third catalogue of Liu Hsin. The first commentator on Mencius, Chao Ch'i, lived in the later Han period (A. D. 108-201). Cf. Legge, *Chinese Classics,* Vol. II, Prolegomena.

[32] Miura, *History of Chinese Ethics,* Chinese edition, p. 309. European scholars are of the same opinion, e.g. Wilhelm, *Hist. Chinese Civilization,* pp. 177, 178.

[33] Cited by Forke, p. 221.

[34] Forke, p. 234; *Hsüntse,* pp. 111 f.; *Works of Hsüntse,* pp. 213 f. Bk. 19 of Hsün Tzu, on *li,* is almost identical with Ssu-ma Ch'ien's treatise on the *Rites.* Chavannes, in his translation, has marked long passages as taken from Hsün Tzu.

[35] Cf. Duyvendak, pp. 66 f.

[36], [37], [38], [39]. Duyvendak, pp. 174, 181, 190, 256, respectively.

[40] Ssu-ma Ch'ien, chap. 74, sect. 14, trans. by Dubs, *Hsüntse,* p. 31.

[41] Cf. Duyvendak, p. 84.

CHAPTER II

CONFUCIANISM UNDER THE CH'IN AND EARLY HAN EMPERORS,
221-140 B. C.

When Ch'in Shih Huang conquered the last feudal state in 221
B. C., he was faced with an even greater problem than those which
had been caused by war. Having conquered the country, he had to
govern it, and he realized that soldiers alone were not sufficient for
the task. At once he set himself to apply the reforms which had
already been practised in his own state of Ch'in.[1]

It is apparent that the rulers of Ch'in had made a considerable
effort to prevent the characteristic Confucian doctrines, particularly
the political theories, from spreading in their state. There had been
no such attempt in the other states, and the country contained a
large amount of Confucian sentiment and a considerable number of
Confucian scholars. In view of later events it is safe to say that they
ran into the thousands. With these men and their views Ch'in Shih
Huang had to reckon. It is apparent that at first he tried to conciliate
them.

The table of officials of the Ch'in and Han dynasties [2] gives a class
of officials called *po shih*.[3] Chavannes translates this term *les lettrés
au vaste savoir*. There is no reason for assuming that all these
scholars were members of the various Confucian schools, but as the
Confucians were above all else students of the past, and stood for
the conservative, historical point of view, it is probable that a number,
even a majority, of the *po shih* were recruited from their ranks, for
the action of the *po shih* under Ch'in Shih Huang was characteristically Confucian. The term *Confucian* is a western designation, and
the Chinese usually call the school the *Jü Chia,* or literati,[4] for whom
Confucius is the model and chief. Therefore the term *po shih* must
not be taken as synonymous with the followers of Confucius, because
many Confucians were not honored by the title, and some of the
po shih were probably scholars of other schools.

These *po shih* appear to have had an advisory capacity and were
librarians, but otherwise the title was honorary only. In Ssu-ma

Ch'ien, a critic of the emperor also attacks these officials, saying that they were content with their title and were not employed in the business of government.[5] There were seventy of them. At least once Ch'in Shih Huang listened to their advice, and the same is true of his successor, Erh Shih Huang. On both of these occasions they, or their spokesmen, gave advice which was unpalatable to the emperor, with disastrous consequences for themselves, but the fact that they were permitted to speak at all, and that the office existed, indicates that the Ch'in rulers realized the literati were a factor which could not be ignored, and that the emperor made an attempt to secure their help in carrying out his plans.

These scholars play an important part in two of the significant events of the reign of Ch'in Shih Huang, which must be considered because they affected, or have been held to have affected, the Confucian movement. These events are known in Chinese history as the Burning of the Books and the Burying of the Scholars.

In the year 213 B. C., Ch'in Shih Huang gave a great feast in the palace at Hsien-yang, his capital, near the modern Hsi-an fu. The seventy *po shih* were present. One official made a complimentary address, which he concluded by saying that from the beginning of history no one had ever equaled the prestige and virtue of the emperor. This was blasphemous to the Confucians, with their respect for the past, and one of the *po shih* at once replied to it. He remarked that the Yin and Chou dynasties had lasted for so long because the rulers had employed the feudal system, giving fiefs to the members of their families and their chief supporters, whereas Ch'in Shih Huang, though possessing "all within the seas," had not surrendered any of his authority. The *po shih* implied the possible consequences by mentioning two historical incidents, one of a subject who had murdered his ruler, and the other of three families who had partitioned their state between them. He concluded by accusing the first speaker of flattery, and of encouraging the faults of the emperor. It would be difficult to imagine a more distasteful piece of advice than this characteristic Confucian speech must have been to Ch'in Shih Huang. Nevertheless the emperor did nothing immediately, but considered the matter.

Then the great minister and member of the School of Law, Li Ssu, pupil of Hsün Tzu with Han Fei, spoke. He pointed out that the Five Emperors [6] and the three preceding dynasties had not imitated nor slavishly followed each other. Times had changed. The stupid scholars were incapable of understanding the great work which Ch'in Shih Huang had accomplished. Formerly the lords had valued and attracted the vagrant scholars, but now the land was united under a single rule and pacified, while the people applied themselves to agriculture and industry, receiving all the instruction they needed from the officials of the emperor. The scholars studied the past in order to belittle the present era, and were the cause of continual trouble, just as in former times the lords made trouble for the ruler, because they used their private studies to disparage the decrees of the emperor. They were useless and dangerous. Li Ssu then proposed that the official histories of the feudal states which Ch'in had absorbed, save those in the possession of the *po shih,* and all private copies of the *Odes,* the *Book of History,* and the writings of the "Hundred Philosophers" should be burned, with heavy penalties for those who failed to obey the command. The emperor approved, and the decree was carried out.[7]

It should be noticed that nothing is said about the punishment of the *po shih* who made the speech to which Li Ssu replied, that there were considerable exceptions to the proscription—works on medicine, divination and agriculture, as well as the official history of Ch'in—and that copies of all the books were preserved by the *po shih.* The books to be destroyed were those which were appealed to by the Confucians in support of the feudal system, the histories of the former feudal states which might be used to keep alive sectional feeling, and the disputes of the various philosophic schools. It was the inclusion of the *Odes* and the *Book of History* which was the chief cause of the condemnation of Ch'in Shih Huang by later Confucians.

The speech of Li Ssu is not strikingly original, but is characteristic of the School of Law. For more than 150 years the Legalists had been saying that these books should be burned, but this was the first opportunity for putting their desire into practice.

The second event, the Burying of the Scholars, presents difficulties to the modern student. The account in Ssu-ma Ch'ien runs as follows. Ch'in Shih Huang had patronized certain magicians or adepts from the states of Ch'i and Yen, which bordered the Yellow Sea. These men claimed to be scholars, and to be able to discover the elixir of immortality. They even persuaded the emperor to send expeditions to find the drug, and to discover fairy islands in the eastern sea where the immortals lived. On these men he expended large sums of money, and gave them much honor. In spite of this, two of them publicly criticized the emperor and fled before they could be punished. Ch'in Shih Huang was angered and seems to have held all the scholars responsible, perhaps for sharing their views. An examination was held by the censors, in the course of which the unfortunate scholars accused one another, and as a result several hundred were executed.[8] The difficulty in this passage lies in the two characters which Chavannes translates as meaning that the scholars accused each other.[9]

Nothing in Ssu-ma Ch'ien suggests that this was a deliberate attack upon the Confucians only. If his account is to be accepted, the action of the emperor was directed mainly against magicians or adepts, and how many of the unfortunate men buried alive were Confucians it is impossible to determine. The fact that there was sufficient common ground for scholars and magicians to be included in one class indicates a great difference from the scholars of the early Confucian period. There was a group of nature philosophers during the last century of the Chou period,[10] and from this time on there were experiments in alchemy associated with what would now be regarded as wild philosophical speculations. The men who conducted them were often learned, just as in the beginnings of science in Europe, and it is probable that most of the men executed by Ch'in Shih Huang could not be called genuine Confucians.

The generally accepted point of view in China, adopted by many European scholars,[11] has been to connect these two events and to interpret them as a persecution of the Confucians. The T'ung chien kang mu,[12] for instance, says that the criticism of the emperor was directly due to the Burning of the Books. The inquisition of the scholars followed on this, and was so cruel that the heir to the throne protested and was banished, the whole affair being an instance of the malignity of the emperor and Li Ssu.[13] The account in Ssu-ma Ch'ien is much more reasonable. The two events are not directly connected, and the emperor not only considers before giving his decision in favor of Li Ssu, but when criticized later complains that he had collected and patronized the scholars, only to find that they were disloyal.

A critic of the thirteenth century of our era, Ma Tuan-lin, wrote, "According to the table of officials of the Western Han Dynasty, the po shih were the official historians of Ch'in. They must have had many students, to whom they handed down the history of past times. Though Ch'in had these officials, their pupils were hated and even killed at times. Ch'in Shih Huang asked the censors [14] to examine these students, and many were killed." [15] The emperor caused melons to be planted on a hill in winter, and invited the scholars to see the prodigy. About 700 went, and were slaughtered there.

He adds, "Under Erh Shih (the successor of Ch'in Shih Huang), the students of the *po shih* were summoned to discuss the situation created by the rebellion of Ch'en Sheh. Their advice was distasteful to the emperor and several tens were executed, but Su Sun-t'ung flattered the emperor and thus escaped. This shows that there were scholars, although Ch'in tried to destroy them." This story is not found in the section of Ssu-ma Ch'ien dealing with Erh Shih Huang. Su Sun-t'ung later became an adviser of the first Han emperor, Kao Tsu.

A contemporary scholar, Lu Ssu-mien, comments on this passage, "Though Ch'in ill-treated these men, there was a continuous line of scholars, and classical studies were not entirely destroyed. The office of *po shih* was continued, though there was no formal education." [16]

Hsieh Wu-liang, in his history of Chinese philosophy, says that although Ch'in burned the books, the *po shih* continued to exist, and under the early Han, there were still many *po shih* of the Ch'in period. When the rebellion started against Ch'in, the Confucianists of Lu took the sacrificial vessels to Ch'en Sheh. One of Ch'en's *po shih* was K'ung Chai, who had been a Ch'in official, but had resigned after the Burning of the Books. Su Sun-t'ung and T'ang Ch'ang, both of whom served under Han Kao Tsu, were old *po shih* of Ch'in.[17]

Hu Shih remarks that the failure of philosophy under the Han is not to be attributed to Ch'in Shih Huang. K'ang Yu-wei [18] and Ch'ui Shih [19] hold that the *po shih* were acquainted with the various philosophic schools, but Hu Shih differs from them, considering that as most of the *po shih* were probably Confucians, they were not interested in other systems of thought. On this question, which is not of much importance here, it seems likely that Hu Shih is wrong, since those Confucians about whom something is known, such as Hsün Tzu, were very well acquainted with other current philosophic systems, and eclecticism was the fashion of the time.

Hu Shih also points out that the catalogue of the imperial Han library is in itself a conclusive proof that the Burning of the Books was a failure.

Most of the "scholars" killed by Ch'in Shih Huang, he maintains, were *fang shih*.[20] This term, usually translated "magician," though "adept" is a better word, is applied to Taoists and later to Buddhists. In any event, even though many more scholars had been killed than was actually the case, the number existing at the time was so large that real philosophy would not have been affected.

Hu Shih considers that the failure of philosophy from the Ch'in period onward was due to four reasons. First, there was the logic of skepticism which had been developed by Chuang Tzu in the closing days of the Chou period. Second, there was a tendency to discredit theoretical reasoning. Third, there was the absolute power of the emperor, which was not as favorable to the development of ideas as the conditions under the warring feudal states. Finally, there were the superstitions of the *fang shih,* or adepts.[21]

The analysis of Hu Shih needs only one comment. The adepts were not ignorant men. On the contrary, they were frequently the most learned and enlightened men of the time, and as such were classed by Ch'in Shih Huang with the literati. In China, as in Europe, the beginnings of science were associated with many ideas which are now considered superstitions, such as physiognomy, the appeal to the stars to foretell the future, and the search for the philosopher's stone or the elixir of life. Paracelsus was a magician, Roger Bacon was considered one, and even Francis Bacon had notions which seem peculiar in the founder of modern science. In the Han period Huai Nan Tzu would illustrate the same tendency.[22] From Han Wu Ti on, many of their theories were accepted by Confucians, and the aspect of Confucianism was considerably altered.

While the general policy of Ch'in as a feudal state had always been unfavorable to the Confucians and in conformity with the theories of the School of Law, Ch'in Shih Huang, on becoming ruler of an undivided country, realized that he needed Confucian support, and endeavored to conciliate the scholars by giving honorary titles and by listening to their advice. Even after the debate which resulted in the decision in favor of the Legalists, the office of *po shih,* given mainly to Confucians, was continued, although the emperor could not permit them to destroy the chief political reform for which he was responsible, the abolition of the feudal system. The destruction of the books was intended to be only partial, extending to privately owned copies of books which were considered politically harmful, and cannot be considered as effective. The killing of the scholars was only indirectly connected with the Burning of the Books, and was chiefly due to the emperor's anger at being deceived and publicly criticized by men whom he had honored and subsidized. The reign of Ch'in Shih Huang was antagonistic, but not fatal, to literature, scholars, and philosophy; and the difficulties in the way of development found in the succeeding period were only in part due to the acts of the First Emperor.

Ch'in Shih Huang died in 210 B.C., and within a year rebellion had commenced. There followed a period of civil war until in 202 B.C. Han Kao Tsu was firmly seated on the throne. During the struggle occurred a catastrophe which was probably as disastrous for literature as the Burning of the Books. This was the complete destruction of the Ch'in capital, Hsien-yang, in 206 B.C., by Hsiang Yu. In cruelty and wantonness it far exceeded anything that Ch'in Shih Huang did after he became emperor. It is said that the conflagration lasted for three months, and even the tombs of the Ch'in rulers were violated and their corpses outraged.[23] It may be assumed that this disaster, as well as the seven years of civil war, were equally responsible with the acts of Ch'in Shih Huang for the difficulties of the Han scholars in the ensuing period.

When Liu Pang emerged in triumph from the struggle, and, as Kao Tsu, became the first ruler of the Han dynasty, his primary task was to restore order and reorganize the government. In general he continued the policies of the Ch'in emperors, his chief change being a modified restoration of the feudal system in place of what is called the *chün hsien* system. This won him the support of the Confucians, but neither Kao Tsu nor his rival Hsiang Yu can be regarded as the deliberate avenger of the Confucians, nor as championing their point of view. As Hsiang Yu lost, he need not be discussed, but it may be pointed out that while Kao Tsu had Confucian advisers, such as Lu Chia and Su Sun-t'ung, his chief friend and counselor, Chang Liang, was a Taoist.

Liu Pang was a rough soldier who had won the empire on the battle-field and made no pretense to scholarship. Even before he became emperor, he had the reputation of disliking scholars, and the Confucian Li Yi-chi had to handle him very carefully in order to overcome his prejudice.[24] His companions during the civil war, who became his lords and ministers later on, were likewise uninterested in literature and scholarship, and continued to exert influence long after Kao Tsu's death, the most able, Ch'en P'ing, lasting into the reign of Wen Ti.

It is true that while on a tour of the country following his accession, during which he appears to have followed the example of Ch'in Shih Huang in visiting places of local interest and worshiping at local shrines, he sacrificed at the grave of Confucius, but it is an exaggeration to hold that this made him a real Confucian.

His repugnance to the Confucian ideas is shown by his refusal to withdraw the decree of Ch'in Shih Huang against the ownership of the proscribed books. A scholar who admired the *Odes* and *History,* Lu Chia, approached the emperor in an endeavor to have the decree repealed. "But the latter, though he sacrificed to Confucius for political reasons, detested the scholars. He was angry, saying that he had conquered the empire on his horse, and could hold it without the *History* and the *Odes.* Lu Chia then wrote an essay which he presented to the emperor, who read it and liked the books better, but would not repeal the decree." [25] Kao Tsu is even said to have shown his dislike of scholars by behaving whenever he met one in a very pointed, but unmentionable, manner.[26] However, the work of recovering the classics began even under Kao Tsu. One of his most important ministers, Hsiao Ho, erected a building in which he collected the debris of old books, an easier task since they were written on slips of bamboo.[27]

The situation under Han Kao Tsu may be summed up in the words of a modern Japanese scholar, Takakuwa. "Han Kao Tsu came from the common people, and his nobles and ministers likewise. They were not familiar with the rites and the rules of propriety, and therefore the court was not well regulated. Su Sun-t'ung (the old *po shih* of Ch'in), persuaded the emperor to fix the ritual of the court. The system of Ch'in was followed in administration and law. The *chün hsien* system was abolished, however, and the feudal system revived, with the emperor's family and favorite officials as the new nobility. . . . The theories of Huang Lao,[28] and Han Shen [29] still predominated." [30]

The remaining reigns before Wu Ti may be dismissed in a few words. The ill-fated Hui Ti repealed the edict of Ch'in Shih Huang against the *Odes* and the *History,* which had remained in force up to that time, in the year 191 B. C.[31] The empress Lu was interested only in the advancement of her own family, which was destroyed, however, by Wen Ti. Under Wen Ti and Ching Ti the country enjoyed relative peace, and the Confucians began to make headway once more. Many of the great scholars of the reign of Wu Ti had already achieved reputations under these preceding reigns. The office of *po shih* was continued, and both Wen Ti and Ching Ti appointed old Confucians to this position, treating them well, but they themselves favored the doctrines of Huang Lao.[32] The Confucians appear to have been growing in political importance, and the Han emperors before Wu Ti, like Ch'in Shih Huang, were obliged to take them into account; but on the whole, Taoist influence predominated at the court, and the legalistic policy of Ch'in was continued. Such an important scholar as Ssu-ma T'an, the father of the great historian, openly preferred the Taoist school.[33] This was the situation when Wu became emperor in 140 B. C.

A word should be added about the state religion of the Ch'in and early Han emperors. It is evident, if Ssu-ma Ch'ien is to be accepted, that the religion of Ch'in differed considerably from that of the more essentially Chinese states. There is no reason why Ssu-ma Ch'ien should not be accepted on this matter, since the Ch'in records were expressly excepted from the burning of the books, and moreover his family came from Ch'in. There is also other evidence. Human sacrifice at funerals was customary in Ch'in, and was looked upon with horror by the more conservative Chinese, as is shown by the *Tso chuan*.[34] It is further recorded that in Ch'in a girl was sacrificed, probably once a year, to the god of the Yellow River.[35] Many of the wives and concubines of Ch'in Shih Huang were immolated at his grave.[36] There is also evidence for the sacrifice of cripples and witches to avert calamity.[37] It does not seem that the Han emperors continued these practices, though immolation at graves appears later in Chinese history.

There were other religious customs of Ch'in which were adopted by the early Han emperors. The *Book of History,* which may be taken to represent Chinese custom, at least of the early Chou period of about 1000 B. C., presents a theory which is almost monotheistic in the worship of Heaven. In Ch'in, as early as the eighth century B. C., the chief religious worship of the state seems to have been devoted to certain heavenly emperors, called *ti,* whose number was later fixed as five, corresponding to the five planets. In the late Chou period the term *Shang Ti* was applied in the plural to these gods.[38] A Confucian list of these emperors in an appendix to the *Book of Changes* includes Yao and Shun, the rulers with whom the *History* begins, but in Ch'in a list of five names, associated with colors, does not include any names honored in the *History*. These gods had shrines or holy places sacred to them, to which the rulers journeyed for worship, and the dates of the founding of these holy places are recorded.[39] The section *Yüeh Ling* in the *Book of Rites* gives an account of this theory and of the yearly practice.

There were four such shrines in Ch'in previous to the Han period, all located in Yung, in the present province of Shensi. Han Kao Tsu, who as Liu Pang had controlled this area, adopted bodily the state worship of Ch'in, and even added a shrine in order to bring the number to five.[40] In the opinion of Doré, Kao Tsu was a skeptic, and appeared religious only for political purposes,[41] but this does not seem to be a necessary interpretation, even though it may be admitted that his action was intended to secure support from the inhabitants of Ch'in. These sacrifices in the holy places of Ch'in were continued by Wen Ti and even by Wu Ti, the patron of the Confucians.[42] Eventually the older Confucian custom of a worship of Shang Ti in the singular, or Heaven, was restored, but the theory of the five emperors made a permanent impression on Chinese religion, and was continued by Taoism. One of these five was the Yellow Emperor. Ch'in had always been under Taoist influence, and the Yellow Emperor came to be associated with Lao Tzu to such an extent that the title of Lao Tzu's work, now known as the *Tao teh ching,* was called the *Huang lao,* or "Words of Huang Ti and Lao Tzu," during the Han period. The result of all this was the intrusion of what we may regard as a foreign element into Chinese religion which affected the cult of Confucius during succeeding centuries. The eclecticism of the Han period felt no inconsistency between devotion to the Confucian canon and these non-classical ideas and practices.

NOTES

[1] Ssu-ma Ch'ien chap 6, is devoted to Ch'in Shih Huang. For generally accepted statements concerning Chinese history, any standard history may be consulted; see, for example, Cordier's *Histoire générale de la Chine;* Conrady, *China,* in Ullstein's *Weltgeschichte;* and Wilhelm, *Hist. of Chinese Civilization.*

[2] Chavannes, *Mémoires historiques,* Vol. II, Appendice I, p. 515. The table in Chavannes is taken from the *Ch'ien Han Shu,* chap. 19, with additional items from the *Hou Han Shu,* chaps. 34-38.

[3] 博士.

[4] 儒家. This is the official designation for the followers of Confucius, that is, of the classical school of thought.

[5] *Mém. hist.*, Vol. II, p. 178 f. Ssu-ma Ch'ien also has the story of the protest of the heir to the throne, and his banishment to the Great Wall. The prince definitely mentions Confucius as the inspiration for the views of the scholars. The criticism of the two scholars does not mention the burning of the books.

[6] There are different lists of the Five Emperors, or *Ti*, 帝. They are found in an appendix to the *Book of Changes*, in the sect. *Yueh Lin* of the *Book of Rites*, the *Bamboo Books*, and the chapter on the *Feng and Shan Sacrifices* in Ssu-ma Ch'ien. They are mythological rulers of the period preceding the opening of the *Book of History*.

[7] *Mém. hist.*, Vol. II, p. 169 f. The speeches have been translated in full by Legge, *Chinese Classics*, Vol. I, Prolegomena, and by De Mailla, *Histoire générale de la Chine*, Vol. II, pp. 401 f., as well as by Chavannes.

[8] *Ibid.*, p. 181.

[9] *Ibid.* Note 2 discusses the translations of Legge, Möllendorf, H. Giles, and Parker. See also the opinion of Wang Ch'ung, that the killing of the scholars and the burning of the books were not connected. Forke, *Lun Hêng, Mitt. des Sem.*, Vol. XI, p. 100.

[10] Forke, *Geschichte chin. Phil.*, pp. 499-520. The chief of these was Tsou Yen, who was the head of a school which developed the theory of the five elements.

[11] For example, by Legge, *Chinese Classics*, Vol. I, Prolegomena. Wilhelm (*Chinese Civilization*, p. 172), says the Confucians championed the cause of the magicians.

[12] The *T'ung chien kan mu* is a history of China, founded on a work by Ssu-ma Kuang which was published in A. D. 1084. De Mailla's work is mainly a translation of it.

[13] De Mailla, Vol. II, p. 402.

[14] 御使.

[15] Ma Tuan-lin, in the *Wen hsien t'ung k'ao*, Vol. XL, sect. 18. Quoted by Lu Ssu-mien, Vol. II, p. 65.

[16] Lu Ssu-mien, *Po hua pen kuo tsu,* or *History of Chinese Civilization*, Vol. II, chap. 8, sect. 1, pp. 65 f. With the exception of Ma Tuan Lin, these Chinese scholars are of the present generation.

[17] Hsieh Wu Liang, *Chung kuo cheh hsioh tsu*, or *History of Chinese Philosophy*, chap. 2, sect. 1.

[18] K'ang Yu-wei, *Hsin hsioh wei ching k'ao*, Vol. I. Quoted by Hu Shih.

[19] Ch'ui Shih, *Ssu chi t'an yuen*, Vol. III. Quoted by Hu Shih.

[20] 方士. Dr. Chiang K'ang-hu considers "adept" a better translation.

[21] Hu Shih, *Chung kuo cheh hsioh tsu*, chap. 12, sect. 3, pp. 384 f.

[22] Carter, *The Invention of Printing in China*, contains chapters on the part played by Buddhist and Taoist charms in the development of printing. Charms seem to have been the first things printed, and the oldest printed documents extant are Japanese Buddhist charms.

[23] *Mém. hist.*, Vol. II, p. 283.

[24] De Mailla, Vol. II, p. 435.

[25] *Ibid.*, p. 514, quoted by Cordier, *Hist. gén. de la Chine*, Vol. I, p. 222. It is Lu Chia who in this passage makes the first use of the famous Confucian argument which was so effective in the hands of Tung Chung-shu. "If the rulers of Ch'in had followed the canon . . . would the empire have fallen into your hands?"

[26] Takakuwa, *Chung kuo wen hua tsu,* a Chinese edition of his *Lectures on Chinese Civilization.* When Han Kao Tsu met a scholar, he urinated to show his contempt.

[27] Couvreur, *Li ki,* Vol. I, p. xii. Quoted by Cordier, Vol. I, p. 222.

[28] Huang Lao is a phrase combining the names *Huang Ti* ("Yellow Emperor") and *Lao Tzu.* It was the Han name for the book now called the *Tao teh ching.* Synonymous with "Taoism."

[29] A similar shortening of the names Han Fei and Shen Pu-hai, and here practically equivalent to the School of Law. For Han Fei and Shen Pu-hai, see Forke, *Geschichte chin. Phil.,* pp. 447, 461.

[30] Takakuwa, pp. 70, 72.

[31] De Mailla, Vol. II, p. 527. Cordier, Vol. I, p. 222.

[32] Takakuwa, p. 108.

[33] Chavannes, *Mém. hist.,* Introd., p. 50.

[34] Tso chuan. Legge, *Chinese Classics,* Vol. V, V, xix, 4; X, xi, 9.

[35] Tschepe, *Histoire du Royaume de Ts'in,* pp. 7, 57, etc., and De Groot, *Religious System of China,* Vol. II, sect. 9.

[36] *Mém. hist.,* Vol. II, p. 195.

[37] Legge, *Sacred Books of the East, Li ki,* Vol. XXVII, p. 201.

[38] *Mém. hist.,* Vol. I, pp. 59, 60, note 1.

[39] *Ibid.,* Vol. III, pp. 420, 422, 423.

[40] *Ibid.,* p. 449. There are two generally accepted lists of the five emperors. (a) That of the regular *annales,* Fu Hsi, Shennung, Huang Ti, Shao Hao, Chuan Hsiu, who was followed by Yao and Shun. Liu Hsiang accepts this list. (b) That of the *Bamboo Books,* which is accepted by Ssu-ma Ch'ien, of Huang Ti, Chuan Hsiu, K'u, Yao and Shun. *Mém. hist.,* Vol. I, Introd., p. 188 f.

[41] Doré, *Superstitions,* Vol. XII, pp. 1109-1114. Cordier, Vol. I, p. 221.

[42] *Mém. hist.,* Vol. III, pp. 457, 462.

CHAPTER III

HAN WU TI AND THE CONFUCIAN TRIUMPH

The reign of Han Wu Ti (141–87 B. C.) is one of the most important in the history of China. Externally it is marked by wars against the Hsiung-nu more or less successful, by the embassies of Chang Ch'ien which brought the Chinese into contact with the nations of Central Asia, and by expansion to the south. It is probable that there had been an increasing foreign influence and a resulting borrowing of foreign culture in China from the last days of the Chou period, as Chavannes has shown in the case of the musical tubes or pipes, which seem to have been of Greek origin and were introduced into China from Turkestan.[1] The journeys of Chang Ch'ien and the intercourse resulting from them not only widened the interest of the Chinese enormously, but resulted in noticeable changes in Chinese culture, such as the importation of foreign plants and animals. In the realm of ideas the most important result of this expansion was the eventual introduction of Buddhism, but this was later than the reign of Wu Ti. The suddenly increased interest in foreign peoples probably aided the eclectic spirit of the times, and was in turn fostered by it.[2]

Internally, the reign was marked by the formation and fixing of the Chinese state in approximately the form in which it was to survive until recent times. Without discounting the influence of Ch'in Shih Huang, it may be said that Wu Ti was the greatest single factor in the formation of a unified government and people.[3] Ch'in had destroyed the feudal system, substituting in its place political divisions called *chün* and *hsien,* the former including a number of the latter.[4] Although the Han emperors had revived a modified form of the feudal system, they had in general followed the administration of Ch'in, and Wu Ti strengthened the central government by appointing advisers who resided at the courts of the nobles, reporting to the emperor somewhat in the fashion of the *missi dominici* of Charlemagne or of the modern British residents at the courts of Indian princes. After 127 B. C. the fiefs were still further weakened

33

by allowing the lords to provide for their younger sons out of their patrimony.⁵ While the larger divisions of the empire have varied, the *hsien,* or districts, first established by Ch'in, have survived until the present. Numerous other internal policies of Wu Ti, such as the standardization of currency, need not be mentioned here.

In some directions Wu Ti continued the policy of Ch'in Shih Huang, even more than his predecessors, but in others he marks an entirely new departure. Of these changes the chief were his patronage of the Confucians and his adoption of certain Confucian principles of government. One of the essential Confucian political dogmas was that the wise or learned should be allowed an important share in the business of government.⁶ Another was that one became wise through study, that is, by the study of books under a properly qualified teacher. A third was that the books which should be studied were what had already come to be called the Five Canons: the *History,* the *Odes,* the *Book of Changes,* the *Rites* (sometimes the *Canon of Music*), and the *Spring and Autumn Annals.* It is the application of these three ideas which made the Chinese state peculiar, resulting in the most remarkable system of education that the world has known, considering the period during which it flourished and the results it achieved, and also in the distinctive position occupied by the scholar or educated man in Chinese society and in the state.⁷ If Wu Ti had merely been following Ch'in Shih Huang in his policy of a strong central government, he was widely at variance with. him in the adoption of these Confucian principles.

Wu Ti and Ch'in Shih Huang had some characteristics in common, and the situations which they faced were not entirely dissimilar. Both were men of great ability, showing understanding and determination. Both were able to select men of the highest caliber for their assistants. They were even alike in their weakness, for both were credulous to a degree. Each found himself the ruler of an enormous empire, which he realized could not be controlled by force alone, and each one had to deal with the Confucian party as representing an important section of public opinion. Each emperor called an assembly of scholars to advise him, but while Ch'in Shih Huang rejected that advice, Wu Ti accepted it, and was justified in the event.

In order to understand the difference in the action of the two rulers it is necessary to mention some differences as well as the similarities in the two situations. Of these the most important is the fact that Wu Ti had the advantage of time; that is, he had the benefit of Ch'in Shih Huang's experience. The Ch'in empire had gone to pieces immediately after its founder's death in a debacle so awful and complete as to leave little of Ch'in except the name. This argument was used with great force by the Confucians of the Han period and was of weight even with the earlier emperors who had been opposed to the Confucian doctrines. Su Sun-t'ung told Han Kao Tsu that if Ch'in had adopted the Confucian system, Kao Tsu would never have become emperor. Hui Ti had abolished the edict against the books, and both Wen Ti and Ching Ti had appointed Confucians to office, though opposed to their teaching. It remained for Tung Chung-shu to put the argument in its final form in his answers to the questions of Wu Ti. Ch'in had outraged public opinion in the frank immorality of its political principles, in the completeness of its departure from custom, in its opposition to education and the classic literature, and in the cruelty of its punishments. As a result, Ch'in had disappeared. In the time of Ch'in Shih Huang the argument was all the other way. Then Li Ssu could point to the fact that it was Ch'in which had adopted the principles of the School of Law and had conquered the empire with them. In the time of Wu Ti the Confucians could point to the destruction of Ch'in as a proof that its doctrines, while they might lead to success in time of war, could not safely be used as the basis of a permanent government.

In the second place, the emperor and the scholars were not so far apart in the days of Wu Ti as they had been under Ch'in Shih Huang. In the latter case the resentment due to the conquests of the semibarbaric state of Ch'in still existed, not only in the minds of the scholars, but in the fear of the emperor that the classic books and the feudal annals would keep sectional feeling alive. Under Wu Ti this condition had disappeared. The chief objection to the earlier emperor had originally been his failure to give fiefs to his family and supporters. This objection hardly applied to the Han rulers, who had brought back a modified form of the feudal system. Yet when Wu Ti attacked this system by permitting the lords to divide their land among their families, he does not appear to have aroused any protest from the Confucians. By the time of Wu Ti, the feudal system was no longer an issue with the literati; and in this, as in a number of other respects, the ideas of Ch'in Shih Huang eventually prevailed. The Han rulers were more careful of public opinion than the

Ch'in, and were not forced by circumstances into such sweeping innovations.

A third reason for the changes made by Wu Ti is to be found in his credulity. De Mailla begins the account of the reign of Wu Ti as follows:

"After the ceremonies of installation of Wu Ti and the funeral of his father . . . the young emperor,[8] impressed by the prodigies and unfavorable omens which had been so frequent in the last year of his predecessor, resolved to remedy the abuses of the government and to find a way of bringing the empire to its highest point of splendor." [9] The unusual phenomena included an eclipse, an earthquake, severe thunder-storms, and a red appearance of the sun and moon which lasted five days.[10] The five planets behaved in unexpected ways, and the moon traversed a constellation with which it was not usually in conjunction.[11]

It was the universal opinion in China, as in other ancient countries, that such phenomena constituted omens of tremendous importance and necessitated radical changes in the state if evil were to be averted. Moreover, the character of Wu Ti was particularly apt to be impressed by such omens. All his life he was given to excessive religious practices, he sought the elixir of life, and he patronized the Taoist adepts to such an extent that he allowed them to estrange him from the heir-apparent by an intrigue which eventually resulted in the death of the prince.[12] It was consistent for him to feel that these omens forced him into some new policy of state, and the most obvious change was the one he actually made, the reversal of the policy of his predecessors by the official adoption of the three Confucian ideas already mentioned. There is no reason for supposing that these prodigies were invented after the event, for the Chinese were very careful in their astronomical observations.

Another reason for the emperor's change of front was probably his own love of ceremony and ritual. "When the emperor Wu Ti took the power, he redoubled his attention to the sacrifices to the gods." [13] The treatise of Ssu-ma Ch'ien on the Feng and Shan sacrifices describes the elaborate sacrificial arrangements made by Wu Ti and his repeated ceremonies, which surpassed anything attempted by previous rulers.[14] Now Confucius himself had been noted for his care and attention to ceremonial, and an entire book of the *Analects* is devoted to a minute description of his behavior in such matters.[15] By the Han period, the sage was regarded as the last word on ritual, and even the Taoist Huai Nan Tzu refers to him as the perfect example of ritual correctness.[16] One of the distinguishing marks of the Confucian school had always been its emphasis upon propriety and the observance of the proper rules for behavior under any circumstances. A long list of instances might be made showing the extent to which the Confucians carried this principle, but perhaps one will be sufficient. Tzu Lu, the personal disciple of Confucius, was stabbed with such force that his cap fell off. He remarked, "The superior man does not allow his cap to be disarranged even in death," adjusted it once more, and died.[17] Hsün Tzu in particular had stressed the importance of *li,* or correct behavior, and his influence was predominant in the early Han period. The result was that the Confucians were the authorities whenever matters of ritual and ceremony were in question, and an emperor who loved these things would naturally turn to them for guidance.

Lastly, it may be noticed that the effect of the prohibitive policy of Ch'in Shih Huang and his successors seems to have had an opposite effect from the one intended. The Burning of the Books increased the interest in them, and even before the edict had been withdrawn, the attempt to recover them had commenced. The action of Lu Chia and Hsiao Ho under Han Kao Tsu has already been mentioned. It would be impossible here to attempt a study of the rising tide of Confucian sentiment under the Han rulers before Wu Ti, but one of the proscribed books may be taken as an illustration. The *Odes* had been burned, yet even before the accession of Wu Ti there were already four different texts of the *Odes* known. The first was that of a scholar of Lu named Hsin P'ei, who had many disciples, and who not only interviewed the first Han emperor, Kao Tsu, but survived until the reign of Wu Ti. The second was that of Yüan Ku, who was one of the *po shih* of Han Ching Ti. The third was that of Han Ying, who was a *po shih* of the emperor Wen Ti and wrote an explanation of the text. The fourth is the "Text of Mao," which eventually became the standard. Mao Heng was a pupil of Hsün Tzu, and he communicated the text of the *Odes* to another Mao, Mao Chang, who was a *po shih* at the court of Ho Chien Wang, a noble of the reign of Wu Ti. All these men founded schools.[18] This list of scholars might be greatly increased, but it can be seen that even before Wu Ti the tide of Confucianism was increasing instead of decreasing under rulers who had little interest in its doctrines or were opposed to them. Considering similar cases in history of the failure to suppress ideas by force and legal action, it may be assumed that the policy of Ch'in Shih Huang actually stimulated the Confucian movement and contributed to its eventual triumph.

The reasons which we may suppose influenced Wu Ti in his adoption of some of the Confucian ideas can be summarized in the order of their probable importance. First, the destruction of the Ch'in empire, which indicated that the principles upon which it was founded needed some change before they could be used as a basis for a permanent government. Second, the growing Confucian sentiment, which made what had been a party· in opposition under earlier rulers the logical group to which the ruler would turn if he made a change. Third, there was the character of Wu Ti himself, loving the ceremonies for which the Confucians were the chief authorities, and apt to be influenced by the unusual natural events which occurred just before his accession. Finally, there was the gradual lessening of the differences between the literati and the emperors, so that with the passage of time an adjustment became easier.

There is still a fifth reason given for the changes made by Wu Ti, and as it is a widespread opinion in China at the present time, it must be considered. This is, that Confucian doctrines were adopted by the emperor for purely political reasons, because they emphasized the subservience of subjects to the ruler, or in other words, that Confucianism was aristocratic, and increased the power and prestige of the emperor and the ruling class. It may be admitted that Confucianism is aristocratic, and that it not only considers the loyalty and obedience of a subject to his prince as one of the fundamental virtues, but assumes that all the common people need do is to follow the example and precepts of their superiors. But having admitted this, it remains improbable that the fact was of much influence in Wu Ti's decision. In the first place, it is a mistake to read into the minds of men of the second century B. C. the thoughts of the present generation when the struggle of social classes is so much discussed. There was no such dispute in the time of Wu Ti. In the second place, if Confucianism exalted the authority of the ruler, so did all the other systems which existed at the time. The chief opponents of the Confucians were the Legalists, and yet the School of Law made the emperor even more powerful than he would have been under a Confucian system of government. As a matter of fact, the Confucians required the emperor to possess the qualities decreed by Heaven for the position, Mencius, in particular, justifying the killing of the last ruler of the Yin dynasty because he did not live up to the standard, being a "thief and a ruffian." [19] It is not likely that Wu Ti abandoned the policy of his predecessors and of Ch'in Shih Huang because of the aristocratic nature of the Confucian doctrines.

On the other hand, it is quite likely that this fifth reason may have been a deciding factor in the minds of later emperors who supported Confucianism, particularly the Manchus. It may have influenced the late Empress Dowager, Tsu Hsi, in the honors she paid to Confucius, and have been behind the ardor of the monarchist K'ang Yu-wei in his advocacy of Confucianism as a state religion. The republican movement in China is suspicious of Confucianism, but it is a mistake to read these modern struggles back into a period when they did not exist.

It is always convenient for historians to assign the changes of history to definite dates and events, when in reality the changes are gradual and sometimes imperceptible. Chinese historians are not always above this temptation. In the present instance it is their custom to consider the changes made by Wu Ti as a sweeping reversal of policy. A more accurate statement would be, perhaps, that the changes made by Wu Ti in adopting Confucianism were somewhat like those made by Constantine when he adopted Christianity; that is, the strength of Confucianism, like that of Christianity, had been slowly growing until in each case the emperor simply made official a fact which was forced upon him by circumstances. This view does not, however, detract from the importance of the emperor's action in either case.

Neither is it fair to consider Wu Ti as only an opportunist, who took advantage of the strength of the Confucian party to ally himself with it. There is no evidence that Wu Ti was insincere in the limited adherence he gave to the Confucian doctrines, and it is likely that he really believed them to be capable of sustaining a government better than any others he knew.

What Wu Ti actually did was this. Shortly after he came to the throne, he collected the leading scholars of the empire together in a sort of advisory council. The emperor himself addressed the meeting three times, and the replies were made by Tung Chung-shu as the representative of the literati.[20]

The *Ch'ien Han shu* says, "Tung Chung-shu was a native of Kuang-chou. He devoted himself to the study of the *Spring and Autumn Annals,* the *Canon of Filial Piety,* and the *Odes,* acquiring fame as a scholar during the reign of Han Ching Ti. He taught many pupils and influenced numbers who did not even see him. His behavior and speech were always in accordance with the rules of propriety. The emperor Wu sought to collect the scholars of the country, and of these Tung Chung-shu was first." [21]

Tung Chung-shu does not seem to have been personally ambitious in politics, nor to have held great positions in the empire. He was the tutor of two of the young Han princes and produced remarkable improvements in their conduct. He also held a number of minor appointments, but on the whole preferred to devote his life to study and writing. His influence was not due to any position he held in the government, but solely to his personal character and to his reputation as a scholar and teacher. The fact that he was chosen to speak for the literati of the whole empire indicates the respect in which he was held by his contemporaries. His influence during the Western Han period may be indicated by the fact that more than 100 years later it was considered remarkable in Yang Hsiung that he did not imitate the style of Tung Chung-shu. His name is particularly associated with the *Spring and Autumn Annals,* upon which he wrote voluminously, and he is the chief figure in a period remarkable for the number and brilliancy of its scholars.[22]

One of the editors of the Ch'ien Lung edition of the *Twenty-four Histories,* Ch'i Shao-nan, after discussing various dates when the conference between Wu Ti and the scholars might have taken place, fixes on the year 136 B. c., four years after Wu Ti ascended the throne, when he was twenty years of age.[23] The effect of the conference may be described in the words of the *Ch'ien Han shu.*

"Following this discourse, the emperor appointed Tung Chung-shu to office. . . . He used *li* and *yi* [24] in advising the emperor, who had great respect for him. Order ruled throughout the land, and the emperor's commands were obeyed. During the long period of the influence of Tung Chung-shu, the teaching of Confucius was spread throughout the country and was understood by all men. Scholars were developed, schools established, and learning was patronized by the state. Tung Chung-shu was the cause of all this." [25]

The importance of these statements is not so much that they are true, as that they represent the official Chinese point of view. The emperor did not always take the advice of the Confucians. On the contrary he frequently ignored it, as in the search for the elixir of life.[26] Neither was there perfect order throughout the empire. The rebellion of Huai Nan Tzu occurred shortly after the conference.[27] It is impossible to believe that all men understood the teaching of Confucius, nor to forget that Tung Chung-shu was only one among a brilliant galaxy of scholars, all of whom contributed to the general result. Nevertheless the questions of Wu Ti and the replies of Tung Chung-shu constitute the most important single source for our understanding of the situation at the time of the adoption of Confucianism by the state.

An immediate result of the conference was the appointment of the *po shih* of the Five Classics in 136 B. C., the same year that Ch'i Shao-nan assigns as the date of the meeting.[28] There followed an intense interest in the recovery of the canonical texts, more intense because now the investigation was under the patronage of the emperor himself, and of great nobles like Huai Nan Wang, or Huai Nan Tzu, and Ho Chien Wang.[29] The recovery and fixing of the texts of the older literature lie outside this study, and even such romantic incidents as the finding of the old books in the wall of a house by K'ung An-kuo, a descendant of the sage, must be ignored.[30] Commentaries and explanations began to be written, great names of the past were assigned to more recent work, and what the scholars of the age lacked in originality they made up in diligence and in research which was not always critical. Some texts, like that of Mencius, caused little trouble,[31] while others, like the *Book of History,* are in dispute to the present day.[32] A vast reverence for the past became a style which lasted in China until the present generation and was one of the most marked characteristics of the country for 2,000 years, while the origins of almost any institution or custom were assigned to remote antiquity. The age was credulous, and even a scholar of the first rank, such as Ssu-ma Ch'ien, can hardly be used without confirmatory evidence. Sharp lines can no longer be drawn between different schools of thought, and writers borrowed ideas at random without acknowledgment. It was a period of brilliant achievement in almost every direction, setting precedents which have lasted almost to the present. Among the great names not already mentioned are Kung-sun Hung, Ssu-ma Hsiang Yü, Tung-fang So, Chu Mai-ch'en, and Mei Kao.

Tung Chung-shu seems to have had the confidence of two of the chief ministers of Wu Ti, and through them recommended two scholars, Chao Kuan and Wang Tsang, who were appointed to high office. But the Empress Dowager, who was partial to the doctrines of Taoism, intrigued against them so successfully that both were accused and executed. One of the ministers who had recommended them on Tung Chung-shu's advice was obliged to retire from public life temporarily, but after the death of the Empress Dowager in 135 B. C. he was recalled to power. This was the only check which the new policy of the emperor appears to have met.[33] From that time on members of the literati were established in high office.

The immediate result of the emperor's change of policy was an intense interest in the classics. A later development was the founding of schools in which the classics were studied, the examination of the graduates for appointment to official position, and eventually the opening of the highest civil offices in the state to men whose only qualification was scholarly attainment and mental ability.

Judged by either earlier or later standards, it is doubtful whether there were many pure Confucians during the Han period. There are at present in the Confucian temple, where the great disciples of all ages are honored, the names of eleven men of the Han period of 400 years. This is a small number, considering the large number of famous scholars who flourished during the period, and of these only four belong to the reign of Wu Ti. Of these eleven, seven are obviously placed in the temple because of the part they played in preserving and fixing the canonical texts. On the other hand, there are thirty-four names representing the 300 years of the Sung period. It has been said in criticism of the Sung Confucians that they departed from the interpretation of Confucianism current in the Han period. But it is also true that the Han Confucians, like the scholars of all the schools, were influenced by other lines of thought than those which descended from Confucius.

A large amount of scientific speculation was accepted by the Confucians, which may be illustrated by the theory of the elements developed by the school of Tsou Yen in the closing century of the Chou period,[34] although the Confucian school was not scientific. Han science was inextricably mixed with philosophy and religion in a manner which would have horrified Confucius. The theory of the Five Emperors, or *Ti,* which so far as we can tell was entirely unknown to Confucius, was not only accepted without protest by the

Confucians, but read back into a prehistoric period for which there was no evidence whatever in the Confucian classics. The elaborate sacrifices of Wu Ti, for which there was no precedent in the *Odes* and the *History,* and his recognition of new gods,[35] which was directly opposed to the teaching of the sage, were accepted without protest.

The *Book of Rites*—considered a Confucian classic, although a compilation of the Han period—contains a section, the *Monthly Observances,* which is almost identical with a section in the Taoist Huai Nan Tzu.[36] In it each season has a divine ruler, one of the Five *Ti,* with a secondary or attendant spirit. There is no authority for this in the ancient literature. Moreover, the use of the term *Shang Ti* in the plural [37] changes the monotheistic theory of the *Book of History* into polytheism.

The most striking change in the Confucianism of the Han period is that Confucius himself, who had said that to worship a spirit which does not belong to one is flattery,[38] was deified and worshiped, his disciples receiving sacrifices with him. All this shows the eclectic nature of the Confucianism of the Han period.

In spite of these new elements, the essential Confucian doctrines were preserved, and their adoption by the state may be said, on the whole, to have been permanent. In other words, the Confucian theory worked well in practice.

What did it add to the state which resulted in the relatively high and permanent civilization of China?

It produced a great literature, and a little later the Confucian Hsü Shen by his dictionary fixed the actual form of the language. The classical literature, expressed in ideographs which have not changed in 2,000 years and which are not written according to a fluctuating pronunciation, has been the greatest single preservative and unifying force in Chinese civilization. The Confucian classics, which became the subject of study in the schools, are of a singularly high moral standard, and the virtues which they teach are based on the fundamental institution of the family. While the Confucian ideal expressed in this literature may have hindered the development of science, its conservatism, its moral interpretation of history, and its insistence upon the five relationships has given the stability and permanence for which Chinese civilization is peculiar. The Chinese are not a homogeneous race, but include very diverse elements. That they appear unified to outsiders is owing largely to the effects of the language and literature to whose development and standardization the Confucians have made the greatest single contribution.[39]

The adoption of Confucianism by Wu Ti put into practice a theory which has often been dreamed of in other lands, but seldom realized, the participation of the wise and learned in the business of government. The later development of the schools and the system of public examinations for appointment to office created an intellectual aristocracy which did not stand aloof from public life, but put the best minds of the nation at the service of the state. High office and high education have been united in China to an extent never reached in any other country. Nearly all the thinkers in the history of China have also been practical men of affairs, and nearly all the military leaders and politicians have been men of culture. Perhaps a comparison with an incident of occidental history may bring out the point. The Englishman Wolfe, on the night before he captured Quebec, recited Gray's "Elegy." An American general would probably not have known of the poem's existence, and had he known, would have been unable to appreciate it. A Chinese general would have written the poem himself. This remarkable union of education, culture, and administrative ability, which has resulted in emperors who wrote creditable poetry, poets who planned campaigns and won battles, and philosophers who could administer a province, has been largely the result of the continued practice of the Confucian doctrines.

Takakuwa says, "Wu Ti was a genius, and his reign a period of prosperity. Since Ch'in Shih Huang, knowledge and art[40] had been neglected, while the theories of Huang Lao and Han Shen still predominated. When Wu became emperor, he summoned the scholars. He discouraged the study of the philosophers and revived Confucianism.[41] He founded the *T'ai hsioh*[42] and established the *po shih* of the Five Canons. He summoned many literary men to court. Huai Nan Wang and Ho Chien Wang Teh searched for the old books of Ch'in.[43] The reason *Hsioh shu*[44] did not flourish (before Wu Ti) was because of the late civil war and the resulting disorder, and when peace was restored, other things were more immediately important, so that the revival of the classics and literature lagged behind.[45]

"Under Wu Ti, Wei Kuan and T'ien Feng[46] became ministers. They persuaded the emperor to discard the doctrines of Huang Lao and Han Shen, and to respect the *Jü Hsioh* (the canon). Kung-sun

Hung and Tung Chung-shu, students of the *Spring and Autumn Annals,* revived the *T'ai hsioh* and the Five Canons. The Confucianists had charge of the examinations. Those who wrote books might offer them to the government, copyists were appointed to collect and copy the books . . . and the whole country encouraged the Confucians. An unfortunate result of this revival was the formation of many parties and schools of thought. However, the *Jü Hsioh* was established at this time." [47]

Lu Ssu-mien, in discussing the Confucianism of the Han period, says, "The reason for the predominance of the Confucians, according to modern scholars, was because Confucius knew the relation between ruler and subjects." That is, the Confucian system was satisfactory to a monarchy. Lu Ssu-mien disagrees with this view for two reasons: first, because the idea that Confucianism benefited a monarchy is a late idea, and was not current under the Han; second, because all the philosophic systems supported a monarchy, as all had been developed under a monarchical government.

"Wu Ti was in much the same position as Ch'in Shih Huang. Having secured the kingdom by war he could not keep it by war and summoned the scholars to secure peace. The Confucian system fostered education, and was therefore best suited to bring peace." [48] Lu Ssu-mien also emphasizes Wu Ti's love of ceremony. He concludes by remarking that later rulers simply followed the precedent of Wu Ti.

NOTES

[1] Chavannes, *Mém. hist.,* Vol. III, Appendice, 2, pp. 630 f. Besides his own researches, Chavannes reviews the work of Amiot, Van Aalst, and other European scholars in this field.

[2] For the importation of foreign plants into China see Laufer, *Sino-Iranica.* Hirth, *China and the Roman Orient,* treats of the general intercourse. For a discussion of the possible date of the introduction of Buddhism, see Pelliot, *Meou-tseu,* Chavannes, *To'ung Pao* (1905), pp. 546 f., and Maspero, "Le Songe de l'ambassade de l'empereur Ming," in the *Bull. de l'Ecole françoise,* Vol. X, pp. 95 f. Han emperors after Wu Ti regularly imported Persian horses. It is very difficult to show the diffusion of ideas. Chavannes is of the opinion that in addition to the musical tubes, it is likely that the calendar as reformed by Wu Ti and the practice of alchemy had a western origin. See also Cordier, *Hist. gén.,* Vol I, pp. 224 f.

[3] Compare Seufert, "Urkunden zur staatlichen Neuordnung unter der Han-Dynastie," *Mitteilungen des Seminars für Orientalische Sprachen* (1922), p. 3.

[4] 郡縣.

[5] Cordier, pp. 238, 224.

[6] Seufert, *op. cit.,* p. 3. See also Franke, *Studien zur Geschichte des konfuzianischen Dogmas und der chinesischen Staatsreligion.*

[7] The founding of the schools and the examinations for the selecting of officials are described in chap. V.

[8] Wu Ti was sixteen when he mounted the throne.

[9] De Mailla, Vol. III, p. 1.

[10] De Mailla, Vol. II, p. 590.

[11] Ssu-ma Ch'ien, chap. 11, gives these other events. The thunder-storm was considered a prodigy because it occurred in February. Chavannes, *Mém. hist.,* Vol. II, p. 508, note 4.

[12] *Ch'ien Han shu,* chap. 6. De Mailla, Vol. III, pp. 83 f.

[13] Ssu-ma Ch'ien, chap. 12. Chavannes, Vol. II, p. 511.

[14] Ssu-ma Ch'ien, chap. 28. Chavannes, Vol. III, pp. 413 f. See also the *Hou Han shu,* chap. 17, p. 2, translated by Chavannes in *Le T'ai Chan,* pp. 158 f. Wu Ti is even said to have imported the elephant and the rhinoceros for sacrifices.

[15] *Analects,* Bk. 10.

[16] *Huai Nan Tzu,* Bk. 12. De Harlez, *Textes taoistes,* p. 205, *Annales du Musée Guimet,* Vol. XX.

[17] *Tso chuan,* Ai Kung, fifteenth year. Translated by Legge, *Chinese Classics,* Vol. V, Pt. 2, p. 843.

[18] This summary is taken from Legge, *Shi King,* Prolegomena, pp. 9-12.

[19] Mencius, I, 2, 8.

[20] *Ch'ien Han shu,* chap. 56. See also De Mailla, Vol. III, pp. 2 f., for a somewhat different version.

[21] Introduction to chap. 56 of the *Ch'ien Han shu.*

[22] Besides the account of Tung Chung-shu in chap. 56 and references to him in other places in the *Ch'ien Han shu,* as in chap. 6, the annals of the reign of Wu Ti, there are articles on him in the *Chung kuo jen ming ta tsu tien,* a Chinese biographical dictionary, p. 1311; in Giles, *Chin. Biog. Dict.,* p. 791; in Mayers, *Chinese Reader's Manual,* p. 224, etc.; and an account in De Mailla, Vol. III, pp. 2 f.

[23] Quoted by Seufert, p. 5.

[24] 禮誼. It is difficult to render these characters into English. The first may be translated as "correct behavior," the second as "what is proper and right," or as "friendly intercourse."

[25] This is the conclusion of chap. 56 of the *Ch'ien Han shu.*

[26] Compare the story in De Mailla (Vol. III, p. 22) of the minister who broke in upon Wu Ti's experiment and drank the elixir of life himself, maintaining that if the elixir were genuine, he could not be punished, while if it were false, he should be rewarded for exposing it.

[27] The date of the suicide of Huai Nan Tzu is disputed, Mayers gives the year 122 B.C., but De Harlez gives two dates, 91 and 87 B.C.

[28] Chavannes, *Mém. hist.,* Vol. II, Appendice 1, p. 515.

[29] There are biographies of both these men in the *Ch'ien Han shu* and in the *Chung kuo jen ming ta tsu tien,* and accounts in European works like De Harlez, *Textes taoistes,* pp. 171 f., and Legge, *Shi King,* Prolegomena, p. 11.

[30] See Legge, in the Prolegomenas to his translations of the *Book of History* in the *Chinese Classics* and the *Sacred Books of the East.* The *Ch'ien Han shu* gives a biography of K'ung An-kuo, and there are notices in general books like Giles and Mayers. It is very doubtful whether at present we have K'ung

An-kuo's version of the *History,* that which goes by his name being probably a later forgery.

[31] See Legge, *Chinese Classics,* Prolegomena to Vol. II.

[32] There is a good discussion of the textual problems connected with the *History* in Vol. I of Chavannes, *Mém. hist.,* chap. 3 of the Introduction, although it does not give the latest views of Chinese scholars.

[33] Slightly different versions of this incident are given in Chavannes, *Mém. hist.,* Vol. III, pp. 461 f., and De Mailla, Vol. III, pp. 7 f.

[34] Forke, *Chin. Phil.,* pp. 503 f.; Chavannes, *Mém. hist.,* Vol. I, Introd., p. 144. Wilhelm finds in Tung Chung-shu a combination of Taoist natural philosophy and Confucianism (*Chinese Civilization,* p. 172).

[35] For instance, the "Princess of the Spirits," *Mém. hist.,* Vol. III, p. 462, and his sacrifices to the T'ai Yi, or Great Unity, *ibid.,* pp. 466 f. See Wilhelm (*Chinese Civilization,* p. 171), who sees evidence of influence from the south.

[36] The *Yueh Lin,* or *Monthly Observances,* of the *Book of Rites,* is almost identical with Book 5 of Huai Nan Tzu, the *Shih Tzu,* or *Law of Time.*

[37] *Mém. hist.,* Vol. I, pp. 59, 60, note 1. *Shang Ti* is singular in the ancient texts, and the Han and later commentators identify it with the polar star, but it is used in the plural in connection with the late theory of the Five Emperors.

[38] *Analects,* II, 24.

[39] Compare Chi Li, *Formation of the Chinese People,* chaps. 6 to 8.

[40] 學術. It is difficult to render these two words into English. *Hsioh* usually means "to study" or "learning," and *shu* usually means "methods," but the phrase as a whole signifies "culture."

[41] 儒學. *Jü Hsioh,* the Chinese name for classical learning or the Confucian school.

[42] 太學. A school or college.

[43] See the biographies of Huai Nan Tzu and Ho Chien Wang in the *Ch'ien Han shu,* chaps. 44 and 53, respectively.

[44] It is preferable to use the romanized characters for this difficult phrase. See note 40.

[45] Takakuwa, pp. 72 and 95.

[46] The two ministers already mentioned as the friends of Tung Chung-shu.

[47] Takakuwa, p. 108 f.

[48] Lu Ssu-mien, Vol. II, p. 77.

CHAPTER IV

Tung Chung-shu on the Art of Government [1]

The emperor Wu said, "I have received the throne from the former rulers, and I should put their principles into practice, but the responsibility is so great that I cannot sleep. I wish to perfect the state, and so I collect the scholars and the loyal men of the country to discuss thoroughly the Great Principle.[2] I am happy that you have come to advise me.

"I have heard concerning the *Tao* of the Five Emperors and the three kings, that they governed peacefully and without disagreement among the lords, while music was heard throughout the land. In the time of Chieh and Tsou this *Tao* was lost, and there was much disorder.[3] During 500 years scholars tried to bring back into practice the principles of the ancient kings, but the evil was too great, and at last the government was destroyed. This was decreed by Heaven.

"My endeavor is to decrease punishments that evil may become less. Then the people will be happy, harvests good, and virtue will extend to the corners of the four seas. You know the *Tao* of the ancient rulers better than I. Reveal it to me and conceal nothing. Help me to adopt the good and correct the evil, so that a good government may be created for future generations. Do your best, hide nothing from me, and I myself will diligently examine these things."

Tung Chung-shu replied, "Your majesty's words are righteous. You wish to search the decrees of Heaven and to know the condition of the people. In these endeavors no one can compare with you, and I can only give you my knowledge of former times, gained by the study of the *Spring and Autumn Annals*. By applying the principles of this book to the present, I observe that the government is not satisfactory, so that we may be unable to obtain or keep *Tao*. Famine and other calamities occur, sent by Heaven as a punishment. Our leaders do not realize this, and ascribe disasters to evil influences, for they cannot see the kind and loving heart of Heaven. If you wish to make the country peaceful, you must do your best, and try to understand all things. Follow *Tao,* and *Teh* will increase.[4]

"In the *Odes* it is said, 'Never be idle, early or late.' [5]

"And in the *Canon of History*, 'Be zealous, be zealous!' [6]

"These quotations illustrate my meaning.

"*Tao* is the way by which man succeeds. Benevolence, righteousness, correct behavior, and music are the tools of *Tao*.[7] The ancient rulers died, but because of their principles, their descendants enjoyed peace for hundreds of years. The causes of this were correct behavior, music, and education.[8]

"An emperor must know how to use the music of former rulers, for it is the music of virtue.[9] Such music can change customs and educate the people. It came from harmony between the people and their rulers. Why is it that although the rulers prefer peace and hate disorder, disorders continue? It is because the right men are not used, and no one knows how to apply *Tao*. At the close of the Chou period the government was weak, not because *Tao* did not exist, but because the ruler did not know how to apply it.

"Confucius said, 'Man can increase the degree to which *Tao* is applied, but *Tao* cannot apply itself.' [10] Therefore the prosperity of the country depends upon us. It does not depend upon the decree of Heaven, for even that can be changed.

"I have heard that great men appear by the decree of Heaven, the people coming to them as children go to their parents. That the people adhere to a man is a sign of his success.

"In the *Canon of History* it is said, 'The fish jumped into the boat.' [11] Such signs [12] show the appointment of Heaven.

"Thus Chou Kung says, 'Heaven rewards him.' [13]

"And Confucius, 'If the ruler is righteous, he receives a reward from Heaven.' [14]

"These things occurred because the ruler was good and virtuous. In later generations the state decayed, and the kings could not control the nobles. The teaching of virtue was abandoned, and cruel punishments were instituted. Even this was a failure, until the morale of the state was ruined, while evil accumulated before the eyes of Heaven. If the ruler and the people do not agree, the harmony of *Yin* and *Yang* will be disturbed, and evils will arise, famines and disturbances.

"Confucius said, 'The virtue of a superior man is like the wind, while the virtue of an inferior man is like the grass. The movement of the grass follows the motion of the wind.' [15]

"Yao and Shun practised virtue, and therefore the inferior men became benevolent and long-lived. The superior men educate the inferior men, who listen to their instruction, and are like clay in the hands of a potter, or gold under the working of a smith.

"I have studied in the *Spring and Autumn Annals* what a great ruler should be. The essential is uprightness. The ruler follows uprightness, and is close to Heaven. The principle of government is to follow the action of Heaven by governing with uprightness, for the ruler must act as Heaven acts.[16]

"The *Tao* of Heaven summons the *Yin* and the *Yang*. *Yang* signifies virtue, while *Yin* signifies punishment or killing. To emphasize virtue is to aid growth. *Yang* is the source of life in the spring, while *Yin* destroys in the fall. From this we can see that Heaven also emphasizes *Yang*. *Yang* is used to give life, and is assisted by *Yin*, for without *Yin*, *Yang* is not complete. The ruler merely carries out the intention of Heaven, and so he should endeavor to develop virtue and education, not depending upon punishment. To depend upon punishment would be like relying upon *Yin* to give growth during the course of the seasons. A state which relies only upon punishment opposes Heaven, and therefore the great rulers of ancient times were opposed to punishment. On the other hand, recent rulers have abolished education and the teaching of virtue, and have established a ministry of punishments, which shows on what they depended.[17]

"Confucius said, 'If you punish without educating the people, that is cruelty.'[18]

"A year is a unit, and exhibits the greatness of all things.[19] It must have a foundation of unity, in order that all may prosper, and therefore a ruler of men, like the year, must unify his heart, making it upright, for if his heart is rectified, the state will have unity and uprightness. Then the officials will follow his example, the people also, until the whole world will be upright and things far and near will possess unity. In such a land, evil will hardly appear, *Yin* and *Yang* will be harmonized, wind and rain will come at the right seasons, while life will be peaceful and the people settled in good order. Harvests will be plentiful, even the grass and trees will flourish, and the whole world will be richly nourished.

"The four seas have heard of the great virtue of your majesty. Sages and great men come to you. This is the sign of the *Tao* of a ruler.

"Confucius said, 'The phoenix does not appear, the river sends no plan. It is a sign of my end.'[20]

"Your majesty controls all within the four seas, having great authority and power, as well as ability. Your actions are high, and your grace abundant. You understand clearly, while your intention is good. You love the people and respect scholars, so that you may be called the ideal ruler.

"Yet this is not enough. Education is needed, for without education you cannot make the people upright. They are selfish and seek their own profit, as water seeks its level.[21] You must educate them, even as you build a dam to stop the flow of water. If you establish education, evil will vanish; while if you abolish education, evil will grow, and even punishments will not prevent it; for the dam will be broken. The ancient rulers knew this, and so they emphasized education as the first duty of a government. They established colleges in the capital and schools in the district cities. They turned the people gradually toward benevolence, stimulated what was right, and modeled them by good customs. Therefore they had little need of punishment, and the people observed the law. Education was general, and the customs were beautiful. When a righteous ruler ascends the throne, evil customs are swept away, and wrong practices eliminated.

"Reinforce education. When education is well established, the ruler and his descendants will be prosperous. This is why the Chou dynasty had five or six hundred years of prosperity. Toward the close of the dynasty the principle was lost, and so the government was destroyed. Ch'in succeeded Chou, and did not change the bad administration. Indeed, it actually became worse, because Ch'in abolished education, closed the schools, burned the books, and destroyed the mores of the people,[22] trying to do away with the *Tao* of the ancient sages. They were proud of their own ability, yet they ruled only fourteen years and then their government perished. In all history there have been no such evils as those which filled the time of Ch'in. The wickedness has not been cleansed away even now, and the government is still rotten.

"Confucius said, 'Rotten wood cannot be carved, and excrement cannot be used to make bricks.'[23]

"Han has succeeded Ch'in. If you wish to reform the state, which is in such a condition, you must find a way to eliminate the evil. Be careful, or you will be like one who tries to cool hot soup by adding boiling water, or like one carrying burning wood to beat out a fire.

Here is a stringed instrument of music with its strings disordered and broken. To obtain music from it, one must restring the instrument. The state needs to be reformed, and without a complete reformation even a sage can do nothing. From the beginning of the Han there has been little change.

"As the ancients said 'You stand beside the water, looking at the fish. Better go back and make a net.' [24]

"This dynasty has already ruled for more than seventy years. If you do not wish things to continue in their present condition, you must reform the government; for when the government is good, there will be no disturbances, and happiness and blessings will come to you.

"The *Odes* say, 'Things suitable to the people bring happiness from Heaven.' [25]

"Your majesty has attempted to reform the government, trying to free the state from disease. Happiness and prosperity are gradually increasing. Therefore these five virtues, benevolence, righteousness, correct behavior, wisdom, and faith,[26] should be practised by every ruler; and if you do this, you will receive blessings from Heaven and from the spirits, while your good administration will spread to the four corners of the world, and all will be benefited."

When the emperor heard this, he was greatly surprised and said, "I have often heard that Yao and Shun governed easily. It seemed as if they did nothing, and yet the land had peace. On the other hand, in the days of the Chou, Wen Wang worked day and night without sleep,[27] and again the land had peace. Are there different ways of governing? Why should some have rest, while others labored always, and what was the difference between them? During the time of Ch'eng and K'ang,[28] no punishments were inflicted for forty years and the prisons were empty, while under the Ch'in many punishments were inflicted and multitudes were killed. What is the weakness of punishment?

"I have a great responsibility and think on these things day and night. I try to be worthy of my great predecessors by making the state strong. In order to do this I must use the scholars and employ great ministers. I myself plough the field that I may set an example to the farmers.[29] I practise filial piety and brotherly love, I comfort those who labor, and I am merciful to the poor and to orphans. Even though I do these things, it seems as if good and evil were still mingled in the state like the *Yin* and *Yang* throughout the universe, and few are relieved. I seek the reason, and you scholars, who know the past and the present, should tell me all, for then we can discuss these things together without concealment."

Tung Chung-shu replied, "I have heard that Yao and Shun received the decree of Heaven, taking it as a responsibility, and not for their own pleasure. They exiled or killed evil men, and employed good men and sages. Thus they secured great ministers to help them govern. With such helpers education was developed, the land became prosperous and the people peaceful. Charity and happiness abounded, while the behavior of all was according to propriety and the *Tao* of the mean.

"Therefore Confucius said, 'When a good ruler ascends the throne, a generation is needed in order to make the government good.' [30]

"When Yao had been on the throne seventy years, he gave the power to Shun. The throne did not pass to his son, because the people followed a good man. Shun used Yü. He enjoyed peace because his state had already been organized by Yao. On the other hand, Tsou disobeyed Heaven and was cruel, killing great men and maltreating the people. Such men as Po Yi and T'ai Kung [31] retired from the government, while good men fled to the sea. The state fell into disorder, and the people were in danger. For this reason the nation was taken from Yin and given to Chou. Wen Wang obeyed Heaven and treated great men as his teachers, so that they gathered around him, serving in the government. As he loved the people, the country came to him naturally. That is why T'ai Kung fought for Chou. At that time Tsou was still on the throne, dreaming and bewildered in the midst of disorder. The people were in distress, and there was pain in the heart of Wen Wang, so he arose to pacify the country. That was why he worked so hard. Later Confucious wrote the *Spring and Autumn Annals,* recording all things, in order to show the righteousness of the uncrowned rulers. [32]

"I have heard that the details of the government show the difference between the ability to govern and the lack of it. It is like a knowledge of values. During the time described in the *Spring and Autumn Annals,* the customs were changed, while the palaces and banners showing rank had to be regulated by law. This shows the change from earlier times.

"Fine jade without carving is nevertheless beautiful, and there

are men among the people who have wisdom without receiving a
formal education, but common jade needs carving.

"A good emperor tries to learn while he is still young, so that
when he becomes mature, he will be able to employ the right men,
and undertake the responsibility for the state. High position is an
opportunity to display virtue.

"Your majesty wishes to secure scholars. The way to do this is to
establish an imperial academy,[33] for then there will be a place to
develop and attract them. Schools are the means of education. If a
province has many people, but few who study, the *Tao* of the ruler
will disappear. I beg your majesty to establish an imperial academy
and bring great scholars to teach the people. Give examinations
in order to select the best, and you will be able to secure learned men.
The governor of a province and the magistrate of a district are the
teachers of their people, and they should encourage the spread of
education. If these teachers are not efficient, education will not develop, and your principles will not reach the people. When there are
no able officials, the people will receive less and less education, and
the officials will resort to cruelty in order to preserve order. The
people will become poor, weak, and without means of employment.
Then disturbances will occur, which you do not want, while even the
Yin and *Yang* will be confused. These troubles will be due to the
lack of educated officials.

"In ancient days, Yao and Shun worked hard at all times in order
to train men for service in the government and to employ the right
men as officials. The positions to which men were appointed depended upon their ability. I beg your majesty to examine my words."

The emperor said, "I have heard that if one is to speak concerning Heaven, he must first know men. If one speaks about the
ancients, he must first know the present.[34] I have examined the
records of the ancient rulers, both good and bad, trying sincerely to
reform the state. You ministers have knowledge of the principles
of *Yin* and *Yang*.[35] You are familiar with the doctrines of the sages,
yet it seems that our knowledge is not adequate for the present
situation. The principles of the three dynasties were different each
from the others, and none was complete. If their principles endured
so long without change, it was because of *Tao*. We will discuss *Tao*
only, then. It can be both constructive and destructive. We should
have information about *Tao,* study it, grasp it, and put it into
practice.

"In the *Odes* it is said, "The ruler should not seek his own comfort. He should hold *Tao* and practise it, for then the spirits will listen to him and help him.' [36]

"I will be such a ruler, and you ministers should understand this *Tao*."

Tung Chung-shu replied, "I have heard that Tzu Hsia said, as recorded in the *Analects,* 'To have a beginning and an end, that is the sage.' [37]

"Your majesty has been so good as to listen to your scholars and ministers. You have examined their words, as well as the examples of former times. We cannot compare with you.

"You speak of those who know Heaven because they know men, and of those who know the ancients because they know the present. I understand Heaven as the origin [38] of all things, which it covers and holds. It created the sun, moon, rain, and wind, that they should be in harmony with Heaven. It made *Yin* and *Yang,* winter and spring. The sages are merely the agents who exhibit Heaven and establish *Tao,* cultivate universal love and destroy selfishness. They spread virtue and benevolence, and increase love. They develop what is right and correct behavior as a way leading to love.[39]

"Spring is the time of growth, corresponding to benevolence, which is the practice of love.[40] Summer is the time of maturity, and corresponds to virtue, which is a form of nourishment. Frost is fatal, while punishment also is a killing. The principles of nature and those of government are the same. *Tao* is the principle of Heaven and of man.[41]

"When Confucius wrote the *Spring and Autumn Annals,* he examined Heaven above and man below, the past and the present. If you understand the *Spring and Autumn Annals,* you can understand present conditions. In this book are found accounts of disturbances, evil customs, strange signs, and the mistakes of governments. You can study the actions of men, good and bad, like the progress of the seasons.

"In ancient times there was a ministry of education, and the people were educated with virtue and goodness. If the people were educated, the prisons would be empty. Now such education is neglected, the people abandon good behavior and work only for selfish ends and profit. Accordingly, punishments are heavy, so that in one year many thousands are imprisoned, and we cannot use the ancient methods of government.

"A real ruler simply listens to Heaven and follows its decree. He educates the people continually and upholds the law in order to maintain the distinctions of the social order. Listen to Heaven, educate the people, and enforce good laws. If you can do these three things, the foundation on which you build will be strong.

"The man who has received the decree of Heaven [42] is separated from other men. He should have the proper attitude toward his family, while he must deal kindly with his ministers and with the people. He must be reverent to the aged, generous to youth, dignified and courteous to all men. Such a man is superior, and he is nourished by Heaven.

"Confucius says in the *Book of Filial Piety,* 'Heaven gives life, and of all the forms of life, the highest is man.' [43]

"If you know the nature of Heaven, you know that as a man you are superior to all other living species. Realizing this, you will know benevolence and righteousness, and will emphasize correct behavior and conformity to one's position in society.[44] Then you will be in harmony with *Tao* and in accord with the law of the universe.[45] You will be called a superior man.

"Confucius said, 'If you do not know the will of Heaven, you cannot be called a superior man.' [46]

"I have heard that great things come from the accumulation of small ones. The sages thoroughly master principles and then examine details. In this way Yao and Shun rose from small beginnings to become rulers. It was not done in one day, but gradually. What a great man does affects every one, because he has mastered detail.

"The *Odes* say, 'Wen Wang was always careful in his daily routine, Yao practised his *Tao,* and Shun continued his filial piety.' [47]

"Accumulate goodness, and your name will be great, your virtue will increase, and you will be of value. This is the *Tao* to prosperity. The slow growth of goodness may be imperceptible, like the evaporation of oil, and unless you examine details, you will not notice it. This is why Yao became a great ruler, and Tsou a bad one. Tsou employed evil advisers, killed good men, and as a result evil increased day by day until the government was in disorder, yet still he thought of himself as the sun in the sky. The end was the destruction of the government, and its weakness was not produced in one day. Even in times devoted to pleasure, order should be maintained. This is called *Tao,* and the opposite of *Tao* is trickery.[48] When there is no trickery for 10,000 generations, that is *Tao.*

"The *Tao* of the ancient rulers spread over all, but if the government is not wise in its administration, *Tao* cannot be manifested. The anicent rulers developed *Tao* in order to suppress trickery. That the *Tao* of the three dynasties differed was not because *Tao* changes, but because it must be applied differently under different circumstances. The three dynasties all made the people upright, following the decree of Heaven. If you do this, the other things that you desire will follow naturally. Why should we change the *Tao* of Yao? There is no need. The form of administration may change, but the principle (*Tao*) never changes.

"Confucius said, '*Yin* followed the ritual of Hsia; wherein it took away or added may be known. Chou followed the ritual of *Yin*; wherein it took away or added may be known.' [49]

"You must realize that *Tao* comes from Heaven,[50] and since Heaven does not change, *Tao* does not change either. Yü followed Shun, as Shun followed Yao, but there was one *Tao* for all. In times of disorder *Tao* was lost.

"Your majesty is seeking to restore the *Tao* of the great rulers, using scholars as your advisers. In my judgment, the present does not differ essentially from the past. Good increases and evil diminishes without effort in times of peace. If the ruler be blessed, the people should have happiness also, according to their degree. But if you are not satisfied with what you have and endeavor to take away the possessions of the people, you will be cruel. When the people are impoverished and disorders arise, you will be forced to resort to punishments.

"The nobles should be satisfied with what they have, and the people also should have their share. This is the *Tao* of Heaven and of the ancients. Adopt this principle yourself, and the nobility will follow, while if the ruling class loves to deal rightly, the people will do likewise. On the other hand, if you and the nobility think only of your own profit, the people will be corrupted; for the emperor and the great officials are examples for the people.

"To think of your own benefit is the characteristic of the inferior man, while to seek righteousness is the mark of a great man. At present every one has his own idea of what should be done and of what *Tao* is, while the emperor does not know how to choose among them. Even the ministers of state do not understand the principles of the canonical books, and the teachings of Confucius are mistakenly applied in such a way as to destroy *Tao*.

"My meaning is that all that is not in the six sciences [51] and the canon of Confucius should be discouraged, and the teaching and spread of these doctrines hindered, in order that false and corrupted principles may be stopped. Then the general guidance can be uniform, and classifications clear. The people will know what is expected of them."

The replies of Tung Chung-shu are typically Confucian. The interpretation of history as showing the will of Heaven, the position of Heaven itself as a monotheistic principle, the denial of fatalism, the close connection between the actions of men and natural events, the emphasis on education and the position of scholars in the government, the importance of the virtues, and the repeated statement that punishments are a failure as a means of bringing peace, are all characteristic Confucian doctrines. The use of education as a correction of man's inherent selfishness is clearly traceable to Hsün Tzu. Tung Chung-shu makes much of the failure of the theories of the School of Law as practised by Ch'in, more than is apparent in this translation, for many of his historical illustrations have been omitted. It was the Legalists who insisted on severe punishments, and who opposed both education and common-sense morality. The document is also valuable as showing the ancient Chinese ideas of the state. The influence of Meh Ti is obvious in the paragraph on universal love and the creation of all things by Heaven. The use of the word *Tao* is Confucian and not Taoist, and the righteous rulers used as examples are those mentioned in the *Book of History*. In the last paragraph Tung Chung-shu states clearly the principle which was soon after put into practice in the government system of educaton, that nothing but the Confucian writings should be encouraged and taught. The result of this was the oblivion of important thinkers like Meh Ti until very recent times and the sterility of Chinese thought for a long period. The position of the scholar was exalted, but only that of the orthodox scholar, and the most brilliant man of the Han period, Wang Ch'ung, received neither encouragement nor attention. He had the hardihood to criticize Confucius.[52] Yet it is obvious that the ethical ideal of Tung Chung-shu was very high, and that his arguments were effective speaks well both for Wu Ti and for Chinese civilization.

The *Ch'ien Han shu* was begun by Pan Piao, who died in A. D. 54, continued by his son Pan Ku, who is generally considered the author, and completed by his daughter, Pan Chao, after the death of Pan Ku in A. D. 92.[53] There is no reason why important speeches like those of Wu Ti and Tung Chung-shu, even though they were made 200 years before the *Ch'ien Han shu* was actually written, should not have been carefully preserved. The ideal picture of education under the early rulers given by Tung Chung-shu, however, does suggest the *Chou Li,* or *State Handbook of the Chou Dynasty,* which appears to have been unknown to the writers of the second century B. C., and which modern scholars consider to have been composed or edited from earlier material during the time of Wang Mang about the beginning of the Christian era.[54] Pan Ku was at one time impeached on the grounds that he had falsified history, but was released through the influence of his brother, the famous general Pan Ch'ao.

NOTES

[1] This chapter is an abridged translation of chap. 56 of the *Ch'ien Han shu,* or *History of the Former Han Dynasty.* The passages omitted are mainly historical references and illustrations, or elaborations of the argument. Portions of the chapter have been translated into French by Du Halde, *Description ....* *de l'Empire de la Chine,* Vol. II, pp. 474 f.; Wieger, *Textes historiques,* Vol. I, pp. 453 f.; and De Mailla, Vol. III, pp. 2 f., who gives a version found in the *T'ung chien kang mu.* The chapter has been translated into German by Pfizmaier, *Sitzungsberichte der phil.-hist. Klasse der Kaiserl. Akademie der Wissenschaften zu Wien,* Vol. XXXIX, pp. 345 f., and by Seufert, in *Mitt. des Sem. für Orientalische Sprachen,* 1922, pp. 1 f. This English translation was made independently and then compared with Seufert and De Mailla.

[2] 大道. Seufert translates this difficult term here by *Grundgesetz,* and elsewhere by *Norm, Princip* and *Weg.* The *Tsu yüan* gives thirteen different meanings for the word *tao.* In this translation it has sometimes been rendered as "principle," but the word *tao* is usually retained, as it is a technical term of Chinese philosophy, and the meaning is usually made clear by the context.

[3] The last rulers of the Hsia and Yin dynasties, respectively, used as bad examples in the *Book of History.*

[4] This distinction between *tao* 道 and *teh* 德 is Taoist rather than Confucian, and is based on the *Tao teh ching* of Lao Tzu. *Tao* is the principle, and *teh* the manifestation of the principle in behavior. *Teh* usually means "virtue," or "good qualities," and in other places has been so translated.

[5] *Odes,* Legge, *Chinese Classics,* Vol. IV, p. 543. The references to the Odes and the *History* are to the paging of Legge in Vols. IV and III, respectively, of the *Chinese Classics,* where both the Chinese text and the translation are given. This translation is independent, and does not always follow Legge.

[6] *History,* p. 74.

[7] The virtues as the tools of *tao* is Confucian, and not Taoist, usage.

[8] 教化. Seufert translates *chiao hua* as two terms, *Lehre und Bildung.* It is really a phrase with a single meaning, and here has been translated as "education."

[9] See D. L. Phelps, "The Place of Music in the Platonic and Confucian Systems of Moral Education," *Jour. N. China Branch of the R. A. S.,* Vol. LIX, p. 128 f. The Confucians considered music to have a close connection with morals, and to have an elevating or degenerating influence, depending on its character.

[10] *Analects,* XV, 28. This famous passage has always offered difficulties in translation, and the versions of Legge, Soothill, Ku Hung Ming, Couvreur, and Zottoli are unsatisfactory. The translations of Legge and Soothill do not make good sense, and the latter apologizes for the "apparently fallacious aphorism" (Soothill's *Analects,* p. 754). This translation is based on Chu Hsi's commentary, and certainly seems to be the meaning of Tung Chung-shu. Seufert translates *tao* here by *Wahrheit.*

[11] This quotation is not in the present text of the *Book of History,* but occurs in chap. 4 of Ssu-ma Ch'ien (Chavannes, *Mém. hist.,* Vol. I, p. 226). The story is that while Wen Wang, the founder of the Chou dynasty, was crossing a river, a white fish jumped into his boat. White was the color of the Yin rulers, and the incident was taken to mean that the kingdom would fall into the hands of Wen Wang, as eventually happened.

[12] 符, *Fu,* a wooden tally. The piece of wood was divided into two equal parts, and when these were held together and matched perfectly, it was a guarantee of the authority of the bearer. Here the meaning is that when unusual events are followed by changes in the state, the omens are indications of the will of Heaven. This is a characteristic Confucian doctrine.

[13] This quotation is not in the present text of the *Book of History.*

[14] *Analects,* IV, 25.

[15] *Analects,* XII, 19. This quotation shows the essentially aristocratic nature of Confucianism.

[16] There is also a comparison between the uprightness of the ruler and the action of Heaven through the beginning of the year with the spring, which seems forced to a modern mind. The Chinese make a close connection between the government of the state and the progress of the seasons.

[17] This is an attack on the School of Law. The paragraph is a typical example of ancient Chinese reasoning.

[18] *Analects,* XX, 2, 3.

[19] Seufert (p. 22, note 5) gives a somewhat different version of this difficult passage.

[20] *Analects,* IX, 8.

[21] This is the well-known doctrine of Hsün Tzu, that the nature of man is evil. Hsün Tzu, chap. 23. Dubs, *Works of Hsuntze,* p. 301 f.

[22] 禮 . *Li* may be translated as "correct behavior," as it is used by Hsun Tzu, as "ritual,' and as "propriety." Here "mores" seems to express the meaning best.

[23] *Analects,* V, 9.

[24] This quotation is not in the present *Book of Odes.*

[25] *Odes,* p. 481.

[26] The present list of five virtues commonly used in China is benevolence, *jen* 仁 ; righteousness or justice, *yi* 義 ; correct behavior and ritual, *li* 禮; knowledge or wisdom, *chih* 智; and faith or loyalty, *hsin* 信. The earliest appearance of this series that I have noticed is in the T'ang Confucian, Han T'ui-chih. The list of Tung Chung-shu is the same, except that for the second virtue another character with the same reading and approximately the same

meaning is used, the character 誼. Various lists of virtues are found in the *Analects*, Mencius, Hsün Tzu, and in other places (see Seufert p. 27, note 2).

[27] Yao and Shun are the rulers with whom the *Book of History* begins. Wen Wang was co-founder of the Chou dynasty with his son Wu Wang. Chou Kung, or the Duke of Chou, was another son of Wen Wang. Their date is about the twelfth century B. C.

[28] Ch'eng and K'ang were the grandson and great-grandson of Wen Wang.

[29] The ploughing of the sacred field by the ruler was one of the most ancient Chinese customs. It took place at the beginning of the spring.

[30] *Analects*, XIII, 12.

[31] Po Yi and his brother are famous examples of loyalty who lived near the close of the Yin period (*Analects*, V, 22, and Chavannes, *Mém. hist.*, Vol. I, p. 217). T'ai Kung Wang was the advisor of Wen and Wu, and the founder of a feudal house under the Chou (Mencius, IV, 1, 13, and Chavannes, *Mém. hist.*, Vol. I, p. 222). T'ai Kung took service with the new dynasty, Po Yi would not.

[32] 素王 . This title, "uncrowned king," is said to have originated as a Taoist term for the ideal rulers. It is grouped with the "nine masters," also a Taoist phrase. Neither has an historical basis (Chavannes, *Mém. hist.*, Vol. I, p. 179). From the Han period on it has been a designation of Confucius himself. If Chavannes is right, the phrase shows a borrowing from Taoism by the Confucians. See Seufert, p. 33, note 1. However, a passage in Mencius (IV, 2, 21, 3) indicates that the title is really Confucian.

[33] 太學.

[34] That the present and past are so connected that knowledge of one necessitates a knowledge of the other has always been realized in China, at least since Confucius. This fact is the basis for the study of history.

[35] The idea of *Yin* and *Yang,* the principles which make up the universe, is philosophic rather than religious. For this and other scientific ideas of the ancient Chinese, see Forke, *World Conception of the Chinese.* Sometimes the expression *Yin and Yang* is used inclusively in the sense of the English "everything."

[36] *Odes*, p. 366.

[37] *Analects*, XIX, 12, 2.

[38] Seufert uses the word *Ahnherr*, which is more expressive than the English.

[39] This paragraph clearly shows the influence of Meh Ti, both in the account of creation and in the doctrine of universal love. Meh Ti, more than Confucius, represented the older Chinese religious point of view. Dr. Hu Shih tells me that he believes a large amount of Mician doctrine was incorporated into Han Confucianism.

[40] The Chinese uses two terms which are almost synonymous, *jen* 仁 , and *ai,* 愛. *Ai* includes the idea of sexual love, but *jen* does not. The word *ch'un* ("spring") is also used for "love."

[41] It is noticeable that Tung Chung-shu does not make a triple distinction here—Heaven, Earth, and man—which is an old Chinese category. The use of Heaven only as opposed to man is more characteristic of Confucianism, though the other phrase is also used by Confucians.

[42] That is, the emperor, or Son of Heaven.

[43] *Book of Filial Piety*, sect. 9.

[44] 節 *chieh*, "to conform to one's position in society," is not ordinarily included in the list of cardinal virtues. It is, however, essential to the aristocratic

social conception of Confucianism. A man should conform to the social rules for "that state of life in which it has pleased God to call him."

[45] 理 *li*, "law." This term was taken up by the Sung Confucians and made a central idea of their system.

[46] *Analects*, XX, 3. 命, *ming*, "the decree, will, or appointment of Heaven," is sometimes used in the sense of "fate," a deterministic principle, and sometimes as "that which happens without man's causing it to happen" (Mencius, V, 1, 6, 2). There is a short discussion of the use of this term by ancient Chinese thinkers in my article in the *Open Court*, June, 1929, pp. 355 f. The latter use is more characteristic of Confucians.

[47] *Odes*, p. 433.

[48] 癖 *pi*. Seufert translates this term by *Veränderung und Störung*. The Chinese character implies that it is a disease or defect. *Tao* is constant and self-sufficient, while *pi* is changing, disorderly and opportunist.

[49] *Analects*, II, 3.

[50] This is the Confucian position, and is directly opposed to Taoism, which holds that Tao preceded and created Heaven.

[51] 六藝 . Seufert translates the term by *Wissenschaft*. The six sciences or liberal arts were correct behavior or propriety, music, marksmanship, chariot-driving, the study of books, and arithmetic or numbers. The phrase is sometimes used for the six classics. *Tsu yüan*, sect. 子, p. 291.

[52] Wang Ch'ung, chap. 33, translated by Forke, *Lun-Hêng*, in *Mitt. des Sem.*, Vol. XI, p. 1 f.

[53] Wylie, *Notes on Chin. Literature*, p. 17. Giles, *Chin. Biog. Dict.*, pp. 610, 611.

[54] For instance, K'ang Yu-wei, in the *Hsin hsioh wei ching k'ao*.

CHAPTER V

THE DEVELOPMENT OF THE SCHOOLS

From references in the canon, particularly the *Book of History,* the *Book of Rites,* and the *Chou Li,* or *Regulations of Chou,* an account can be compiled which indicates an amazing educational system said to have existed at the beginning of the Chou period, about 1000 B. C., and reaching back to the legendary Shun. On the whole this account has been accepted by Chinese scholars, and even as late as 1915, Dr. Kuo P'ing-wen, in his work *The Chinese System of Public Education* reconstructs an elaborate system of schools on the basis of this evidence.[1]

Modern scholars have been very critical of these sources, especially K'ang Yu-wei and Hu Shih. The *Book of Rites* is admittedly a Han compilation, and its sections are of uneven and questionable antiquity. The last is also true of the *History.* K'ang Yu-wei believed that the *Regulations of Chou,* though pretending to recount conditions under the early Chou rulers, was actually unknown to the writers of the second century B. C., and was probably an idealistic forgery of the period of Wang Mang at the beginning of the Christian era.[2] Thus modern criticism is questioning the sources on which the picture of the ancient Chinese educational system was based.

The *Encyclopedia Sinica* [3] apparently alludes to Dr. Kuo's book and remarks sarcastically, "We are expected to believe that each hamlet had its hall of study, each village a school, and each department of a state a college. Every day all the inhabitants of each village, men and women, in the morning and in the evening, received instruction in the halls of study. Truly a golden age!"

It is not necessary for us to choose between complete agnosticism and unquestioning acceptance. Admitting that many of the sources are of doubtful authority and that others admit of more than one interpretation, so that there is not very much reliable information about real schools in ancient China where literary attainments were taught, it is still a safe assumption that there must have been schools of some sort. It is known from archeological evidence that writing existed in China at a time before the Chou dynasty. It is hard to see how the art could have continued unless it had been taught in schools of some sort. To take one instance: Confucius told his son to study the *Odes*. Either Confucius taught the boy himself, or some one else did, and in either case a school is implied, at least for the children of the upper classes.[4] It is safe to take the position of Maspero,[5] and to assume that while the classical account certainly idealizes the situation, schools in China must be approximately as old as the art of writing.

It is generally admitted that by the times of Confucius and Mencius such schools as existed were private ventures, without government supervision or aid.[6] Confucius himself and his followers always stood for education, but the feudal period with its continual warfare was not a time for the development of an educational system. The School of Law, whose doctrines dominated the period of the Contending States and of the Ch'in dynasty (third and fourth centuries B. C.), was opposed to education. From the time of Shang Yang the Legalists reviled the schools, and particularly the study of such Confucian books as the *Odes* and the *History*.[7] In spite of this, learning increased, and while we know only the results of more advanced study as shown in the literary remains of the time, the literature itself implies a large amount of private elementary instruction. There is no discussion of private schools in the canon, except in the more advanced sense in which Confucius and others were followed by disciples. Confucius presupposed a knowledge of the *Odes, History,* and *Rites* in his scholars, before—to quote his language to his son— they would be worth conversing with. We have little information as to how they secured that knowledge. It might be said of this period that we have a detailed knowledge of the faculty, but are ignorant of the students. It is evident that in the Ch'in and early Han periods, the *po shih* had numbers of students, but they were not recognized by the government, and under the Ch'in they had a hard time of it.

In general, it may be said of the reliable references to the ancient system of education [8] that they tell us practically nothing about literary instruction, and are concerned with the practice of archery, chariot-driving, the correct behavior at various ceremonies, and moral teaching.[9] We may assume a certain amount of literary instruction from the continuation of the art of writing and from literary remains. From the time of Confucius onward, there must have been a large number of private schools, in which at least the boys of the upper class learned to read. It does not seem worth while to enter into a discussion of such institutions as the *Pi yung* college, the *P'an kung* of the nobles and the *Ming t'ang* of the ruler. These institutions unquestionably existed under the Han, and are said to be much older. The buildings were certainly used for other purposes besides education, though they may have contained schools.[10]

Hsün Tzu gave a great, though not immediately effective, impetus to education. His doctrine that the nature of man is essentially evil carried as a corollary the idea that man became good by education, and passages frcm his works when compared with the actual practice in the Han schools show that he is to be regarded as the source of many of their educational ideas. It is curious that the educational methods of Chinese schools from the Han period on, with their repetition of the canon and emphasis on memory work, have been so much the opposite of the teaching methods of Confucius, who "skilfully led men on," and who, when he turned up one corner of the subject, expected the student to turn up the other three.[11] Confucius became the model for scholars, although the schools ignored his methods of education. This change in methods may be traced directly to Hsün Tzu.

"Study should never stop . . . iron must be ground on the whetstone to be sharp; the superior man must make his learning broad and daily examine himself in order to have his knowledge exact and his actions without blemish. . . . If he never hears the wisdom handed down by the former kings, he will not know the greatness of knowledge."[12]

"What should one study? How should one begin? The art begins by reciting the classics and ends in learning the rites. . . . Study until death and do not stop before, for the art of study occupies the whole of life; to arrive at its purpose, you cannot stop for an instant. . . . The *Book of History* records political events. The *Odes* regulate sounds so that they should attain the normal and not go beyond it. *Li* deals with the great distinctions of society through rules; it is the unifying principle of general classes of action. Study advances to *li* and stops there. . . . The reverence and love of elegance of *li*, the harmony of the *Book of Music*, the broad knowledge of the *Odes* and the *Book of History*, the subtleties of the *Spring and Autumn Annals*, are the completion of all creation."[13]

"The superior man knows that his knowledge is not complete . . . so he recites the classics sentence by sentence in order to make them a part of himself."[14]

"The function of the *Odes*, the *History*, the *Rites* and the *Music*, is certainly not for the ordinary man to understand."[15]

"The original nature of man is evil, so he needs to undergo the instruction of teachers and laws, then only will he be upright . . . man to-day is without good teachers and laws, so he is selfish, vicious, and unright-eous." [16]

"If a man is without a teacher or precepts, he will exalt his original nature; if he has a teacher and precepts, he will exalt self-cultivation. Original nature is not good enough to set itself up as the ruler of a person-ality. Choices and rejections and habitual practice are the means of de-veloping original nature. . . . Therefore the possession of a teacher and precepts is the greatest treasure a man can have." [17]

Such passages were the inspiration for the Han system of educa-tion, and indicate both its methods and its subject-matter.

It may be assumed that the *po shih* of the early Han rulers con-tinued to have pupils, but the central government took no recognition of education until the decrees of Wu Ti which followed the recom-mendations of Tung Chung-shu. Yet the chief credit for the found-ing of schools should go, not to Tung Chung-shu, but to another man who is almost unknown outside of China. This is a provincial official of the reign of Ching Ti (149–140 B. C.), named Wen Weng.[18] His biography is given in the *Ch'ien Han shu.*

"Wen Weng was a native of Lu Chiang.[19] He was studious as a young man and knew thoroughly the *Spring and Autumn Annals.* The district magistrate recommended him and eventually he was made governor of a part of Szechuan in the reign of Ching Ti.[20] He was benevolent in his administration and encouraged education. On taking up his post he dis-covered that the district was uncivilized, the culture resembling that of the Man barbarians,[21] so he tried to educate and improve the people. He selected a number of minor officials who showed ability, supervised their education himself, and later sent them to the capital to study under the *po shih* there.[22] . . . A few years later these men returned, and were appointed to higher positions. In Ch'eng-tu, Wen Weng established a de-partment of education [23] administered by these trained men, and invited boys of the outlying districts to come and study under them. The best students became candidates for official positions, while those of lesser ability received an honorary title.[24] On Wen Weng's official visits throughout his district he took these students with him, and honored them in various ways, such as allowing them the privilege of entering his official residence by a special gate. As a result the people respected the students and desired to become scholars themselves, the wealthy even paying for the privilege. Civilization therefore improved, and the schol-ars were equal to those of the district of Lu.[25] The Emperor Wu established schools in the provinces, but the system of government education really began with Wen Weng. He died in Szechuan. The officials and the people erected a temple [26] in his memory, and sacrificed to him at the seasons of the year. Even now (after 200 years) the people of Szechuan love culture and education, and this is due to the work of Wen Weng." [27]

This passage is interesting not only as showing the beginnings of the government system of education and the appointment of officials, but also as a chapter in the spread of Chinese civilization, in whose history Wen Weng deserves an honorable place as a great provincial administrator. By peaceful means he changed a semi-barbaric country into a center of civilization. Szechuan first came under Chinese control in 316 B. C., when it was conquered by Ssu-ma Tso, a general of the state of Ch'in.[28] As Ch'in opposed education and schools, it may be assumed that the country remained largely barbarian until the time of Wen Weng. Some of the land is very fertile, particularly the valley in which Ch'eng-tu is situated. The The circumstances were favorable for the development of civilization, but this does not take away from the achievement of Wen Weng. Since his day the province has always been important. In the period of the Three Kingdoms, the third century of our era, it was able to contend on equal terms with the rest of China. It has been independent at various times, and in the tenth century of our era the art of printing was developed there. It is said that Wen Weng is still honored as the patron saint of the province.[29]

The best account of the Han system of education in a European language is that of Biot, published in 1845.[30] It gives a good account of Wen Weng and his system of schools, promotions, and titles. It adds that he supported his students during the time they were at school, that he built a dormitory for them, and that the subjects studied were the Confucian canons, Confucius and Mencius being mentioned by name. According to Chi Ku, a scholar of the T'ang period,[31] the college of Wen Weng was located in Yi-chou, the modern Ch'eng-tu, and the gazetteer of this district stated that the hall of study of Wen Weng contained pictures or images of the sages and scholars of antiquity. The vessels and instruments used in the official sacrifices and the tablets of precious stone were kept there. The T'ang Annals—this reference is indefinite—are said to quote another passage from the Ch'ien Han shu, which says, "Wen Weng gave the people regular methods of speaking and writing." [32] Biot also translates a eulogy of Wen Weng by Ma Tuan-lin.[33]

In concluding this account of Wen Weng it should be said that the official plan of the Confucian temple issued in later ages, and the Tsu yüan, a modern source-book of words and phrases,[34] quote a work called the Wen Weng K'ung miao t'u ("Plan of the Confucian Temple"), by Wen Weng, as the ultimate authority on such questions as the number of disciples of Confucius. This work, which now appears to have been lost,[35] is not mentioned in the list of books given in the *Ch'ien Han shu*. This is not conclusive, for a work by Wen Weng might have existed, but not have been considered of sufficient importance to catalogue. While the number of personal disciples may have been fixed at seventy-two by Wen Weng himself, by placing that number in his hall of study, it is probable that the Plan of the Temple belongs to a later period. There is no evidence that the hall of study was called a *K'ung Miao,* which is a much later term.[36]

There is a passage in the *Ch'ien Han shu,* the biography of Chia Shan, which ascribes the founding of the *T'ai hsioh,* or imperial academy, to the second year of Wen Ti, 178 B. C., but this is probably a mistake, for the more authentic documents of the history, the *pen chi,* or Annals of the Emperors, give the following sequence of events. Following the conference of scholars in 136 B. C., at which Tung Chung-shu made his appeal for the founding of schools, Wu Ti appointed the *po shih* of the Five Classics. In 128 B. C., the emperor again appealed to the scholars of the country, and received a memorial whose advice he followed by allowing the feudal lords to divide their lands among their children and families, thus weakening the feudal system.[37] It is evident that the scholars aided the emperor in his desire to limit the power of the nobles.

The next step was in the same direction. In 124 B. C., Wu Ti acceded to the request of Tung Chung-shu by founding the *T'ai hsioh,* or imperial academy, for the study of the classics. It was located in the capital. The details are given by Ssu-ma Ch'ien, in a section not translated by Chavannes, and the immediate request was made by Kung-sun Hung.

Kung-sun Hung had a bad reputation in his youth. He was a native of the present province of Shantung. At the age of forty he reformed and became an ardent student of the *Spring and Autumn Annals.* Eventually he became a *po shih* under Wu Ti, and made his petition for the founding of the academy at a meeting of the *po shih* connected with matters of ritual. It was reported to the emperor and approved.

The *T'ai hsioh* was administered by the *Po shih kuan,* or Board of Scholars, and under Wu Ti contained fifty students, called *ti tzu.*[38] They were drawn exclusively from the royal domain; that is, from the land under the immediate authority of the emperor and not controlled by the nobles. It is apparent that they were intended to be a further check on the power of the nobility. The instructors were *po shih,* and the academy was under the supervision of the *T'ai ch'ang,* or minister of rites.[39] The students were exempt from taxation and were supported by the state. They were required to be of irreproachable morals, and were examined every year. The schedules for the amounts of grain given for their support, their titles, promotion to official position, and presentation to the emperor are given.[40]

The academy proved so successful that it was steadily enlarged under the successors of Wu Ti. Under Chao Ti (86–74 B. C.) the number of students was raised to 100. In 50 B. C., Hsüan Ti raised the number to 200, and in 48 B. C., Yüan Ti added twelve more. This emperor exempted from taxation all who knew the canon, appointed *po shih* to lecture on the books, and finally raised the number of students to 1,000. In 8 B. C., a petition was presented to the emperor Ch'eng, pointing out that Confucius was said to have had 3,000 disciples, and that the number of *ti tzu* should be raised to this number. The suggestion was followed. Under Ai Ti (6–1 B. C.) the *ti tzu* were excused from their studies for three years following the death of their parents; that is, during the required period of mourning.[41]

Biot translates an edict of Ch'eng Ti in 25 B. C., which is typical of the imperial attitude. It states that the *T'ai hsioh* was founded for the purpose of transmitting the sacred ways of the ancient rulers, and for the moral and intellectual improvement of the empire. The scholars should study and make clear things ancient and modern in order that they might be initiated into the principles of administration. They were in charge of the *po shih,* received support from the state, and were regularly examined.[42]

The method of examination was curious. The questions, which involved the explanation of classical passages, were written on two tablets of different size. The candidates shot at the tablets until they had touched one with an arrow, on which they were allowed to answer the questions on the back. The rewards and titles were fixed by schedule, and varied with the size of the tablet touched.[43] The biographies of the *Ch'ien Han shu* record a number of instances of men who secured promotion by means of this test. In the reign of P'ing Ti (A. D. 1–6) there are the records of forty graduates in class one and twenty in class two.[44]

It seems unnecessary to go further into detail concerning the schools. The system was extended to the provinces and the feudal domains, and an edict of the year A. D. 3 told the names of different kinds of schools in districts of various sizes. In the smallest a teacher was appointed who lectured on the *Book of Filial Piety*.[45] Biot gives a list of twenty-one edicts, covering a period from 196 to 1 B. C., concerning the discovery and promotion of scholars and officials, usually addressed to the *yü ssu*, or Censors, and the *po shih*. They have been partially translated by Du Halde, and often follow some unusual natural disturbance, like an earthquake or an eclipse. The emperor deplored the negligence of the government in finding men of merit and ordered that they be discovered and recommended, so that the wrath of Heaven might be appeased.[46] Five edicts from 106 to 35 B. C. are cited which deal with the examinations.[47]

Ma Tuan-lin quotes a Han document to this effect: "The Grand Historian examines the scholars. They must be able to write at least 9,000 characters, and be capable of acting as historians and secretaries." [48] They were also examined on the canon—the *Book of Changes,* the *History,* the *Book of Filial Piety,* and the *Analects* being mentioned by name. Candidates for the position of *po shih* were also examined on their filial piety and conformation to the rites.[49] The emperor himself occasionally visited the schools, and such visits were carefully recorded.

Under the last weak rulers of the Western Han toward the close of the first century B. C., the real power gradually passed from the family of Liu, which had furnished the rulers of the Han dynasty, to that of Wang, the family of the Empress Dowager. Most of the Wang were proud, dissolute, and otherwise corrupt, but Wang Mang won a reputation for scholarship in the canon, for filial piety, for simplicity of living, and for his patronage of the learned. Eventually he drew to himself almost absolute power under a puppet emperor, and his plans for taking the throne became clear. A messenger from Heaven appeared to an official of Shantung, announcing a change of dynasty, and verified his statement by a miraculous well which was discovered the following day. Then in A. D. 8 a written message, assumed to be supernatural, was found in the temple of Kao Tsu, the first Han ruler, saying that as the Liu family had become degenerate, a new dynasty would begin. This message from the ancestor of the Han was considered conclusive, and Wang Mang openly proclaimed himself emperor and the founder of a new line. His rule lasted until A. D. 25, when the Liu family rallied, Wang Mang was killed, and the emperor Kuang Wu began the dynasty of the Eastern Han.[50]

It is curious that two men who contributed so much to the development of the Chinese state, Ch'in Shih Huang and Wang Mang, should be regarded by the Chinese with the greatest abhorrence, the former as a tyrant, the latter as a hypocrite and usurper. It is only recently, in an interesting essay by Hu Shih, that any Chinese has endeavored to do justice to the great qualities of Wang Mang.

His general policy would now be called a kind of state socialism. The government maintained monopolies in salt, iron, wine, coinage, and other things. He endeavored to abolish slavery, to fix the prices of necessary commodities, and to put into practice reforms about the ownership of land which seem to resemble similar experiments now being made in Russia. He was ahead of his time. The changes he advocated were too great, even though Tung Chung-shu had suggested some of them. His officials were corrupt, and abuses crept into the system, until at last Wang Mang lost his life in a struggle which depopulated one of the most flourishing districts of the empire and necessitated the new emperor's moving his capital to the east.[51]

Hu Shih makes the statement that Wang Mang founded a national university.[52] Hu Shih's essay is not documented, but it is certainly not correct to imply that Wang Mang founded the higher education. He did, however, build dormitories for 10,000 students, an unprecedented number, and Lu Ssu-mien says that he was the first ruler to do this.[53] In the disorders which closed the reign of Wang Mang these scholars were scattered, but they were patronized again by Kuang Wu, who also transported 2,000 wagon-loads of books from Ch'ang-an to his new capital at Lo-yang, reopened schools, and again appointed the *po shih* of the Five Canons. Under his successors, Ming Ti and Hsün Ti, more dormitories were built for the *T'ai hsioh,* until under Hsün Ti (A. D. 126–145) the number of students reached 30,000, though Takakuwa estimates that not more than a third of these could be called real Confucians.[54] Toward the close of the eastern Han period the scholars were persecuted by the court eunuchs.[55]

The period of Wang Mang is also important because, if K'ang Yu-wei is correct, it was at that time that a number of books which pretend to represent a much earlier date were actually written. Of these the most important for this discussion is the *Regulations of*

Chou. This work describes a Utopia the scene of which is placed in the past instead of the future, and presents an ideal form of government. The section *Ti kuan* ("Ministry of Earth"), gives an account of the moral instruction of the people, and the section *T'ien kuan* ("Ministry of Heaven") treats of the examination and promotion of officials. The scheme of education is so broad as to include special instruction for the blind. There is no reason to suppose this system was ever put into practice in ancient China, but the *Chou li* is of great importance because in succeeding ages it represented the model for educational organization. If it approximates the system of Wang Mang, he is highly to be praised. It is evident without making this assumption that Wang Mang did a great deal for education and for the scholar class. In this he was aided by a number of able men, two of whom, Yang Hsiung and Liu Hsin, stand very high in the history of Chinese scholarship.

This sketch indicates the way in which the Han educational system originated and developed. It was copied and approximated, and its precedents were followed by succeeding dynasties until recent times. Of course, the history of the schools is uneven and varies with the general conditions throughout the country. A large system of schools requires wealth and good order. It may be said as a general formula that under strong rulers who could enforce peace, such as are to be found at the beginning of each dynasty, the schools flourished, and under the weak emperors toward the close of a dynasty, the schools fell into decay, while in times of civil war and foreign invasion they occasionally vanished altogether. The tradition of learning was never completely lost in China, and when the public schools disappeared there were always scholars who carried on private instruction, so that even in the ages of disorder and uncertainty which followed the final downfall of the Han there was no such intellectual darkness as that through which Europe passed after the destruction of the Roman Empire in the west.

Along with the development of the schools there was the growth of a privileged scholar class, largely supported by the state and exempt from taxation. By entering this class a man not only received honor, respect, and more material rewards, but it became possible for him to enter upon a career of government service, with the highest positions in the state as an ultimate goal. It is not surprising that education has been popular in China.

All this is important in a study of the cult of Confucius, because the sage has been worshiped in the main by the scholar class only, and because that worship seems to have developed in the schools. The next step is to consider the worship of the spirits of men in ancient China, and to see how, granting the position of Confucius as the example and model for scholars, and the creation of the scholars as an important and separate element in society, the worship of the sage became almost inevitable.

NOTES

[1] P. W. Kuo, *Chinese System of Public Education,* published by the Columbia University Press in 1915. The text is in English. Chaps. 1 and 2, pp. 7 f., deal with the ancient system of education. Although it is only fair to Dr. Kuo to say that his main interest is in modern education, to which these opening chapters are merely an introduction, his treatment is very uncritical. The book is a doctor's thesis, and does not represent Dr. Kuo's more mature work. Nevertheless it is almost the only treatment of the subject in English.

[2] 新學偽經考, by K'ang Yu-wei. It has not been translated. The thesis is that parts of the *History,* Mao's *Commentary on the Odes,* the *Commentary of Tso-ch'iu Ming* on the Spring and Autumn Annals, the *Chou li,* and other works supposed to be much earlier, were really forgeries of the period of Wang Mang. His point of view is largely accepted by Hu Shih in his *History of Chinese Philosophy* 中國哲學史大綱, the text of which is in Chinese, and in his English essay on Wang Mang in the *Jour. N. China Branch of the R. A. S.,* Vol. LIX, pp. 218 f.

[3] *Encyclopedia Sinica,* art. "Education," pp. 153 f.

[4] *Analects,* XVI, 13.

[5] H. Maspero, "The Origins of the Chinese Civilization," translated by C. W. Bishop from *Annales de Géographie,* No. 194, XXXV Année, Mar. 15, 1926, in the *Smithsonian Report* for 1927, pp. 433-452. "These little hamlets... had each an altar to the god of the soil, a school, and a market" (p. 444). And in note 21 on the same page, "We know this organization only under the purely theoretical shape in which it is described by certain late rituals with Utopian tendencies."

[6] *Encyclopedia Sinica,* p. 154.

[7] For unfavorable references to schools and education, see Duyvendak, *Book of Lord Shang,* pp. 174, 181, 185, 190, 191, 256. The author is indebted to Mr. L. Tomkinson for references in Kuan Chung and Han Fei to the same effect. Liang Ch'i-ch'iao, in 先秦政治思想史, points out that the Legalists did hold that the people should be taught the law and that they used the regular officials, the army, and the prisons in this way.

[8] Mencius (I, 1, 7, 24) refers to schools. The *Odes* (IV, 2, 3,) refer to ponds before buildings which later were considered to have housed schools. the *Book of Rites* (chaps. 4 and 5) gives less reliable references to schools.

[9] Dr. Kuo (chaps. 1 and 2) gives a general account of the subjects taught.

[10] The *Ming t'ang* 明堂 was the prerogative of the ruler, and was used for audiences.   The *Pi yung* 辟雍also belonged to the ruler, and had before it

a circular pool, while the *P'an kung* 泮宮 of the nobles had semicircular pools, which are copied in temples to Confucius. The last two were probably used for bodily exercises in the Chou period, which later caused them to be considered parts of a system of schools. In the *Pi yung* the ruler feasted the old men. In A.D. 56 Kuang Wu built at his new capital of Lo-yang a *Ming t'ang, Pi yung,* and *T'ai hsioh,* located together near the palace, and called collectively the "Three Pavilions." Ts'ai Yung thinks the three were separate establishments, but Ma Tuan-lin believes the names were used interchangeably (*Wen hsien t'ung k'ao,* chaps. 40, 26, 30, cited by Biot, pp. 153, 172).

[11] *Analects,* IX, 10, 2; VII, 8.

[12], [13], [14], [15], [16], [17] These notes refer to Dubs, *Works of Hsüntse,* pp. 31, 36, 40, 65, 302, and 114, respectively.

[18] 文翁 . The biography of Wen Weng is found in the *Ch'ien Han shu,* chap. 89, sect. 59. Biot gives a French translation. This translation was made independently.

[19] 陸賈 . In the present province of Anhui.

[20] 舒 . Shu was an ancient term for a part of the present province of Szechuan.

[21] 蠻夷 . *Man Yi* is a term for the aboriginal tribes of southern China. Biot says that Wen Weng found himself among these barbarians, but the Chinese text actually says that he found the culture of Shu to be like that of the Man Yi (Biot, pp. 121 f.).

[22] At this point there is a passage dealing with the support of the students. Biot simply says that Wen Weng gave them silver. The text says that he bought some quantities of the products of Szechuan and sent them to the *po shih,* probably for the tuition of his students.

[23] 學官 *Hsioh kuan.*

[24] 孝弟力田 . Literally, "Moral Agriculturist." It implies that they continued as farmers, though the title shows that they had received instruction in morals, probably in the *Book of Filial Piety.*

[25] Confucius was born in the state of Lu, and naturally the district was the center of Confucian learning. The name lingered on into the Han period, and is still used as a literary name for the province of Shantung. This sentence therefore implies high praise.

[26] 祠堂 . *Ssu t'ang.* The Chinese have a number of different terms that we would translate by the word "temple." This expression is applied to ancestral temples and buildings in memory of great men. Shryock, *Temples of Anking and Their Cults,* Appendix I.

[27] *Ch'ien Han shu,* chap. 89, sect. 59.

[28] *Chang kuo tseh,* or *Chronicle of the Fighting States,* Japanese edition, p. 7, cited in Chi Li, *Formation of the Chinese People,* p. 240.

[29] *Chung kuo jen ming ta tsu tien,* a biographical dictionary, p. 56.

[30] E. Biot, *Essai sur l'histoire de l'instruction publique en Chine* (Paris, Duprat, 1845). Biot's essay is based on two Chinese compilations of the Sung period, the *Wen hsien t'ung k'ao* by Ma Tuan-lin, of the fourteenth century A.D., and the *Yü hai,* or *Sea of Jade.* In Ma Tuan-lin, chaps. 40-42 deal with the establishment of the *T'ai hsioh.* or imperial academy, the *Kuo tzu chien,* a school for the sons of nobles, and the other educational establishments of the Han. Chaps. 43 and 44 deal with the sacrifices and ceremonies instituted in the schools in honor of the ancient masters. Chap. 45 records imperial visits

to the schools, and chap. 46 describes the district schools. Chaps. 28-39 deal with the choice and presentation of officials. The *Yü hai* was published anonymously in 1340. Chaps. 111 and 112 treat of the schools, chap. 113 of imperial visits and the honors paid Confucius and his disciples in the schools, and chaps. 114 and 115 of the choice of officials. Only the *Yü hai* is documented.

[31] Biot does not give the Chinese characters, and the author has been unable to find any account of this scholar.

[32] *Ch'ien Han shu,* chap. 28, the *Ti li chi,* or description of earth.

[33] Biot, p. 126. Ma Tuan-lin, chap. 46, sects. 6, 5.

[34] *Tsu yüan,* sect. 子, p. 18, art. on the Seventy Disciples. The reference in the temple plan is translated later.

[35] The Curator of the Gest Chinese Research Library at McGill University and Mr. Hummel, who is in charge of the Chinese section of the Library of Congress, have been unable to find any trace of the work.

[36] The catalogue of books in the *Ch'ien Han shu* is in chap. 30, sect. 10.

[37] Biot, p. 102.

[38] 弟子 *ti tzu* indicates both a disciple and a learned man.

[39] 太常. Under the Ch'in dynasty this official was called the *Feng ch'ang* 奉常. *T'ai ch'ang* is the Han term. The position was abolished under the Manchu dynasty. *Tsu yüan,* sect. 丑, p. 233.

[40] Biot, p. 103. The original source is Ssu-ma Ch'ien, chap. 121.

[41] Biot, p. 112 f. The original sources for these decrees are the opening chapters of the *Ch'ien Han shu,* the *pen chi,* or imperial annals, the chapters bearing the emperor's name.

[42] Biot, p. 113, after the *Ch'ien Han shu,* chap. 10.

[43] Biot, p. 115.

[44] Biot, p. 116.

[45] Biot, p. 128.

[46] Biot, pp. 135, 136. Partially translated in Du Halde, Vol. I, p. 489.

[47] That calamities occur when the right men are not employed in the government is a characteristic Confucian doctrine. In these edicts the emperor often blames the negligence of the feudal princes for this condition. As a matter of fact, the scholars were a check on the nobility.

[48] Biot, p. 140. Biot's source is *Ma Tuan-lin,* chap. 35.

[49] Biot, p. 147, taken from *Ma Tuan-lin,* chap. 40, sect. 25.

[50] In the *Ch'ien Han shu,* chap. 99, sects. 1-3, deal with Wang Mang. This brief account is taken from the essay by Hu Shih, already cited.

[51] Chi Li (*Formation of the Chinese People,* p. 263) quotes a document of the third century A. D. to the effect that the three metropolitan districts "within the passes" were entirely depopulated. The imperial library was almost entirely destroyed (Wylie, *Notes on Chinese Literature,* p. xiv).

[52] Hu Shih, "Wang Mang," *Jour. N. China Branch of the R. A. S.,* Vol. LIX, p. 220.

[53] Lu Ssu-mien, Vol. II, p. 66.

[54] Takakuwa, p. 110.

[55] Biot, pp. 189 f. There has always been bad blood between the literati and the eunuchs.

CHAPTER VI

THE WORSHIP PAID TO THE SPIRITS OF MEN IN ANCIENT CHINA

It is a difficult task for us to understand the religious thoughts and practices of such a people as the ancient Chinese. We have become accustomed to a monotheistic definition which assumes an enormous gulf between God and His creatures. We define certain practices and ceremonies as belonging peculiarly to God, and therefore as being inappropriate and blasphemous when applied to men. We forget that the distinctions which we make, however real to us, are nevertheless arbitrary, and that a different nation with a different culture may reasonably adopt other systems of classification. A Christian may bow before the altar, and shortly after, bow on meeting a friend. To a non-Christian, who might conceivably argue that he must regard his friend as a god because his behavior had been the same in both cases, he would reply that the idea which lay behind the action was entirely different in the two instances. The same logic applies to the ceremonial behavior of the Chinese. They offer food and other gifts to their living friends, to their ancestors, to the memory of great men, and to unquestioned divinities. The actions with which these gifts are offered are much the same. It does not necessarily follow, however, that this similar behavior implies similar ideas and motives. That the sacrifices to ancestors are similar to the sacrifices to Heaven is not in itself proof that the ancestors are gods.

What is a god? How are gods to be distinguished from mere spirits? It can hardly be a difference in the quality of the attributes, because gods have the same qualities as men, or at least men are unable to conceive of gods except in terms of their own personalities. Do gods differ from men only in quality; that is, do they possess the same attributes as men, only in higher degree? Such a conception makes any distinction between gods and men merely arbitrary. It is customary to take refuge in some such term as *supernatural*, but on analysis this word means either "extraordinary and unusual," or else "non-mechanical," and neither meaning helps us. In the study of religions a practical distinction between gods and spirits is made, which, while unsatisfactory to religious men, is useful on the whole. A god has a cult and receives worship, while a spirit does not. This works fairly well for undisputed cases, but it fails when applied to such a religion as that of China, because the Chinese have different categories from our own. Moreover, the use of any ceremony as a test of divinity is defective because ceremonies give no assurance of the spirit in which they are performd nor of the motive behind them, and these are the essence of religion.

These remarks are a necessary introduction to the subject of this chapter because the question is often asked, Do the Chinese consider Confucius as a god, or their ancestors as divine? Indeed, occidentals have engaged in long and bitter controversies over these points. Any decision on these questions is arbitrary, and is apt to rest on western conceptions rather than on those of the Chinese when the decision is made by occidentals.

The point to be made is that this study is not concerned with such questions at all. If the word *worship* is used, it is not with the idea of prejudging such an issue, but because in English usage the word may not only be used to designate ceremonies addressed to gods, but may also be used as a term of address to a man, such as a judge, when it indicates only respect and reverence. The authorities of a Christian organization may be forced to decide whether their converts shall be allowed to continue certain ceremonies, but we are not in such a dilemma. In this study it is sufficient to indicate what the Chinese have done, and what they have said in explanation of their actions, without entering upon theological implications which may arise out of these things.

Wang Ch'ung, about A. D. 80, gives an account of the sacrifices of the ancient Chinese, and while the customs he mentions are not of equal antiquity, they were all practised under the Han, and some go back to the beginnings of Chinese history.[1]

"According to the *Li chi,* the emperor sacrifices to Heaven and Earth, the feudal princes to the mountains and rivers (of their territory), the ministers and high dignitaries to the Five Genii,[2] the scholars and the common people to their ancestors.[3] From the offerings to the spirits of the Land and Grain[4] down to those in the ancestral hall, there is a gradation from the Son of Heaven to the commoners.

"The *Book of History* says that a special sacrifice was made to Shang

Ti, a pure one to the Six Superior Powers, a sacrifice on high to the Mountains and Rivers, and a sacrifice to the various spirits round about.[5]

"Wood was burned on the great altar as a sacrifice to Heaven, a victim was buried in the great pit as a sacrifice to Earth. A red calf was immolated, and a sheep buried in bright daylight as a sacrifice to the Seasons, and they approached the sacrificial pits and altars to offer sacrifice to the Heat and the Cold. In the imperial palace a sacrifice was made to the Sun, and in clear night they sacrificed to the Moon. Oblations were made to the Stars in the dark hall, to Water and Drought in the rain hall, and to the Four Cardinal Points at the four pits and altars.

"The mountain forests, the valleys of the rivers, and the hills and cliffs can emit clouds and produce wind and rain. All these curious phenomena are regarded as spirits. The ruler of the world sacrifices to all the spirits, the princes only as long as they are within their territories, but not when they have left them.[6]

"Such are the official sacrifices according to usage and the prescribed rites. The emperor treats Heaven like his father and Earth like his mother. Conformably to human customs he practises filial piety, which accounts for the sacrifices to Heaven and Earth. In the matter of Mountains and Rivers and the subsequent deities the offerings presented to them are in appreciation of their deserts. A living man distinguishing himself is rewarded, ghosts and spirits which are deserving have their sacrifices. . . . The spirits of the Land and Grain are rewarded for their kindness in letting all the things grow."

Although Wang Ch'ung might be described as a monist and hardly as a religious man, his account is typically Chinese, and it is at once apparent that his approach to the whole question is different from that usually found in western religions. It is certainly a sounder method for the study of the history of religion. Although all these gods might be classed as nature divinities, the sacrifices to them are explained on human grounds. We honor our parents and men who have rendered great services, therefore we should honor the spirits whom we assume to lie behind natural forces and objects. As a matter of fact, this is what happens in any religion, and the rules of behavior among men, announcements, praise, congratulations, requests, apologies, and thanks, are paralleled in the relations of men and gods. According to Wang Ch'ung, man behaves toward the gods in a certain way because he behaves in the same way toward other men. "If we love some one in our heart, we give him to eat and to drink, and if we love ghosts and spirits, we sacrifice to them." [7]

"Two motives are underlying all sacrifices: gratitude for received benefits and ancestor worship. We show our gratitude for the efforts others have taken on our behalf, and worship our ancestors out of regard for their kindness. Special efforts, extraordinary goodness, merits, and universal reforms are taken into consideration by wise emperors, and it is for this reason that they have instituted sacrifices. An oblation is offered to him who has improved the public administration, who for the public welfare has worked till his death, who has done his best to strengthen his country, who has warded off great disasters, or prevented great misfortunes." [8]

The *Li chi,* from which this last sentence is quoted, took its form in the first century B. C.,[9] and therefore the practice of honoring great men by sacrifices may be at least as old. Nothing is said to indicate that men so honored were considered to belong to the same class as the nature spirits.

"The ancestors in the ancestral temple are our own kindred. Because, while they are alive, it is customary to maintain our parents, this duty cannot be shirked when they are dead. Therefore we sacrifice to them, as though they were still alive. Ghosts are treated like men, for it is the living who attend the dead. For man it is usual to reward good deeds, and to maintain the nearest relatives, whence the duty to requite the kindness of the ancestors and to sacrifice to them has been derived.

"When the dog which Confucius had bred was dead, he requested Tzu Kung to bury him. 'I have been told,' he said, 'that one does not throw an old curtain away, but uses it to bury a horse, and that an old cart-cover is not thrown away, but used to bury a dog. I am poor, and have no cover to wrap him in.' Then he gave him a mat, and bade him not to throw the dog down with his head first." [10]

Wang Ch'ung then cites a story from Ssu-ma Ch'ien,[11] of a man who had promised to give his sword to a prince. When he returned from a journey the prince was dead, but he hung his sword on a tree over the tomb in order to keep his promise. The *Lun Heng* continues,

"Those who make offerings in recognition of special merits, are animated by the same sentiment as Confucius, when he interred his pet dog, and those who sacrifice, lest they should evade a former obligation, have the same tenderness of heart as Chi Tse, who hung up his sword over the tomb." [12]

Wang Ch'ung has been quoted, not only because he represents the best Chinese opinion on these questions in the first century of our era, but because he is a thinker of the first rank whose analyses are worthy of respect. It can hardly be questioned that the mere offering of sacrifices to a man is not necessarily a proof that he is regarded as a god by the Chinese. Further evidence is necessary as to why the sacrifices are offered and what the position of the recipient of the gifts is supposed to be.

The worship of ancestors, which Wang Ch'ung considers one of the main types of sacrifice, is already in existence at the opening of Chinese history, and the references to it in the canon are too numerous· even to list.[13] This worship is a part of what might be called the Chinese family complex, which is to be found in almost every feature of Chinese culture. Not only do such obvious matters as the laws of inheritance and the holding of land depend upon the organization of the family or clan, but the influence extends into trade, where families control certain industries and trade processes are held as family secrets. Politics is honeycombed with nepotism, the criminal law is based upon family relationships, and in every direction the family is met sooner or later. This is especially true of the Chinese moral sanctions; for although ancestor worship itself appears to have no connection with morals, since a man receives or offers sacrifices without respect to his ethical qualities, the whole system of Chinese morality has been built up upon the fundamental virtue of filial piety. This applies not only to modern China, but as far as we know, to ancient China also, in which the feudal system and the organization of the state, as well as the private life of the individual, were based upon the rules of family life and governed by them.

Thus the worship of ancestors is seen to be a part of a very complex whole, and in order to understand it thoroughly a knowledge of the entire civilization of China is necessary. The fundamental idea is the unity of all bearing the same surname (which descends through the male side), and sharing the same blood. It includes both the living and the dead, and is maintained not only by custom, tradition, and the law of the state, but by extraordinary records, which in the family of Confucius himself extend for more than eighty generations.

The ceremonies connected with the worship of ancestors fall naturally into two classes, those connected with death itself, and those which were a part of the regular and continued cult of the dead. There are already detailed accounts of the services at funerals and of the ceremonies used in the regular worship of ancestors in European languages, so that it seems unnecessary to go over the ground again.[14] It is important to notice that although the Chinese have many words denoting different kinds of sacrifices varying in the amount and nature of the victims and gifts offered, as well as in their preparation, the way and place in which they are offered, and the occasion, there appears to be no fundamental distinction in the ceremonies themselves between those which are offered to nature deities and those which are presented to the spirits of men. Laufer is of the opinion that the earliest objects of worship used in the cults of nature divinities, apart from the natural objects themselves, like the heavenly bodies, were certain geometrical pieces of jade, many of which are to be found in western museums.[15] In the worship of ancestors, the earliest custom seems to have been the selection of some member of the family, usually a child, who impersonated the ancestors, remaining silent and immovable throughout the ceremony, the blessing being pronounced by an officer of prayer in his name. Later, stones or tablets bearing the name of the ancestor were placed in permanent shrines, the Chou rulers having seven of these, the chief nobles five, and so on to the common people, who placed the tablet of the father in their main apartment. These blocks or tablets were called *chu*.[16] Still later images were introduced, at least in funerals, and Confucius speaks in the strongest disapproval of this practice.[17] Human sacrifice seems to be a late custom which was borrowed from barbarian tribes not earlier than the seventh century B. C., and was practised both at funerals and in the worship of nature deities.[18] This was always opposed by the Confucians so strongly that in the *Book of Rites,* Tseng Tzu is made to say that objects placed in graves should resemble those actually used, but should be themselves unusable, in order that men might not be tempted to immolate human victims in sacrifice.[19] The ceremonies were accompanied by both music and pantomime. There were the offering of the victims and other gifts, libations of wine, bowing and prostrations, and in the ceremonies of the family, there was usually a general feast at the conclusion. Every event of importance, birth, marriage, death, setting out on a journey, and so on, was not only announced to the ancestors, but whenever possible the ceremony connected with the event was performed in their presence.[20]

While there seems to be no necessary connection between ancestor worship and worship of nature gods, there were in ancient China what appear to be attempts to combine the two. From early times it was the custom for the ruler to associate his chief ancestor with Shang Ti in the state sacrifices. Legge calls the ancestor the correlate of Heaven.[21] One of the titles of the ruler was the Son of Heaven;

Heaven is often referred to as the father of all, and doubtless the similarity of the two ideas led to the ancestor's being grouped with Heaven in certain ceremonies.

There was a still closer connection between the two kinds of cults in the worship of the gods of the Land and Grain. These deities were originally folk gods, there being one for every twenty-five families, approximately. The ancestors and the clan grouped men in terms of descent, while the gods of the Land and Grain grouped men in terms of locality. These gods received sacrifices in the open air, and groves of trees are mentioned in connection with the cult. The altars were simply mounds of earth, for the god was the personification of the energies of the soil. It is difficult to differentiate between the god of the Soil and his acolyte, the god of the Grain, for they are nearly always grouped together. When a sacrifice was offered, each family sent one of its members to take part, and afterwards an equable division of the offerings was made among the families constituting the village.[22] It can be seen that there was a resemblance to the ancestral sacrifices, both ending in a general feast, and both using a man or a child to impersonate the spirit. The god was worshiped at eclipses of the sun and in case of floods or drought. On the altar was a stone, called *chu,* which may have been worshiped as the god himself.[23]

The cult of these gods was later taken up by the state, the god becoming identified with the political division.[24] This was the condition of the cult during the feudal period, and each feudal state had its gods of the Land and Grain, who were built into the state religion. The scientific theory of the *Yin* and *Yang* was generally accepted, and these gods, representing the *Yin* principle, had their shrine on the west of the palace, being balanced on the east by the shrines of the ancestors, who represented *Yang.* The idea was carried even further, for rewards were given in the presence of the ancestors, while punishments were inflicted before the gods of the Land and Grain. The *chu* were taken on military expeditions and had to be avoided, all being required to keep out of the way when they were carried forth. These gods are frequently mentioned as synonymous with the state itself, and to sacrifice to them was equivalent to assuming the lordship. Under the Han, the district officials were required to sacrifice to the god of the district.[25]

After the cult became welded to the state religion, it became a custom for the founder of a new line to appoint some one, usually one of his own ancestors, to fill the divine office.[26] Mencius says that the term of office depended on their good behavior; that is, when things went wrong with the crops, and sacrifices were unavailing, new gods were appointed.[27] Chavannes explains how in case of drought, the attitude of the worshipers was humble, but in the case of excessive and unseasonable rain, the gods were rebuked. He quotes Tung Chung-shu's very logical argument on the subject.[28] Nature spirits seem occasionally to have been maltreated when other methods failed to produce results.[29] These gods were clearly nature spirits, but when their cult became incorporated in the state religion, the position of the god of the Land became what might be called a political appointment in the hands of the ruler, and was filled by the spirits of deceased men, who thereupon received sacrifices by virtue of their office. The cult is seen to be a link between the worship of nature deities and that of the ancestors, since the men were not worshiped simply because they were dead, but because they filled a position in the spirit world which paralleled that of the lord or official in this one.

The victims and food which had previously been offered in sacrifice both to ancestors and to the gods of the Land and Grain were divided among the group of worshipers. When both these cults became a part of the state religion, and the ruler or lord wished to show particular honor to some one outside that group, he sent him a portion of the sacrifice as a gift. Such a gift might be a political event of the first importance, as in 344 B. C., when the weak Chou king sent the viands of his sacrifice to his own ancestors to Duke Hsiao of Ch'in,[30] which was tantamount to recognizing him as the chief lord of the kingdom. As the Duke of Ch'in had no connection whatever with the worship of Wen and Wu, this custom, which is at least as old as the Chou dynasty, appears to be a further development of the state religion. The original idea in the worship of the spirits of men was that such worship should be paid only by those within a limited group who were specially obligated to the dead, as in the case of a man's being worshiped by his descendants. As the eating of the offerings was a part of the ceremony, this custom amounts to a limited worship of the spirits of men by others than the group to which the dead belonged.

It is impossible to say exactly when the worship of ancestral spirits by what may be called outsiders began, but by the time of Confucius it had developed to the point where the sage found it neces-

sary to inveigh against it, saying that to worship a spirit who did
not belong to one was flattery.[31] In spite of the attitude of Confucius the development continued.

The Chou ruler Hsüan, who reigned in the latter part of the ninth
century B. C., was the subject of a legend. He was said to have put
to death unjustly one of his generals, who came to be called the
Master of Tu.[32] Some time after this the king assembled his nobles
for a hunt, in the midst of which the dead Master of Tu appeared
in red hat and clothes and killed the king with an arrow. During
the feudal period a cult grew up around this personage, particularly
in the state of Ch'in, where it was a part of the state religion, and
it continued into the Han period.[33] In this case we do not know
whether any one was allowed to sacrifice to the Master of Tu, or
whether the cult was limited to a definite group.

When Ch'in Shih Huang had unified the empire, he made tours
of inspection throughout the provinces, in the course of which he
visited places of local interest and often sacrificed. For instance, in
the southern part of the modern province of Hunan he found a
temple dedicated to the two daughters of Yao, the tradition of Yao
and Shun having been transported to this spot and localized. The
emperor sacrificed to them in the temple.[34] As the emperor by virtue
of his position sacrificed to all spirits, this involved no special departure. Han Kao Tsu continued the custom of touring the provinces,
and in 195 B. C., while in the state of Lu, he visited and sacrificed
at the grave of Confucius.[35] This was probably no more than a
political gesture.

An important step was made by his successor, Hui Ti. In 195
B. C. he ordered that each district and fief of the empire should erect
temples to his father, Kao Tsu, and that sacrifices be offered in
them at fixed times.[36] Before this the founder of a dynasty had received regular sacrifices from his own descendants, the succeeding
rulers, at a single temple erected to his memory. Under the Chou
dynasty, no one else was allowed to sacrifice to him. This instance
of Han Kao Tsu appears to set the precedent for a series of shrines
throughout the empire to a single man, at which any one, provided
he occupied a certain official position, might, and indeed was required
to offer sacrifices.

How soon this practice extended to others besides emperors it is
difficult to say, except that by the time of the formation of the
Book of Rites in the latter part of the first century B. C., less than 200

years later, it was accepted as a regular custom that any great man might receive sacrifices. Indeed, it was assumed that this condition had always existed, in spite of the fact that Confucius had spoken directly against the custom. The instances of the general worship of men in antiquity which were accepted during the Han period do not appear to be historical (for instance, such cults as that of Huang Ti), and it is difficult to find instances of the spirits of men which received general worship, as opposed to the worship of a limited group, such as their descendants, in the Chou period.

The culture and religion of the state of Ch'in were different from those of the rest of China. The cult of the Five *Ti,* which originally were probably the five planets, the establishment of shrines to which pilgrimages were made, the worship of stars and meteors, all appear to have developed there before they spread to the rest of China.[37] These cults were continued and others added under the Han emperors, especially Wu Ti. In nearly every case new cults were attributed to remote antiquity, as in the case of the Feng and Shan sacrifices, and Wu Ti's worship of the *T'ai Yi,* or Great Unity.[38] Tung Chung-shu himself wrote on such subjects, and is given credit for the first use of the dragon in the sacrifice for rain.[39] Organized groups of priests and priestesses made their appearance, and human beings were deified within a short time of their death, as is illustrated by the story of the Princess of the Spirits and her cult under Wu Ti.[40] Miracles and fables were easily accepted even by Confucian scholars, Wang Ch'ung being almost the only exception during the Han period.

Exactly when groups of men with common interests began to select a patron deity it is impossible to say. The oldest trade-god in China is probably Lu Pan,[41] the god of carpenters and allied trades. By the time of Wang Ch'ung, the first century A. D., the fabulous stories about Lu Pan were already so widespread and generally accepted that he found it necessary to argue against them.[42] A large part of these inventions were due to Taoist charlatans who were prominent from the time of Ch'in Shih Huang on. Not only did mythological divinities make their appearance, like Hsi Wang Mu, but historic persons such as Huai Nan Tzu had become gods or genii within a century after their death.[43] The Han period was an age of credulous scholarship, and by the beginning of the Christian era almost any prominent man of the past who was still a force in society was apt to become the focus for a cult and a mythical conception.

In ancient China religion consisted of the cults of nature divinities, in which Heaven is included, and of the ancestors. The worship of men was limited to small groups to which the men had belonged. Toward the close of the Chou period there had begun a development which reached into the Han period and beyond, in which the lines between these two kinds of cults had broken down, men becoming gods and nature gods being considered as men of the past. Great men came to be honored by sacrifices as the reward of their merit, and these sacrifices were paid, sometimes by any one, sometimes by groups, such as the members of a trade, who felt under obligations to the great men. This situation came about the more easily because there had never been any sharp line between the ceremonies performed for the nature deities and those for the ancestors, and because the age was one of boundless credulity and acceptance of the extraordinary and the fabulous.

NOTES

[1] The *Lun Hêng* of Wang Ch'ung has been translated by Forke in Vols. IX, X, and XI of the *Mitt. des Sem. für Orientalische Sprachen*. The account of his life and work is found in Vol. IX, pp. 244 f., and in Forke's Introduction, Vol. IX, pp. 184 f. He was born in A.D. 27 and lived until A.D. 97. While he studied under Pan Piao and was recognized as a brilliant scholar, he occupied only minor posts, and during his later years was poor and neglected. The Chinese themselves have seldom recognized his greatness, and this is in part owing to his criticism of Confucius. These quotations are from the *Lung Hêng*, chap. 42, and the translation is by Forke, *Mitt. des Sem.*, Vol. XI, pp. 125 f.

[2] Wang Ch'ung gives the Five Genii as the outer and inner doors, the well, hearth, and inner hall (*ibid.*, p. 126). There are other lists; see Huang and Shryock, "A Collection of Chinese Prayers," in the *Jour. Am. Oriental So.*, Vol. XLIX, p. 149, note 4.

[3] This sentence is quoted from the *Book of Rites*, chap. *Ch'u li* (Legge, *S. B. E.*, Vol. XXVII, p. 116).

[4] The best studies of the gods of the Land and Grain 社稷, the *Hsieh Chi*, are by Chavannes, "Le dieu du sol dans la Chine antique," published as an appendix to *Le T'ai chan*, pp. 437-525, and Franke, *Studien zur Geschichte des konfuzianischen Dogmas und der chinesischen Staatsreligion* (Hamburg, Friederichsen, 1920), pp. 265 f. *Le T'ai Chan* was published as an unnumbered volume of the *Annales du Musée Guimet* (Paris, Leroux, 1910).

[5] *Book of History*, II, 1,6 (Legge, *Chinese Classics*, Vol. III, p. 33). In ancient China the nature gods had almost no personality. In the poetry of Ch'ü Yüan, of the third century B.C., they become real persons.

[6] *Book of Rites,* chap. *Chi fa.* Legge (*S. B. E.,* Vol. XXVIII, p. 201) gives a somewhat different version, but that of Forke is the more accurate.

[7] *Lun Heng,* Vol. XI, p. 128.

[8] *Ibid.,* p. 130. This last sentence is quoted from the *Book of Rites* (Legge, *S. B. E.,* Vol. XXVIII, p. 208). The commentator K'ung Ying-ta says, "The spirits were men who, when alive, had done good·service and were sacrificed to when dead. From which it follows that what was agreeable to the minds of men would be in accordance with the spirits" (Legge, *S. B. E.,* Vol. XXVII, p. 395, note).

[9] Wylie (*Notes on Chinese Literature,* p. 6) has a brief but excellent account of the work of the two Tai in collecting the *Book of Rites,* and of their sources. The introduction to Legge's translation in the *S. B. E.,* Vols. XXVII and XXVIII, is fuller, and discusses the different chapters.

[10] *Book of Rites,* chap. *T'ang kung* (Legge, *S. B. E.,* Vol. XXVII, p. 196).

[11] Taken from Ssu-ma Ch'ien, chap. 31, 9 (Chavannes, *Mém. hist.,* Vol. IV, p. 15).

[12] *Lung Hêng,* Vol. XI, p. 132.

[13] Addison, in a useful little essay on *Ancestor Worship,* published in Shanghai by the National Christian Council, has collected practically all the references to ancestor worship in the *History,* the *Odes,* and the *Rites.* Unfortunately he omits the ones in the *I li,* which give the ritual of the sacrifices, and the many illustrations which occur in the historical books.

[14] De Groot (*Religious System of the Chinese,* Vol. I), gives a very detailed account of modern funeral customs in Amoy and many historical references. Steele's translation of the *I li* gives the rubrics of the services in the cult of the ancestors.

[15] Laufer, *Jade,* pp. 120 f.

[16] 主 *chu.* There is a good discussion of the *chu* and of the ceremony of putting the dot above the character with blood, in Chavannes, *Le dieu du sol, T'ai Chan,* pp. 476 f. The stones may have been crude images.

[17] Mencius, I, 1, 2, 6. "Confucius said, 'Was not he without posterity who first made wooden images?'" The question of the beginning of the worship of images in China is difficult. Dr. Chiang K'ang-hu believes that the personators of the dead and the tablets came first, but Conrady is of the opposite opinion. Chavannes is rather non-committal. Ssu-ma Ch'ien tells of a ruler of the Yin dynasty, of the twelfth century B. C., who made an image and later dishonored it (Chavannes, *Mém. hist.,* Vol. I, p. 198). The story is not substantiated by any other source. The earliest reference to wooden tablets is also in Ssu-ma Ch'ien, when Wu Wang, the founder of the Chou dynasty, made a wooden tablet for his father, Wen Wang, and carried it on his expedition against Tsou (*ibid.,* p. 224). The custom of putting images of straw or wood in the graves is certainly older than Confucius, but it is probable that geometrical pieces of jade were used even earlier. See also the *Tsu yüan,* sect. 千, p. 191.

[18] The earliest reference to the immolation of men at graves is at the funeral of Duke Wu of Ch'in (*Mém. hist.,* Vol. II, p. 22). The *Spring and Autumn Annals* record that in the nineteenth year of Duke Hsi of Lu, a noble who had arrived late at an assembly was "used" in a sacrifice. Tso-ch'iu Ming comments on this that he was sacrificed instead of an animal, but Ku-liang thinks that they struck the man on the nose till it bled, and smeared the sacrificial vessels with the blood (Legge, *Chinese Classics,* Vol. V, Pt. I, p. 177). In the state of Ch'in a girl was sacrificed to the Yellow River, a practice

imitated in Wei (Tschepe, *Histoire du royaume de Ts'in*, pp. 7, 57, etc., and De Groot, *Religious System of China*, Vol. II, chap. 9). There are no recorded instances of human sacrifices under the Han.

[19] See Legge, *S. B. E.*, Vol. XXVII, pp. 148, 154, 173, and 182.

[20] The *I li* records the presence of the ancestors in connection with practically every ceremony. See Steele's translation, Vol. I, pp. 1, 18, 22, 31, 200, 228, etc.

[21] For instance, the *Odes*, IV, 1, 7 (Legge, *Chinese Classics*, Vol. III, pp. 575, 576). See also Legge, *S. B. E.*, Vol. III, p. 207.

[22] Chavannes, *Le dieu du sol . . . Le T'ai Chan*, p. 440.

[23] *Ibid.*, p. 476 f.

[24] Franke, *Studien . . .*, p. 265.

[25] Ssu-ma Ch'ien (chap. 28, p. 7) records an edict of Kao Tsu in 205 B. C. to this effect. Under the Han these sacrifices were also performed by the feudal lords, but after the rebellion of Huai Nan Tzu they were performed by the emperor's officials in order to weaken the power of the nobility (*Mém. hist.*, Vol. III, p. 454).

[26] At the founding of the Shang dynasty, T'ang did not appoint a new god of the Soil, but continued Chu Lung, the god of the Hsia dynasty (*Mém. hist.*, Vol. I, p. 184, note). He did, however, change the god of the Grain to Ch'i. This is confirmed by the *Ch'ien Han shu*, chap. 5, on sacrifices. As Ch'i was the ancestor of the Chou rulers, he also received sacrifices under that dynasty. In 205 B. C., Han Kao Tsu supplanted the gods of the Land and Grain of Ch'in with those of the Han (*Mém. hist.*, Vol. II, p. 363). Chavannes in a note calls this "the religious consecration of the prize of possession."

[27] Mencius, VII, 2, 14.

[28] Chavannes, *Le dieu du sol . . .*, p. 496. Tung Chung-shu's argument is taken from his work on the *Spring and Autumn Annals*, the *Ch'un Ch'iu Fan Lu*, sect. 74. It is based on the assumption that rain represents the *Yin* principle, while drought is caused by the *Yang*.

[29] Compare *Mém. hist.*, Vol. I, p. 198. Franke (*Studien . . .*, p. 265) cites the *Tso chuan*, the twenty-fifth year of Duke Chuan, as instancing the maltreatment of these gods. The Chinese text indicates that something unusual took place in connection with the gods during a time of prolonged rain. The practice can easily be illustrated in more modern times, and is probably ancient. It is found among other peoples than the Chinese. It illustrates a fundamental difference between the position of nature gods and that of ancestors, for no Chinese would think of insulting or reproving his ancestors.

[30] *Mém. hist.*, Vol. II, p. 63. One of the first rulers of the Chou dynasty, Ch'eng, sent the sacrificial wine to his uncle, the Duke of Chou (Legge, *S. B. E.*, Vol. III, p. 194). The names of ministers yet alive were sometimes placed on banners as a sign that they would share in the sacrifices after their death (*ibid.*, p. 250), but this cannot be called sacrificing to them. The meaning seems to be that in the future life they would enjoy the hospitality of their lord in the same way that they did in the present.

[31] *Analects*, II, 24. Legge, in a note, points out that ancient Chinese ritual provides for the worship of three kinds of spirits, those of heaven, of earth, and of men. This saying of Confucius applies only to the last (*Chinese Classics*, Vol. I, p. 18).

[32] *Mém. hist.*, Vol. III, pp. 443, 446. The story is also mentioned in even greater detail by Meh Ti, *Evidences of Spirits*. See Tomkinson, *Social Teachings of Meh Tse*. p. 101.

[33] The *Ch'ien Han shu* (chap. 28) says, "In Tu, at Po (in the present prov-

ince of Shansi) there are five temples to Tu Chu" (*Mém. hist.*, Vol. III, p. 446, note).

³⁴ *Mém. hist.*, Vol. II, p. 154. The question of influence from southern China, as shown in Ch'ü Yüan, is interesting, but little is known. Wilhelm, p. 171; Conrady, *China*, p. 543.

³⁵ *Ch'ien Han shu*, chap. 1, p. 9L. Wilhelm thinks Kao Tsu went merely out of curiosity (*Chin. Civ.*, p. 172), but the sacrifice indicates more than this.

³⁶ *Mém. hist.*, Vol. II, p. 403.

³⁷ There is a good account of the cults of Ch'in in Ssu-ma Ch'ien's treatise on the *Feng* and *Shan* sacrifices, which is chap. 28 of his *Historical Records* (*Mém. hist.*, Vol. III, pp. 420 f.).

³⁸ *Mém. hist.*, Vol. III, p. 495. See also Legge, *S. B. E.*, Vol. XXVII, p. 386. Wu Ti's sacrifice was in 111 B.C., after the conquest of Nan Yüeh.

³⁹ Wang Ch'ung, *Lun Hêng*, chap. 47.

⁴⁰ *Mém. hist.*, Vol. III, pp. 462, 472. A woman died in childbirth and later appeared as a divinity to her sister, who sacrificed to her. The cult spread, until the grandmother of Wu Ti sacrificed. As her descendants rose to power, the spirit was considered efficacious, and Wu Ti included the cult in the state religion.

⁴¹ Lu Pan, the god of carpenters and mechanics, is said to have been an historical person and a contemporary of Confucius. Among the other stories told abut him is that he invented a chariot which ran by itself. Lu Pan placed his mother in it, whereupon the chariot set off and the lady was never seen again (cf. Laufer, *The Prehistory of Aviation*).

⁴² *Lun Hêng*, Vol. XI, pp. 107, 108.

⁴³ There is a short, but excellent discussion of Hsi Wang Mu in Hirth, *Ancient History of China*, pp. 144 f. The goddess has attracted a good deal of attention from Sinologues. There are quite a few legends about Huai Nan Tzu. See *Lun Hêng*, Vol. X, pp. 118, 119. Chap. 24 contains many such stories.

CHAPTER VII

The Cult of Confucius during the Han Period, 206 B. C.–A. D. 220

The cult of Confucius is a matter different from his life and doctrines, or the development of his school of thought. Its beginnings are obscure, like the beginnings of most customs, and as the cult has been studied only incidentally by European and Chinese scholars, this obscurity has been glossed over by statements which it is difficult or impossible to verify.

There is a Chinese tradition, found in modern works, which has been often accepted by western scholars. The *Encyclopedia Sinica* says, "The Duke of Lu built a temple for him (Confucius), and instituted sacrifices in his honor which were continued until the accession of the First Emperor" (Ch'in Shih Huang).[1] The oldest statement of this sort in a European work appears to be in Amiot's life of Confucius, where it is not documented.[2] Cordier repeats the statement, giving Amiot as his authority.[3] Forke makes it, giving as authority the passage in Chavannes's translation of Ssu-ma Ch'ien which will be considered later, and Doré repeats it without giving any authority.[4] The *Encyclopedia Sinica* rests on the authority of Legge, who says that Duke Ai of Lu erected a temple in which sacrifices were offered to Confucius at the four seasons. At first, he continues, the worship of Confucius was confined to the state of Lu, but in A. D. 57 it was decreed that sacrifices should be offered to him in the schools throughout the country.[5] This sentence covers a development of about 450 years, and gives no reason why a decree should suddenly order general sacrifices. Legge gives as his Chinese source a plan of the Confucian temple.[6] There have been many such plans issued at various times, but all are late, and cannot be considered as authoritative on the origin of the cult unless supported by other evidence.

Without examining the whole literature of ancient China here, it is safe to say that there is no such evidence, and that the temple

93

plan represents a late tradition. There are a number of places where, if there had really been a temple to Confucius in which regular sacrifices were offered by persons who were not his descendants, the fact would certainly have been recorded.

The first of these is in the *Tso chuan,* or commentary on the *Spring and Autumn Annals,* which were continued by the disciples of Confucius for a short time after his death. The *Annals* simply say that Confucius died in the summer of the sixteenth year of Duke Ai. The commentary adds the following narrative.

"The duke pronounced his (Confucius') eulogy, saying, 'Compassionate Heaven vouchsafes me no comfort, and has not left me the aged man, to support me, the One Man, on my seat. Dispirited I am, and full of distress. Woe is me! Alas! O Ni Fu! There is none to be a rule to me!' Tzu Kung said, 'The ruler is not likely to die in Lu. The Master said, that error in a point of ceremony shows darkness of mind; error in the use of a name is a fault. Failure of the mind is darkness; a fault is failure in one's position. The duke could not use the Master when alive; in eulogizing him when dead, he has transgressed the rules of ceremony. In calling himself the One Man he has assumed a name which does not belong to him. In both things the ruler has erred.' "

Not only does this passage not say anything about a temple and worship, but the man who is supposed to have built the temple is condemned. As the passage prophesies the duke's exile, it was probably written after that event, and had there been a temple, the author would certainly have known about it.[7]

The second passage is one in which Mencius describes the mourning of Confucius' disciples.

"When Confucius died, after three years had elapsed, his disciples collected their baggage, and prepared to return to their several homes. But on entering to take their leave of Tzu Kung, as they looked toward one another, they wailed, till they all lost their voices. After this they returned to their homes, but Tzu Kung went back, and built a house for himself on the altar-ground, where he lived alone three years, before he returned home."[8]

Here again, had there been a temple and worship, it would certainly have been recorded. Mencius was writing more than a century after the death of Confucius.

In the *Book of Rites* is a passage, already quoted, which describes what services entitle great men to receive sacrifices after their death. It is immediately followed by a paragraph illustrating this. A number of examples are given, but the men are all mythological characters except the founders of the Shang and Chou dynasties, T'ang, Wen, and Wu. The *Book of Rites* was compiled in the first century B. C. by Confucian scholars, and if there had been regular sacrifices to Confucius for 400 years, the fact would certainly have been noticed, for no better illustration of the practice of sacrificing to great men could have been found.[9]

The Chinese tradition that there was a temple and cult of Confucius during the Chou period is probably based on a passage in Ssu-ma Ch'ien's account of Confucius.

"Together with the disciples and the men of Lu, houses were built near the grave until there were more than a hundred, and the place was called the village of K'ung. Lu transmitted from generation to generation the custom of sacrificing to Confucius at fixed times during the year. Scholars performed the rites of the District Banquet and the Archery Bout at the tomb of Confucius. The building which had formerly been used by the disciples during their mourning was made into a memorial temple by following generations, in which were kept the clothes, ceremonial hat, and lute of Confucius, besides his chariot and his writings. This was continued during more than 200 years until the beginning of the Han. When the emperor Kao visited Lu, he offered the sacrifice of the three victims. When the lords and officials arrived (in Lu), they first visited (the tomb) before taking up their duties." [10]

At the beginning of the second sentence of this passage, Chavannes has put in parentheses the words "the princes of," making it appear that the worship of Confucius was a part of the state religion of Lu from the start. In doing so he must have been following some commentator. Ssu-ma Ch'ien was writing somewhere near the year 100 B. C., before the cult of Confucius had become a state affair. It is probable that after the cult had become part of the state religion, scholars followed the Chinese custom of trying to show that it had always been so, and as this was the oldest passage dealing with the worship of the sage, the word *Lu* is interpreted as meaning "the princes of Lu." From this to the temple of Duke Ai would be an easy jump, even though Ssu-ma Ch'ien says the building was that used by the disciples in mourning. Here also commentators have differed about the passage, as is indicated by Chavannes,[11] and there is no statement that the duke built the temple. However, Ssu-ma Ch'ien does say that there was a regular worship of the sage in Lu beginning almost immediately after the death of Confucius.

Modern scholars are of the general opinion that Ssu-ma Ch'ien is to be used with great caution where he is not confirmed by other sources. He was not always critical, and incorporated into his work statements and passages from questionable sources. In this instance he is not supported by any earlier authorities. Not only in the passages already quoted, but in the mass of literature from the time of Confucius to Ch'in Shih Huang, there is no reference to the worship of the sage by others than his descendants. This is impressive silence, and leads us to ask how far the testimony of Ssu-ma Ch'ien is to be regarded as reliable.

The historian says that he visited the tomb and saw the clothes, lute, chariot, and books of Confucius. If he saw the books, it is a pity that he did not give a list, and it is also hard to understand why, if they had been always preserved in a mortuary temple, the Han scholars had such a hard time in fixing the texts. But when we consider the historian's account of the origin of the cult, the case is quite different. He was in Lu nearly a century after the well-authenticated visit of Han Kao Tsu. A century is long enough for an unhistorical tradition to spring up, and Ssu-ma Ch'ien does not pretend that his account of the origins of the cult rests on anything but tradition. If there had been a well-established cult of Confucius in Lu, with a temple and a library, Ch'in Shih Huang would certainly have destroyed it. This is so obvious that a story was invented, and is cited by Doré from a work of the nineteenth century,[12] to the effect that Ch'in Shih Huang did violate the tomb, and found there a written prophecy of the event, and of his own approaching death. This story has no historical foundation.

The conclusion to be reached from the consideration of these facts is that there is no satisfactory evidence for a cult of Confucius before the beginning of the Han period, apart from his inclusion in the ancestral worship of the K'ung family. When this is supplemented by the mass of literature in which the cult would almost certainly be mentioned had it existed, but in which no reference to it is made, the fact that Confucius himself can be quoted against such practices as the cult would imply, the absence of similar cases of rewarding great men by sacrifices in the Chou period, unless they had been appointed to spiritual offices such as the gods of the Land and Grain, and the very questionable authority of the passage in the *Book of Rites* where sacrifices to great men are authorized—

all this negative evidence leads to the conclusion that there was no cult of Confucius outside his own family before the time of Han Kao Tsu.

The visit of Han Kao Tsu in 195 B. C., while he was making a tour of the country, is told not only by Ssu-ma Ch'ien, but also by the imperial annals of the *Ch'ien Han shu*,[13] and can therefore be accepted as historical, although the *Ch'ien Han shu* may be simply copying Ssu-ma Ch'ien. Kao Tsu was following the precedent of Ch'in Shih Huang, who made a tour of the provinces during which he visited and sacrificed at local spots of interest. Kao Tsu was not a follower of Confucius, nor a member of the literati, but he depended upon the Confucians for political support, and therefore his sacrifice to Confucius was probably a political gesture, as has already been stated.

The emperor is said by both Ssu-ma Ch'ien and the *Ch'ien Han shu* to have offered the *T'ai lao,* or sacrifice of three victims—an ox, a sheep, and a pig.[14] This was a great honor to the sage, and set a precedent. Ssu-ma Ch'ien records that the officials and lords of the state or province of Lu in the Han period visited the tomb before taking up their duties. Although this is not mentioned in the *Ch'ien Han shu*,[15] it may be historical, if the passage is accepted as genuine, because the *Ch'ien Han shu* does not give accounts of local cults, and because there is no reason why Ssu-ma Ch'ien should not be accurate upon a point of contemporary practice. It would be expected that, the emperor having sacrificed in a certain place, his officials would be obliged to follow his example, though probably not offering the same rites as Kao Tsu. If they went to the tomb at all, they performed some ceremony. The whole passage in Ssu-ma Ch'ien is difficult and questionable. There were no more imperial visits under the Western Han dynasty.

The increased respect for Confucius is shown by the eulogy of Ssu-ma Ch'ien.

"In the world there have been many, from sovereigns to sages, who have lived in a glory which ended with their death. But Confucius, though clothed in cloth, has transmitted his fame for more than ten generations; he is considered the chief of scholars. From the Son of Heaven, the princes and lords, all who discuss the six liberal arts follow the precedent of the Master. He may be said to have been perfectly holy." [16]

This was written during the reign of Wu Ti, after the official adoption of Confucian principles. It will be noticed that neither here, nor in any other place, is it said that every one should worship Confucius. Ssu-ma Ch'ien does go further than any one before him in that he places the account of Confucius among the descriptions of the hereditary houses of nobility, where, as a matter of fact, the sage did not belong. This was a recognition of his preëminence among the great men of antiquity, since Lao Tzu and the other philosophers were not so honored.

The next century saw Confucius and the K'ung family actually elevated to the position of hereditary nobles. Biot says that Yüan Ti gave a title to K'ung P'o,[17] a descendent of Confucius, but this is not found in the imperial annals of the reign. According to Ma Tuan-lin,[18] it was in 8 B. C. that scholars obtained for a direct descendant of the sage a title and a grant of land. The scholar Mei Fu petitioned the emperor, pointing out that Wu Wang, founder of the Chou dynasty, had given fiefs to descendants of the Hsia and Shang dynasties where they could continue the sacrifices of their lines, and that the Han dynasty should follow this example. Confucius was descended from one of the last rulers of the Shang or Yin dynasty, and therefore his descendant should sacrifice to T'ang, the founder of the Shang dynasty. The emperor Ch'eng agreed, and appointed K'ung Ho-tsu to do this, with a hereditary fief of 100 li. Mei Fu, after pointing out that the descendants of Confucius were still commoners, says, "It is not the intention of Heaven that so great a man should receive honor only from people of so mean a condition."

This argument applied not only to the Shang and Hsia dynasties, but to the Chou also, which was now extinct. In A. D. I, P'ing Ti repaired the temple at Ch'ü-fu, the home of Confucius, and gave the title of duke to the sage. At the same time he gave the title of marquis to descendants of both Confucius and the Duke of Chou, thus ensuring the continuation of the sacrifices of the lines of the Shang and Chou dynasties.[19] No one seems to have been interested in the sacrifices of Ch'in.

It is further evidence against the existence of a cult of Confucius before the beginning of the Christian era that when a descendant of the sage was ennobled, it was not for the purpose of sacrificing to Confucius himself, but to a much more remote ancestor, T'ang, the founder of the Shang dynasty. In allowing the ancestral sacrifices of preceding dynasties to be continued, the Han emperors were following a precedent at least as old as the Chou dynasty.

The same evidence indicates that it was not the custom under the Western Han and earlier dynasties to honor great men with sacrifices. The *Book of Rites,* as already quoted, says that it was, yet it is impossible to find an instance. The spirits of certain men, usually ancestors, received sacrifices because they had been appointed as the gods of the Land and Grain; others, like T'ang and Wu, because they had founded dynasties and therefore their ancestral cult had become a part of the state religion. Still others, like the Master of Tu and the Princess of the Spirits, because after their death they had been responsible for miracles. But it is impossible to find an instance, in the period before Wang Mang, of a man who received sacrifices from others than his descendants simply because he was a great man. The *Book of Rites* was completed about the close of the Western Han period. It is not quoted as a final authority until the period of the Eastern Han, when anything having the authority of the scholars of the Western Han period was generally accepted, and we have a skeptical critic like Wang Ch'ung quoting the *Book of Rites* as final. Many great men of the Chou and Western Han periods came to have cults connected with them. T'ai Kung, Ch'ü Yüan, and Chang Liang are examples. But these cults cannot be shown to have existed before the Eastern Han period.[20]

If it is true, as we have tried to show, that the custom of generally honoring great men by sacrificing to them developed after the formation of the *Book of Rites,* and not before, the sacrifice of Kao Tsu to Confucius, if it be accepted as historical, may be regarded merely as a political device which followed a precedent set by Ch'in Shih Huang, and not as a part of a cult of Confucius; while the visits of officials to his tomb, as described in the unsupported statement of Ssu-ma Ch'ien, would be in the nature of announcements, such as were commonly made in ancestral temples.

The first mention of a regular cult of Confucius is in A. D. 37. Kuang Wu, founder of the Eastern Han dynasty, had visited the district of Lu in A. D. 29. Instead of visiting the grave of Confucius himself, he sent a minister, who sacrificed. But in A. D. 37 the same emperor gave titles to two descendants of Confucius, making K'ung An marquis of Chao Chia, and K'ung Tzu marquis of Pao Ch'eng. This made two noble branches of the family of Confucius. The

Chao Chia branch sacrificed to T'ang, while the Pao Ch'eng branch sacrificed to Confucius. The sacrifices to T'ang stopped with the reign of Kuang Wu, but those to Confucius continued to the end of the Han dynasty.[21] These sacrifices seem to have been similar to those regularly offered to ancestors, but in as much as they were offered by direct command of the emperor, they were a part of the state religion.

There are three instances of imperial visits to the memorial temple at Ch'ü-fu in the Eastern Han period. It would seem that this temple was the building mentioned by Ssu-ma Ch'ien and repaired by P'ing Ti. Mayers says [22] that P'ing Ti erected a temple in which sacrifices were offered jointly to the Duke of Chou and Confucius. This statement is not found in the Ch'ien Han shu, which says only that P'ing Ti repaired the temple.

The first of the imperial visits was made by Ming Ti in A. D. 72. He was making a tour of the provinces, accompanied by his brother, his son, and a suite of nobles and officials. During the tour he went to the temple at Ch'ü-fu, accompanied by his suite, and sacrificed to Confucius, while his officials sacrificed to the disciples of the sage. Then he sat down, and ordered his son to read from the canon.[23] Unfortunately the Hou Han shu does not state what grade of sacrifice was offered, nor exactly what the emperor did. He may simply have stood before the altar while gifts were presented in his name. There is no record that a prayer or praise ode was offered, and a passage in the T'ang history [24] says that under the Han no prayers were used in the worship of Confucius.

In the passage of the Hou Han shu describing the visit of Ming Ti, it is said that the temple belonged to Confucius and his seventy-two disciples, while an explanatory note adds, "Yen Hui and the others." This is the first instance recording any worship of the disciples, and the number seventy-two raises an interesting point.

The earliest reference to the number of disciples is in Mencius,[25] who says there were seventy. Han Fei gives the same number.[26] Ssu-ma Ch'ien gives accounts of seventy-seven,[27] and is followed by the Family Sayings. Yet the generally recognized number of disciples is seventy-two, for which the Hou Han shu, in the passage just cited, is the oldest historical authority. The temple plans say that the number seventy-two rests on the precedent set by Wen Weng. This is quite possible, and if Wen Weng did not think of the number seventy-two, some one else of the Han period did, but the reason why it appealed to the men of the Han age is apparent. From the time of Tsou Yen in the latter half of the fourth century B. C., Chinese scientific thought was fascinated by attempts to explain the universe in terms of certain numbers, of which the one most used was five. During the Han period mathematical theories were carried so far that the *Book of Rites* gives accounts of five seasons of the year.[28] Chavannes points out that the number seventy-two is connected with these theories.[29] Multiplied by five, the number of the elements and of the planets, it gives 360, considered as the number of days in the year, and so on. The Confucian school was not interested in science, and took its scientific ideas at second hand. These numerical theories were fastened on Chinese thought in the Han period. While they have no connection with Confucius and his early disciples, they were grafted to Confucianism so as to become a part of its system of thought, and acquired the weight of its authority and conservatism. It is safe to say that it was this attractiveness of the number seventy-two which led to the rejection of numbers which had much better authority behind them.

The temple at Ch'ü-fu was visited by Chang Ti in A. D. 85, and by An Ti in A. D. 124. Both emperors sacrificed to Confucius, while their officials sacrificed to the seventy-two disciples. In both cases gifts of money and silk were made to the family of the sage.[30]

The importance of these imperial visits can easily be exaggerated. The state cult of Confucius did not develop from them, though they did give prestige to the Ch'ü-fu temple. This temple, though it became in a sense a national institution, was the property of the K'ung family, and the regular worship there was a part of their ancestral rites. Imperial visits were only occasional, and the custom never became obligatory. A majority of the emperors of China did not go, and there is no trace of such an idea as that it was necessary for an emperor to secure the blessing of Confucius or the approval of any member of the K'ung family for his acts. The authority of the sage has never been required as a religious sanction, nor has a visit to the temple and sacrifice there been considered an imperial prerogative, like the *ti* sacrifice to Heaven. On the other hand, the religious ideas of the Chinese and the preëminence of Confucius from the Han period on have made the spot sacred. It has escaped disaster during times of war and unrest, and has been respected even by foreign conquerors. Its position may be compared to one between that of Mt. Vernon and that of the shrine of St.

Thomas à Becket at Canterbury. With the exception of occasional sacrifices by distinguished visitors, the worship has been ancestral, and there has never developed a Confucian priesthood, save in the sense that every Chinese is a priest in his own home. The family of the sage has always been prominent, and has furnished many distinguished men since the time of Confucius and Tzu Ssu. Although the temple and its cult will be mentioned at times, this study makes no attempt to follow the fortunes of the temple, nor of the K'ung family, which properly belong to a study of ancestor worship.[31]

The growth of the Confucian school has been outlined up to the time of the adoption of some of the Confucian principles by the state. This was followed by the development of the schools and the creation of a privileged scholar class acknowledging Confucius as a model and a final authority. This class owed its prominence, at least in part, to the fact that it made the emperor less dependent upon his family and the nobility. The worship of men developed to a point where, from the time of Wang Mang onward, it was customary to honor the great men of the past with sacrifices. The combination of these circumstances made it inevitable that Confucius should eventually receive worship from the scholars.

It is not known exactly how or when the cult of Confucius began in the schools, beyond the fact that at a certain time an imperial edict made the worship compulsory. It is safe to assume that this edict made general a practice which had already existed in some places. Wen Weng is said to have placed pictures or images of the sages in his hall of study, but the edition of the gazetteer of Ch'eng-tu which was the authority for this statement no longer exists, so that much weight cannot be attached to it. The *Ch'ien Han shu* says nothing about religious ceremonies in the schools under the Western Han, nor do secondary authorities like Ma Tuan-lin and the *Yü hai*. Worship of Confucius may have begun in private schools, and spread from them to those of the state, or it may have been introduced by the head of some government institution and proved so satisfactory that its use was made general. There is no evidence that there was any worship of Confucius in the *T'ai hsioh,* or other government institutions, under the Western Han.

Both Ma Tuan-lin and the *Yü hai* mention that in A. D. 30 a ceremony which seems to have consisted in the pouring of a libation of wine was performed in the district schools twice a year, spring and autumn.[32] The Sui history at a later date mentions a wine ceremony in honor of Confucius in the schools,[33] which may have been the same rite.

The first clear instance of a regular cult of Confucius in the schools is a decree of the third month of the second year of the reign Yün-p'ing, when the emperor Ming ordered that the schools in all the larger cities should sacrifice to the sage.[34] Legge, on the authority of the Temple Record, dates this event in A. D. 57,[35] while the *Yü hai,* cited by Biot, places it in A. D. 58, on the authority of a commentary on the *Book of Rites;* but the date in the *Hou Han shu,* which is the primary source, fixes the event in the year A. D. 59. It is obvious that all three passages refer to the same event. From that time onward, as long as there were schools, the cult was connected with education. The edict of Ming Ti adds that the worship should be paid equally to the Duke of Chou and Confucius. The Duke of Chou was a great man, and is reputed to have been the author of the larger part of the text of the *Book of Changes,* besides being quoted at considerable length in the *History.* From this date, until the T'ang period, he and Confucius appear together as the patron saints of schools and scholars. It is not stated whether there were temples to these men connected with the schools, or shrines, or whether the objects of adoration, tablets, images, or pictures, were simply placed in a hall which was also used for other purposes.

Neither is it clear what was offered, nor how many times a year the sacrifice was made. In view of later practice, it was probably made twice annually, in the spring and autumn, but it may have been at the four seasons, or at the beginning and completion of the school year, or even at each new moon, for at various periods all these times have been associated with the cult. Ma Tuan-lin says that in the district schools a dog was sacrificed to the Duke of Chou and Confucius in A. D. 59.[36] This is enough to show that the ceremony included more than a libation, for the rites in the capital were certainly more elaborate than in the smaller cities.

It may be said in general of all Chinese sacrifices that they vary both with the position of the person to whom the sacrifice is offered, and with the position of the persons sacrificing. On the one hand, the higher the rank of the one receiving the sacrifice, the greater the offerings. On the other hand, the sacrifices offered to the same person would differ with the rank of the one sacrificing. An official would not offer the same sacrifice as an emperor, and the victims presented in a country district would be less than those offered in the capital.

The conclusion to be drawn from the best evidence is that there was no regular cult of Confucius, outside the ancestral worship of the K'ung family, under the Western Han dynasty. The Confucian renascence under Wu Ti did not aim at the establishment of a worship of the sage. The Confucian scholars, like Tung Chung-shu, did not urge it. That later tradition should assume, or endeavor to prove, that there had been such worship, was owing to a trait that the Chinese share with other peoples—the desire to believe that their institutions were of the greatest possible antiquity and that a great man of the past had always held the same position that he came to hold in later times.

There was a cult of Confucius under the Eastern Han dynasty. Between the two dynasties lies the period dominated by Wang Mang, and it is interesting to speculate what part the ideas developed under the usurper played in the growth of the cult. The *Ch'ien Han shu* is antagonistic to Wang Mang, as Chinese opinion has been ever since. The three sections of chapter 99, all of which are devoted to him, contain no direct evidence. There is indirect evidence, however. After Wang Mang assumed the throne, he became involved in political disputes which eventually led to his downfall. It seems evident that in his sweeping reforms he was endeavoring to return to what he believed to be the Chou usage. In doing this he was in the orthodox line of Confucian thought, and he had the support of such Confucians as Yang Hsiung. His petitions, before he became emperor, show a deep respect for Confucius, the canon, and the old Chou customs. He himself, in the earlier stages of his career, was a student who appeared to practise all the Confucian virtues, and he was a patron of scholars and of education. The books, such as the *Chou li,* which some modern scholars think were forged during his period, are idealistic attempts to find a model state in the remote past. It is possible that the idea of rewarding great men by general worship and sacrifices developed under the impression that it was really a return to lost tradition.

This much is certainly true. The acts attributed by historians to the emperor P'ing, a puppet, were in reality the acts of Wang Mang, who ruled the state with the title of Lord Protector of the House of Han. These included the repairing or building of the temple at

Ch'ü-fu, the granting of a posthumous title to Confucius, and the ennobling of a descendant of the sage. There can be no question that he made a great contribution to the development of Confucian sentiment, and possibly to the growth of the cult, but he betrayed the trust implied in his title and has been condemned by succeeding generations. Wang Mang failed, but the Confucian sentiment which he had furthered went marching on.

The evidence presented in this chapter may be summarized as follows. The statement that there was a cult of Confucius in Lu, beginning with Duke Ai, and continuing through the Chou and Ch'in periods, rests on a late tradition, and lacks historical foundation. The account of the sacrifice of Kao Tsu may be accepted as accurate, but Kao Tsu does not seem to have inaugurated a regular cult.[37] A great impetus was given to the prestige of Confucius by Wang Mang, acting through his puppet P'ing Ti, but there is no reason for believing that under Wang Mang any one sacrificed to Confucius except members of his own family.[38] The first definite date when it is known that there was a regular cult of Confucius outside the K'ung family is A. D. 59, when Ming Ti ordered sacrifices to him and the Duke of Chou in the schools. The few instances of sacrifice by outsiders before this are sporadic, and such sacrifices were performed at Ch'ü-fu, whereas the edict of Ming Ti authorized, if it did not create, a general cult throughout the schools of the country. It was this act which took the worship of Confucius outside the K'ung family, and changed Confucius from the model of scholars into their patron saint.

This imperial action did not make Ming Ti and his successors into Confucians in the sense in which a man is said to be a Moslem or a Christian; that is, there was no feeling that the emperor or the scholars should sacrifice to Confucius and to no one else. But there can be no question that under the Eastern Han religion was brought into what had previously been an ethical, political, and philosophic school of thought. The Confucians of the Chou, Ch'in, and Western Han periods revered and followed their master, but they did not worship him.[39]

The cult of Confucius was a hero worship deliberately adopted by the state at the instance of a social group, the scholars, who acknowledged the leadership of the sage. This hero worship occupied a place in the state religion between the cults of nature deities and the worship of ancestors, from both of which it borrowed.[40] While there have been many such cults recognized by the Chinese government, it is very doubtful whether any extant cult can be shown to have existed prior to the cult of Confucius.

In ancient China there were the cults of ancestors and the cults of nature gods. As early as the Chou period the distinction between these two had been partly broken down by the appointment of the spirits of men to the position of gods of the Land and Grain. Ch'in Shih Huang sacrificed to the nature gods of other states than his own, and Han Kao Tsu went one step further by sacrificing to Confucius. Ch'in Shih Huang sacrificed to nature gods who were held to be the spirits of men, but who were really mythological characters, while Han Kao Tsu sacrificed to a man who was no myth, and who was revered by an influential section of society as a master. The acts of these two emperors followed precedents set in the nature cults. The first regular worship of Confucius was by his own family, even though its members were ordered to sacrifice by imperial decrees. The combination of the two, and the constant increase in the prestige of Confucius due to the power of the scholar class, made the inauguration of the cult of Confucius in the schools almost inevitable. The action of Han Ming Ti was the result of a natural and an indigenous development.

NOTES

[1] *Enc. Sin.*, art. "Confucius," p. 128.

[2] Amiot's *Vie de Koung-tsée*, in *Mémoires concernant les Chinois*, Vol. XII, p. 397. Amiot's work was published in Paris in 1786. There is a good list of these early studies in the bibliography of Latourette's *History of Christian Missions in China*. Du Halde and De Mailla are especially valuable.

[3] Cordier, *Histoire générale de la Chine*, Vol. I, p. 156.

[4] Forke, *Chin. Phil.*, p. 109. "Herzog Ai liess dem Konfuzius einen Tempel errichten und befahl, dass seinen Manen viermal im Jahre geopfert wurde." The authority for this is Chavannes (*Mém. hist.*, Vol. V, p. 429), but Chavannes is careful, and does not say this. His passage runs, "(Les princes de) Lou se transmirent de génération en génération la coutume d'offrir des sacrifices à K'ong-tse à des époques fixes de l'année."

Doré, *Recherches sur les superstitions en Chine*, Vol. XIII, p. 93, published in Shanghai, 1918, by the Imprimerie de la Mission catholique at Siccawei.

[5] Legge, *Chinese Classics*, Vol. I, Prolegomena, p. 91.

[6] Legge, in a note, gives his authority as the 聖廟祀典圖考卷 一. Editions of these temple records, not including Legge's authority, are in the Library of Congress, and are listed here in the Chinese Bibliography. The earliest such plan is that attributed to Wen Weng, but none can be accepted as an authority for the time of Confucius. Legge does not give the date of the one he used, but Doré (Vol. XIII, p. 122) says that it was published in 1826.

[7] *Tso chuan,* sixteenth year of Duke Ai (Legge, *Chinese Classics,* Vol. V, pt. 2, p. 846). The passage also occurs, in a shortened form, in the *Book of Rites,* II, 1, 3, 43. The expression "the One Man" should properly be used by the king only. That the duke would not die in Lu is a reference to his exile.

[8] Mencius, III, 1, 4, 13. Legge's translation.

[9] *Book of Rites,* chap. *Chi fa,* or the *Law of Sacrifices,* par. 9 (Legge, *S. B. E.,* Vol. XXVIII, p. 201). The *Chi fa* is based on the *Kuo Yü,* or *Conversations Regarding the States,* a history of the Chou feudal period, 1, 2, 7. "The statements have much perplexed the commentators, and are held to be of doubtful authority" (Legge, p. 202, note 1).

[10] Ssu-ma Ch'ien, chap. 47 (Chavannes, *Mém. hist.,* Vol. V, p. 429). There are descriptions of the Archery Bout and the District Banquet in the *I li,* which has been translated by Steele. The Chinese text of this passage is given in Appendix IV.

[11] *Mém. hist.,* Vol. V, p. 429, note 2. The chief commentators on Ssu-ma Ch'ien are P'ei Yin, 裴駰 Ssu-ma Cheng 司馬貞 and Chang Shou-chieh 張守節. Chavannes (*Mém. hist.,* Vol. I, Introduction, pp. 210 f.) gives an account of their work.

[12] Doré, Vol. XIII, p. 92. Doré gives as his source a modern work called the *Sheng chi t'u* 聖蹟圖 . The phrase that the books of Confucius were kept in the temple is a little ambiguous, but Ssu-ma Ch'ien certainly gives the impression that he saw the actual copies used by Confucius (*Mém. hist.,* Vol. V, p. 435). Possibly the books discovered by K'ung An-kuo were kept there. One is tempted to be skeptical about the whole passage, and to suspect that the text has been tampered with. The ancient Chinese were not relic worshipers. There is no other evidence of a cult of Confucius in Lu. Even if the story of K'ung An-kuo is accepted—and there is some doubt about it—the books he found had not been hidden from Ch'in Shih Huang, who would certainly have destroyed the place if it had been a shrine connected with the literature that he burnt. Probably there is no other instance in ancient China of such ceremonies as the Archery Bout and the District Banquet being performed at any one's grave. There is no historical support for the statement, which is not found in Ssu-ma Ch'ien, that Ch'in Shih Huang interrupted the sacrifices to Confucius.

[13] *Ch'ien Han shu,* chap. I, p. 9L.

[14] There were two grades of sacrifices, the *t'ai lao* 太牢 ("great offering") consisting of an ox, sheep, and pig, and the *hsiao lao* 少牢 ("small offering") also called the *chung lao* 中牢 , consisting of a sheep and pig. Takakuwa (p. 94) says that Kao Tsu offered the lesser sacrifice, but this is contradicted by Ssu-ma Ch'ien and the *Ch'ien Han shu,* both saying that he offered the *t'ai lao.* There are short articles on the two sacrifices in the *Tsu yüan,* sect. 丑, p. 231, and sect. 子, p. 69.

[15] It is not in the imperial annals nor the *Li chi,* nor is there a chapter where one would expect to find it.

[16] The conclusion of Ssu-ma Ch'ien's account of Confucius, chap. 47. This translation follows Chavannes (*Mém. hist.,* Vol. V, p. 435), and may be compared with that in Giles (*Chin. Biog. Dict.,* p. 400), which is less accurate. The term *Chih sheng* 至聖 ("Perfectly holy"), refers to the perfection of Confucius' character, and not to any idea of divinity, which Giles implies. Since Sung Cheng Tsung, this term has been a part of Confucius' title. It first occurs in the famous passage of the *Doctrine of the Mean* (chaps. 30-32),

which has not been mentioned because the commentators disagree as to how far the passage was intended to apply to Confucius. For an account of their opinion, see the notes to Legge's translation (*Chinese Classics,* Vol. I, pp. 291 f.). The text permits both interpretations. According to Legge, Tzu Ssu employed language with reference to Confucius far stronger than any ruler had applied to the founder of his line, which is so unlikely that such orthodox scholars as Cheng K'ang-ch'eng and K'ung Ying-ta have rejected it.

[17] Biot, p. 169. This appears to be a mistake, for there is no reference to it in the annals of the reign of Yüan Ti. That emperor did, however, ennoble a descendant of Chou Kung.

[18] Ma Tuan-lin, chap. 43, sect. 8. Ma Tuan-lin is not documented, but the original source is obviously the biography of Mei Fu 梅福 in the *Ch'ien Han shu* (chap. 67, pp. 1 f.), where the petition of Mei Fu is given in full. He criticizes the Ch'in rulers for not following the ways of Confucius and Chou Kung, so that there was no way of applying *tao* to the rulers, and uses the old distinction between *pa tao* 霸道 "rule by force," the doctrine of the School of Law and of Ch'in, and *wang tao* 王道 "the way of the [ancient] rulers," which did not depend on coercion. Mei Fu goes on to argue that although Confucius was not descended from the Yin rulers in the direct line, it would be proper for his descendants to sacrifice to them. The traditional genealogy of Confucius is given in the *Family Sayings* (sect. 39). The genealogy as collected from different parts of Ssu-ma Ch'ien is given by Chavannes (*Mém. hist.,* Vol. V, p. 284, note 2). It goes back to a representative of the royal house of Yin, who was given the fief of Sung by the founder of the Chou dynasty. The petition of Mei Fu is translated by Du Halde (Vol. I, pp. 496, 497). In the eleventh century, Mei Fu was canonized as a Taoist god (Giles, *Chin. Biog. Dict.,* p. 578). The Chinese text of a part of the petition of Mei Fu is given in Appendix IV.

[19] *Ch'ien Han shu,* chap. 12, p. 29 R. P'ing Ti appointed K'ung Chun as the marquis of Pao Ch'eng 襃成. It is not known how early the Chinese began to give titles of nobility. Takakuwa (p. 35), thinks the feudal system existed under Yao and Shun. Under the Chou dynasty there were five such titles, the first two of which existed under the Shang dynasty. They were *kung* 公, *hou* 侯, *po* 伯, *tzu* 子, and *nan* 男. Various European titles of nobility have been used in translating them. Here, *kung* is translated as "duke," and *hou* as "marquis." Under the Chou, the ruler bore the title of *wang* 王, but Ch'in Shih Huang used a new title, *huang ti* 皇帝, translated "emperor." *Wang* was used as the highest title of nobility under the Han, and is translated "prince." These five grades of nobility are frequently mentioned in the canon. Toward the close of the Chou period, the chief feudal lords usurped the title of *wang,* which led to Ch'in Shih Huang's using a new title, that has been adopted by the sovereigns ever since. A good account of these ranks of nobility is given by Mencius, V, 2, 2. P'ing Ti also gave to Confucius the title *Pao ch'eng hsüan ni kung* 襃成宣尼公 (*Ch'ien Han shu,* chap. 12, p. 20 R).

[20] T'ai kung 太公 (eleventh and twelfth centuries B.C.) was a supporter of the founder of the Chou dynasty, and was rewarded by a fief. Both a mythology and a cult grew p around him, and he is still regarded as having such power over the spirits that the sentence "Chiang T'ai kung is here" is sufficient to keep away evil spirits (Giles, *Chin. Biog. Dict.,* pp. 135, 136).

Ch'ü Yüan 屈原 (332-295 B.C.) was a minister of the state of Ch'u, who committed suicide in despair at the condition of the state. He was the author of a poem, in which sect. 9 contains songs or hymns in honor of nine gods of the state of Ch'u. They are all nature gods. He has since been connected with the Dragon Boat Festival, on the fifth day of the fifth month, which is really a rain festival (Giles, *loc. cit.*, p. 200, and Ferguson, *Chinese Mythology*, p. 85, Vol. VIII of the *Mythology of All Races* series).

Chang Liang 張良 (died in 187 B.C.) was the friend and advisor of Kao Tsu, the first Han emperor. Reputed to be an ancestor of the Taoist line of "popes," he became a prominent figure in Taoist mythology (Giles, pp. 33, 34).

[21] *Hou Han shu*, chap. 1, b, p. 9 R. The titles were given in the fourth month of the fourteenth year of the reign. K'ung Tzu was the son of K'ung Chun, who had been ennobled by P'ing Ti. The passage is cited by Ma Tuan-lin, chap. 43, sect. 9, 5. The Marquis of Pao Ch'eng assisted Kuang Wu at the *feng* sacrifice on T'ai-shan (*Hou Han shu*, chap. 17, p. 2, cited by Chavannes, *Le T'ai Chan*, p. 166). At this sacrifice there were also representatives of the Yin and Chou dynasties.

[22] Mayers, *Chinese Reader's Manual*, p. 112. Mayers' authority seems to be a collection of essays called the *Ji chi lu* 日知錄, chap. 4, art. 大夫.

[23] *Hou Han shu*, chap. 2, p. 12L.

[24] *Hsin T'ang shu*, chap. 15, p. 40L. The word *wen* 文, a written essay, when used in connection with a sacrifice, may be translated "prayer," though in the worship of ancestors and of Confucius no request is ordinarily made. The essay is addressed to the person to whom the sacrifice is made, and is usually an ode of praise. For illustrations of such prayers addressed to various divinities, see Huang and Shryock, "A Collection of Chinese Prayers," *Jour. Am. Oriental So.*, Vol. XLIX, No. 2, June, 1929, pp. 128 f. That no prayer was used in the Han worship of Confucius makes it certain that no requests were made.

[25] Mencius, II, 1. 3, 2.

[26] *Han Fei*, chapter on "The Five Kinds of Maggots," cited by L. Tomkinson, *Early Legalist School of Chinese Political Thought*. As Han Fei was an opponent of the Confucians, this is good evidence.

[27] Ssu-ma Ch'ien, chap. 67. This chapter has not been translated.

[28] *Book of Rites*, chap. Yüeh ling (Legge, *S. B. E.*, Vol. XXVII, p. 249 f.). It is this chapter which is almost identical with a section of Huai Nan Tzu. The fifth season, invented to correspond to the five elements, the five planets, etc., is placed between summer and autumn.

[29] Chavannes, *Le T'ai Chan*, pp. 17, 159.

[30] *Hou Han shu*, chap. 3, p. 15 R. *Ibid.*, chap. 5, p. 20 L.

[31] There was a mound of earth over the grave of Confucius, of uncertain size. The original temple was simply the building used as living quarters by the disciples during their mourning, according to Ssu-ma Ch'ien (*Mém. hist.*, Vol. V, p. 429). It is safe to say that there was no real temple there before the Han period, probably not before the time of P'ing Ti, in A.D. 1. For accounts of the present temple, one of the most magnificent structures in China, see A. C. Forsyth, *Shantung, the Sacred Province of China*, (Shanghai, 1912, Christian Literature Soc.), and Edkins, "The City of Confucius, (*Jour. N. China Branch of the R. A. S.*, Vol. VIII, p. 79 f.). The Chinese authorities, local gazetteers, are given in the Chinese Bibliography.

The *Chung kuo jen ming ta tsu tien* gives accounts of 184 members of the K'ung family. A list of the official heads of the K'ung family is given in Doré (Vol. XIII, p. 106 f.). The *Ch'ien Han shu* (chap. 81, p. 37 L), in the biography of K'ung Kuan, gives a list of the heads of the family for fourteen generations following Confucius. Doré's list stops with the seventy-first generation after Confucius, in 1744. A letter from China received in December, 1929, says that the Nationalist Government has taken away the grants of land which have been the property of the family for many centuries. This has not been checked. There are several thousand in the clan at present, mostly in the neighborhood of Ch'ü-fu. There is no reason to doubt the accuracy of the family records.

The best account of the temple and cult at Chü-fu is *Konfuzius und sein Kult,* by F. X. Biallas.

[32] Ma Tuan-lin, chap. 46, sects. 7 and 8; *Yü hai,* 111, 40; cited by Biot, p. 164.

[33] *Sui shu,* chap. 9, p. 22 R.

[34] *Hou Han shu,* chap. 14, p. 43 R.

[35] Legge, *Chinese Classics,* Vol. I, Prolegomena, p. 91.

[36] Ma Tuan-lin, chap. 43, p. 38 R. From very ancient times the Chinese have preferred pairs where they might have had unity. Rulers sacrificed to the founder of their line as the associate or correlate of Heaven. Wen and Wu were coupled as the founders of the Chou dynasty. In the Han period, Taoism was called the doctrines of Huang (Ti) and Lao (Tzu), while the Legalistic School was called the doctrines of Han (Fei) and Shen (Pu Hai). While this rule was not absolute, there is enough of the practice to show that in associating the Duke of Chou and Confucius together in sacrifices, the Han were following a strong precedent. The duke was the model of Confucius, and it was fitting to group them together. Later, when Chou Kung was eliminated from the cult, Yen Hui was advanced to be the associate of the Master.

[37] The only study of the cult of Confucius in English which is worth mentioning is *A Guide to the Tablets in a Temple of Confucius,* by T. Watters, printed at Shanghai in 1879 by the American Presbyterian Mission Press. It was privately printed and not originally offered for sale. A review of the book in the *Chinese Recorder* (Vol. X) in the year the book was published, says that Watters dates the beginning of the cult with the sacrifice of Kao Tsu.

[38] Mayers' statement (*Chinese Reader's Manual,* p. 112) that Confucius and Chou Kung received sacrifices together in the temple erected by P'ing Ti is based on a secondary source, and is not confirmed by the *Ch'ien Han shu.* Mayers' article, while brief, is very good.

[39] One is tempted to speculate as to whether the introduction of Buddhism into China may have had anything to do with the development of the cult of Confucius. There is absolutely no evidence that it had during that period, and therefore the possibility has not even been mentioned in the text. There is no need to assume it, since the development of the cult can be explained as a combination of hero worship and ideas borrowed from the indigenous ancestor worship and the cults of nature deities. The worship of Confucius followed the pattern of the worship of ancestors, and was at first performed by members of the K'ung family. On the other hand, the sacrifices by Kao Tsu and later emperors followed the precedents set in the cults of nature divinities.

An interesting parallel to the study of the cult of Confucius would be a corresponding study of the transformation of Taoism from a monistic philosophic system into a religion. The Taoists of the Ch'in and Western Han period were combinations of mystics, scientific investigators, and charlatans, but can hardly be called either the priests or prophets of a religion of Tao. Following the development of the cult of Confucius, there was a development of Taoism in the second century A. D. Han Hsüan Ti (A. D. 147-168) is said to have sacrificed to Lao Tzu, and Chang Tao-ling founded a Taoist society,

or church, which still exists. Chang's dates are usually given as A. D. 34-156.
This society, as the Yellow Turbans, played a considerable part in the fall of
the Han dynasty.

⁴⁰ Grube says, "Innerhalb des Staatskultus nimmt nun aber wiederum die
Verehrung des Konfuzius als Heroenkult eine Art Mittelstellung ein zwischen
dem Kultus der Naturgottheiten einerseits und dem Ahnenkult anderseits"
(*Religion und Kultus der Chinesen*, p. 65).

CHAPTER VIII

THE MEDIEVAL PERIOD, A. D. 220–618

The Han empire, weakened by court intrigues and the power of the eunuchs as well as by the rebellion of the Yellow Turbans, had practically ceased to exist before the end of the second century. There followed a period of disorder in which civilization was temporarily beclouded, a time of almost constant warfare between the various divisions into which the country was partitioned and of foreign invaders from the north who settled permanently in China. There was a succession of dynasties, most of which were of short duration, and during the 400 years immediately preceding the founding of the T'ang dynasty, there were only a few decades when the country could be called united.[1]

In spite of the disorder, culture never sank to such depths as it did during the early middle ages in Europe. Advances were made in some directions, notably sculpture and painting.[2] Learning never vanished, books continued to exist, the classics were known, and schools of some sort frequently attempted to conform to the Han models of education. But in general it may be said that culture and civilization were at their lowest ebb since the days of Confucius, and lower than they have ever been since. The worst elements in society were often in control of the government. Good men gave up the attempt to improve political conditions and retired into obscurity.

It is evident that such conditions would not be favorable to the development of the cult of Confucius. That cult depended upon the existence of a cultured scholar class. Such a class implies a group possessing leisure; it can exist only in a country which enjoys wealth and good order, or else in monastic establishments which are respected even by warring factions. The latter possibility was closed to the Confucians, who have never possessed a monastic order or a priesthood, and whose existence depended upon schools. A comparison may make the contrast between the Han and the medieval periods more vivid. Wen Weng sought out scholars, urged them to study, subsidized them, and gave them official positions. Ku Huan (about A. D. 500) was forced to get his education by listening against the walls of buildings in which books were being read. He studied while plowing, and burned chaff at night for light. When he opened a private school he went into the mountains, where education could be carried on. It is not surprising that there were few scholars during this age, and that a period of 400 years is represented in the Confucian temple by only three names. The surprising thing is that scholarship and the cult of Confucius, which was inseparably connected with it, continued to exist at all. Confucianism demands good government and orderly conditions, and just as the Confucians of the closing centuries of the Chou period, like Mencius and Hsün Tzu, found it difficult or impossible to put their theories into practice, so the few scholars of the medieval period found themselves handicapped and neglected.

The conditions were much more favorable to the development of Taoism. Taoism has two sides, one political and the other mystic. Politically it is allied to the absolute authority of the ruler, and in practice to the organization of the state for war and the doctrine that might is right. Mystically, it cultivates non-action, passivity, retirement from the world, and the resumption of a primitive and uncivilized simplicity. From this latter side sprang ascetic practices resembling those of the Indian Yogi with the aim of securing a mystical experience of union with *Tao,* the power of levitation, and immortality. Still later there developed the cults of those who had attained immortality, and other religious features of the Taoist society founded by Chang Tao-lin. As early as the time of Ch'in Shih Huang, Taoists conducted a search for the drug of immortality, and in the period following the Han, specialized in charms and other forms of magic, which probably originated as short cuts to the goal of an immortal union with *Tao.*

Such a complex of ideas as is found in Taoism would flourish in the disturbed and relatively ignorant conditions of the medieval period. The best Taoists would retire from the world to become hermits, or give themselves up to semi-scientific researches for the drug of immortality and the philosopher's stone. From such researches chemistry sprang. The worst Taoists profited by the prevailing ignorance to form secret political societies among the lower classes, encouraged superstitions, myths, and the miraculous, and peddled charms. Even these were of some ultimate good, as they aided in the development of printing. Among the serious Taoists of the period, Ko Hung [3] and Kuan Lang,[4] and the Seven Sages of the Bamboo Grove, who were largely Taoist,[5] made real contributions to Taoist thought. Some men who are considered legitimate Confucians, like Chu-k'o Liang, Wang Pi [6] and Wang T'ung,[7] were greatly influenced by Taoist thought.

But Chinese thought was no longer confined to ideas which were native to China. Buddhism was brought to China at least as early as the year 2 B. C. by an ambassador of the Yüeh-chi, a tribe of central Asia.[8] It does not appear to have been of much importance before the reign of Ming Ti, when that emperor, in A. D. 65, allowed a statue of Buddha to be erected, and the cult began to spread. Ming Ti seems to have done this at the instance of his brother, the Prince of Ch'u, who in turn was influenced by the Taoists, so that Buddhism first gained a real foothold in China through the invitation of the Taoists.[9] The Confucian scholars opposed the "pernicious doctrine" from the first, and the Prince of Ch'u appears to have stood alone at court in his patronage of the new faith. By A. D. 150, Buddhism was patronized by the emperor.

In the medieval period conditions were much more favorable to the spread of Buddhism. Like Taoism, it teaches withdrawal from the world and the emptiness of worldly ambitions and achievements. Its monastic establishments gave refuge to the discouraged and the defeated, while its doctrine of salvation was singularly fitted to the times. It would be neither possible nor appropriate to attempt an account of the spread of Buddhism during this period, of the missionary monks from India like Kumāradjīva and Bodhidharma,[10] of the Chinese pilgrims who followed Fa Hsien to the holy places of India,[11] of the translation of the Sūtras and the development of the monasteries. By the beginning of the sixth century Buddhism was respected and honored both by the dynasty of Wei in the north and by that of Liang in the south, the emperors rivaling each other in the erection of magnificent pagodas.[12] The emperor Wu of the Liang dynasty became so devout that he neglected the affairs of state, to the eventual ruin of his dynasty.[13] It was an age of intense piety, boundless credulity, and terrible misgovernment.[14]

Taoism and Buddhism had many things in common and usually did not oppose each other. It is easy to make general statements about the influence each had on the other, but a careful and adequate study of the interplay of ideas and the borrowing of doctrines has not yet been made. This is more true of the effect of Taoism upon the foreign religion, and especially in the use of Taoist terms in the translation of the Buddhist scriptures. We are still largely ignorant of the development of both religions, and generalizations are more than usually dangerous, but it may safely be said that there was borrowing and influence on both sides.

This is less true with regard to the real Confucians. Orthodox scholars have always opposed Buddhism,[15] but there were few of them in the medieval period, and the new faith was generally successful. Between the Taoists, who borrowed freely, and the Confucians, who tried not to borrow at all, the emperors held a middle place. According to classic precedent, the emperor sacrificed to all spirits. Buddha had become a recognized divinity, and if the emperor sacrificed to Buddha or patronized the monasteries, the scholars, however little they liked it, had to adjust themselves to the situation. When their influence was strong enough, the Buddhists were subjected to relatively mild persecutions; mild, that is, when compared with those suffered by the early Christians, or those which medieval Christians themselves inflicted upon Jews and Moslems. There were few Buddhist or Taoist martyrs, either in the medieval or in later periods. Throughout their long history, Taoism and Confucianism have always had points of contact, and there has never been a time when mutual influence could not be shown. Philosophic Taoism has always been treated by Confucians with respect, though the charlatans and magicians have not. It is not likely that much direct borrowing was made by Confucianism from Buddhism, aside from art. Buddhist influence, where it existed in Confucian doctrine and practice, came through the medium of Taoist and other cults. Laufer has shown that Confucian iconography was modeled on Buddhist art.

This raises an interesting point. It was during the medieval period that the phrase arose which has been so generally translated as "The Three Religions."[16] It is more than doubtful whether the word *religion* adequately renders the sense of the Chinese. The term *religion* itself is hard to define, and while it would apply to this phrase in a broad sense, in the narrow Roman usage of being concerned with the things of the gods, or of being bound or obligated to them, it does not apply. The Chinese term is better rendered by "teaching" or "doctrine" or "school of thought." It is then true that from the medieval period onward there were three main schools of thought, with various subdivisions, in China, but it is not true to say that there were three religions in the narrow, occidental sense.

This can be seen in the study of the large number of extant cults which had their beginnings in the medieval period, and which show the influence of all three "teachings." Of these, the cult of Kuan Ti, so-called god of War, as a part of the state religion, is the most nearly pure Confucian,[17] yet there is no precedent for it in the classics that is adequate to explain all the features of the cult. The cult of T'ai Shan is Taoist, and goes back in its origin to the nature cults of ancient China, yet in its modern form it shows clear Buddhist influence.[18] The cults of Ti Tsang and Kuan Yin are unquestionably Buddhist, yet they show other influences.[19] If this diffusion of influence is true of cults which can be definitely called Confucian, Taoist, or Buddhist, it is still more true of other modern cults which it is almost impossible to classify, and which cannot accurately be put in any one of the "Three Religions." Such are the cults of the Dragon Kings,[20] the City-Gods,[21] and the various trade deities.[22] The origins of these cults can be traced to the medieval or T'ang period, and show a mixture of earlier influences, both indigenous and foreign. The syncretism of the Han period was largely confined to choosing from various native schools, but the advent of Buddhism, to mention only the chief foreign influence, and the confused conditions of the medieval period, combined to make the religious situation still more complex. It must be admitted that we are still largely ignorant of this development.

During the medieval period, and afterwards, emperors who patronized one cult might patronize others as well. Liang Wu Ti may serve as an illustration. He was not only a devout Buddhist, but a great patron of the Confucian scholars, an emperor who restored the position of the classics and founded schools.

The same tendency toward combination and syncretism is found in the philosophers of the time, particularly in a school which endeavored to show that there was no essential difference between the teachings of Confucius, Lao Tzu, and Buddha.

Chang Yung (A. D. 443–497) was an official and favorite of Kao Ti of the southern Ch'i dynasty. He was sent as ambassador to Hue and Annam, and on one occasion he escaped death by bandits because, while waiting for the decision, he wrote poetry. He held that Taoism and Buddhism were alike in that the end of both was quietude and absence of movement. The differences between them

were caused by time and space, that is, such differences were historical and not philosophic, just as a bird, flying over different countries,
might be called by different names in each. While he did not treat
Confucianism in detail, he held that it was founded in *Tao*, like
the others. That the Confucian, Taoist, Mician, and Buddhist schools
disagreed was also owing to their historical differences, and such
conflict was unnecessary. When Chang Yung was dying, he asked
to have the *Book of Filial Piety* and the *Tao teh ching* put in his
left hand and a Buddhist Sūtra in his right.[23]

Ku Huan (about A. D. 500) has already been mentioned. He held
that although Taoism and Buddhism were established in different
ways, they were essentially the same. The end of the former was
immortality, while the end of the latter was freedom from the round
of existence, but although the names differed, the two ends were really
one. Opposites implied unity, and these opposites were combined
and unified by the sages. Therefore Confucius, Lao Tzu, and Buddha
were one, and the apparent differences between them were caused
by customs, rules, and ceremonies, which were outward appearances.
A boat sailed over the water, while a carriage traveled on land, yet
both were vehicles for moving from one place to another. Each had
its use, and they could be interchanged. This last statement led Ku
Huan to formulate an argument which has been used not only
against Buddhism, but more recently against Christianity. While
these teachings were essentially the same, the different circumstances
required that they be used in different ways and by different people.
Men living by the water would use boats, but men living inland
would use wagons. Just so, the customs of the western barbarians
could not be used in China, and the traditions of China could not
be used in the west. If China should take up the western [that is,
the Buddhist] ideas, the family sacrifices, filial piety, and reverence
would disappear. Birds sang, animals roared. They expressed themselves in different ways, for such differences were natural and the
result of differences in nature or environment.[24]

Similar attempts to harmonize the three schools were made by
Li Shih-ch'ien in the last decade of the sixth century,[25] and by
T'an Ch'iao.[26] These ideas persisted even after the revival of Con-
fucianism, and eventually resulted in a cult and temples in which
Confucius, Lao Tzu, and Buddha appeared together on the altar.
The cult cannot be called Confucian in any sense. It was started by

a Buddhist monk, and while it was permitted by the officials for a long time, the Confucians finally secured its suppression by the Manchu emperor Tao Kuang. To place the images of Lao Tzu and Buddha with that of Confucius was regarded as sacrilege by the orthodox Confucians. The cult belongs among the syncretistic sects which have flourished in China from the medieval period on, and need not be considered in a study of the state cult of Confucius.[27]

In such an environment it is not surprising that we have little development of the cult of Confucius. Both the cult and the schools suffered, but the dynastic histories contain statements which show that Confucius and the representatives of the K'ung family continued to receive honors, and to a certain extent the other features of the cult continued.

The Han dynasty was succeeded by the Three Kingdoms (A. D. 220–280). One of these, Shu, owed its existence largely to the efforts of Chu-k'o Liang, one of the three men belonging to the medieval period who have been honored by having their tablets placed in the Confucian temples. Wen Ti, of the rival state of Wei, appointed a representative of the K'ung family to be marquis in A. D. 221. This emperor sacrificed in the temple of Confucius, and ordered the magistrate of Ch'ü-fu to repair the building.[28] According to Ma Tuan-lin, the magistrate was told to build dormitories beside the temple for the accommodation of students.[29]

A little later, in A. D. 240, Fei Ti of the same dynasty, while studying the classics himself, ordered that the T'ai lao should be offered to Confucius.[30]

The Three Kingdoms were succeeded by the Chin dynasty. The same text records that Chin Wu Ti, in A. D. 267, decreed that the T'ai lao should be offered to Confucius at the four seasons, both in the imperial academy and in the district of Lu. The T'ai hsioh, or Imperial Academy, had been reëstablished in that year, after having ceased to exist in the troublesome times of the Three Kingdoms.[31] Four years later, the same emperor gave a lecture on the classics in the T'ai hsioh, and himself offered the T'ai lao to Confucius.[32]

In A. D. 319, the heir of Chin Yüan Ti offered the T'ai lao again to Confucius, but this time it is mentioned that the sacrifice was also presented to Yen Hui, as the associate or correlate of the sage.[33] Immediately following this is the record of the appointment of the representative of the K'ung as marquis, by Chin Ming Ti in A. D. 325.

This closes the records for the Chin dynasty. In 317, after violent disorders, Yüan Ti had moved the capital to the east, and the dynasty was known as the Eastern Chin thereafter. From 325 to the end of the Chin in 419, there are no references to the cult or the schools.

In 386 a new dynasty was set up in the north by Tatar invaders led by the house of Toba, called the Wei dynasty. The invaders adopted Chinese names and Chinese culture to a certain extent, but on the whole their conquests were a blow to civilization in the period following their appearance. Parker says that toward the close of their rule, about 500, they prohibited barren women from praying to Confucius for children.[34] This would show a tendency to make the sage into a popular deity, which would be repugnant to the literati, who probably secured the prohibition. The Wei emperors were patrons of Buddhism, and since they were themselves foreigners in China, their empire formed a link with central Asia through which foreign influences entered, as is shown by the stone sculpture at Yün-kang, Lung-men, and elsewhere.[35]

For 200 years China was divided into northern and southern kingdoms, with the more characteristically Chinese civilization surviving in the south. For the Liu Sung and Ch'i dynasties (420-501) there appear to be no records of the cult of Confucius.

The Ch'i was succeeded by the Liang dynasty, and the long reign of Liang Wu Ti (502-550) probably represents the height of Buddhist influence in China. Sung Yün visited India, and returned with 170 volumes of Sūtras.[36] Bodhidharma, the twenty-eighth patriarch of Buddhism, arrived in China and was received by the emperor.[37] Wu Ti himself not only spent great sums on Buddhism, but actually became a monk, to the horror of the literati.[38] Yet Wu Ti was also a patron of the Confucians, more so than the rulers of the Chin, Liu Sung, and Ch'i dynasties. According to the *T'ung chien kang mu,* he was the first emperor to erect public temples to Confucius, in which sacrifices were offered every year in memory of the sage, though this is not confirmed by the dynastic history.[39] The establishments for scholars had fallen into ruin, but Wu Ti rebuilt them. He sought out men who were educated in the classics and patronized them. His reign marks the revival of culture in China.

The short-lived dynasty of the Northern Ch'i (550-577) emphasized education and opened schools. Confucius received sacrifices under the title *Hsien sheng,* while Yen Hui was given the title *Hsien shih.*[40] These sacrifices were offered twice a year, in spring and autumn. On the first day of the month, which is the new moon, a libation of wine was offered to Confucius, there were lectures on the sage, and the students made an obeisance to him. Any student absent from these ceremonies was punished. Small temples or shrines to Confucius and Yen Hui were placed in the schools, apparently just inside the gate.[41]

The same passage in the Sui history states that under the Sui dynasty (581–618), schools called *Kuo tzu ssu* were reëstablished in the capital.[42] Sacrifices were offered in them to the *Hsien sheng* and *Hsien shih* at the four seasons. There was also an annual festival at the end of the year in honor of Confucius, when wine was offered. In the provincial centers, sacrifices were presented twice a year, while in the lesser districts there was only a yearly festival held after the examinations. The regulations applied only to the students in schools established by the government.

In A. D. 601, Kao Tsu (Yang Chien) of the Sui dynasty issued an interesting edict. The preamble stated that the aim of education was to enable men to understand the five relationships, and that in order to do this, schools had been established. But in the government schools of the capital there were almost 1,000 students, besides many more in the districts. These men were students in name only, and were simply wasting their time. The schools had quantity, where they should have had quality. The edict therefore abolished the *T'ai hsioh* and all schools except the *Kuo tzu ssu,* which was limited to seventy students. Later the title of this school was changed to the time-honored one of *T'ai hsioh.*[43]

Yang Chien was himself an ignorant man, who had conquered the empire, and who considered the scholars useless. This edict concerns more than the establishment or disestablishment of schools. It implies a modification of the system of government, for officials were appointed on the basis of the examinations in the schools.

The edict was not of great effect, however, for it was practically repealed by the next emperor, Yang Ti, in 605. A long edict reviewed the development of education from the Han period on, and without mentioning Yang Chien, stated clearly that the Han system of education ought to be followed. Doubtless the change under Yang Ti was due to the indignation caused by the earlier edict. At any rate, Confucianism emerged stronger than before. The schools were reopened, and in 609, Confucius received the title *Hsien shih Ni Fu*. A third edict eulogized the sage and ordered that special respect should be paid him, while a representative of the K'ung family was given a title. Officials were directed to locate descendants of the sage and report them to the emperor. A little later the same passage gives a similar eulogy and command concerning the Duke of Chou, who is called Chou Wang, a higher title.[44] This closes the record for the Sui dynasty, and for the medieval period between the Han and T'ang dynasties. At the time these edicts were issued, Li Shih-min, who was later to be, as T'ang T'ai Tsung, one of the greatest rulers China has produced, was a brilliant young officer in Yang Ti's army.

The medieval period was not favorable to the development of Confucianism. Beginning with the collapse of the Han and extending through the Three Kingdoms, the Chin, and later dynasties, civilization went steadily down hill. The invasions from the north and northwest added to the confusion, though they aided in the introduction of foreign and principally Buddhist culture. The low point was reached during the fifth century. Taoism and Buddhism flourished, and scholars attempted to harmonize the two with the Confucian system. With the Liang dynasty, during the first half of the sixth century, an improvement began which continued steadily until the advent of the T'ang.

In spite of unfavorable conditions, which caused temporary lapses when the cult of Confucius and the schools do not seem to have existed, the cult did develop. Yen Hui came to be associated with Confucius in worship, new titles were given, the ritual increased, and temples or shrines were erected to the sage. There is nothing in the cult as practised in the schools to indicate direct borrowing from Buddhism.

There is another direction, however, in which Taoist and probably Buddhist influence can be seen—the creation of a Confucian legend.

The Confucian classics, while not entirely free from legendary material, are marked by the relatively small amount of the supernatural and the mythical which they possess, compared with the early literature of other countries. If the story of Confucius' labors as an editor is true, this may be due to the sage himself. While never questioning the reality of Heaven or the spirits of his ancestors, he was skeptical of the miraculous and the extraordinary, never dis-

cussing them. Following in the footsteps of their master, the orthodox Confucians have been singularly free from acceptance of legends.

Nevertheless, the forces which create myths exerted themselves
from the first. The last books of the *Analects* are regarded with suspicion, and seem to show Taoist influence. Lieh Tzu attributes the
power of performing miracles to Confucius,[45] and Chuang Tzu contains a whole series of apocryphal stories about the sage, designed
to show his inferiority to Lao Tzu.[46] These are clearly Taoist. It
is to the credit of the Confucians of the Han and earlier periods
that they did not allow superstitions to grow up about·their master,
although the spirit of the time was favorable to such a growth.

This is shown by Wang Ch'ung. Writing in the latter half of the
first century, A. D., he did not hesitate to criticize the sage, attacked
superstition, and devoted a chapter to the exaggerations of the literati.[47] Therefore the fact that in his criticism of the literati he
mentioned no legends about the person of Confucius is conclusive
evidence that there were none generally accepted by the scholars
of his day.

In the third century a book was produced which had a great influence and has usually been accepted as of a much earlier date.
This was the *Family Sayings,* which purported to give conversations of Confucius and his disciples.[48] This book also contained
practically no legendary element, except in the sense that it could
not be regarded as historical.

There were, however, a number of genuine legends connected
with the sage, and a few may be briefly mentioned. There was the
story of the pilgrimage of the mother of Confucius. Also there were
the stories of the appearance of the unicorn, the inscribed piece
of jade announcing the birth of Confucius as "uncrowned king,"
and the placing of the ribbon on the horn of the unicorn by the
mother. On the night of Confucius' birth, two dragons appeared,
and the five planets were seen as old men. There were supernatural
harmonies, and a voice was heard saying, "Divine harmony strikes
the ear, because Heaven has caused a saint to be born. His doctrine
will be the law of the world." Confucius himself miraculously told
the origin of an arrow, and diagnosed the cause of an earthquake
as a buried image which was later discovered. Being about to die,
the sage turned to the constellation of Ursa Major, when a meteor
descended and turned into a jade tablet. Miracles continued after

124 THE STATE CULT OF CONFUCIUS

the death of the sage. The soldiers of Ch'in Shih Huang, on violating the tomb, found a written prophecy of the event and of the death of the emperor. When Kung Wang of Lu, about the middle of the second century B. C., demolished the walls of the temple, a mysterious music was heard. Lastly, there was a story of the discovery of seven pieces of jade and a bowl of Confucius. An inscription on the bowl recommended Tung Chung-shu for official employment, and also told how a servant had stolen one of the pieces of jade.[49]

These legendary inventions may be dismissed in a sentence. One or two such tales occur in the *Kuo Yü*, and are quoted by Ssu-ma Ch'ien, but the majority are late. Most of them show Taoist, rather than Buddhist, influence, and none has had any effect on the development of the cult.

NOTES

[1] For a general account of this period, see Cordier, Vol. I, pp. 293-406. Among the blows to scholarship were the destruction of libraries at various times. The Chinese consider that there were five great "bibliothecal catastrophes," and three of these occurred during the medieval period. The first was the burning of the books by Ch'in Shih Huang. The second occurred when the imperial library at Ch'ang-an was completely burned during the time of Wang Mang. The third was the destruction of the imperial library collected by the Eastern Han dynasty during the disorders at the end of the second century A. D. when Lo-yang was burned. The fourth happened in A. D. 311, when the library of the Chin dynasty was destroyed. The fifth was the destruction of the library of the Liang dynasty in A. D. 554. For an account of the attempts to collect books and the difficulties due to the general disorder, see Wylie, *Notes on Chinese Literature*, pp. xv-xvii.

[2] Cordier (Vol. I, pp. 364-375) gives a good account of the sculpture of the period. See also H. A. Giles, *Introduction to the History of Chinese Pictorial Art; Pelliot, Notes sur quelques artistes des six dynastie et des T'ang, T'oung Pao*, 2d series, Vol. XXII, pp. 215 f.; and Sirén's exhaustive work, *La sculpture chinoise du Vᵉ au XIVᵉ siècle*.

[3] Ko Hung 葛洪, also known as Pao P'u Tzu 抱朴子, fourth century A. D. Appointed an official in 326, he journeyed to Cochin China to secure cinnabar for his researches. As the author of the *Biographies of the Gods* 神仙傳. and other works, he had great influence on the development of Taoism (Giles, *Chin. Biog. Dict.*, p. 372). There are also accounts of him in De Harlez, *Textes taoïstes*, pp. 75-82; Miura, p. 258; and Ryukichi Endo, *History of Chinese Philosophy*, Bk. 2, chap. 3, sect. 2.

[4] Kuan Lang, 關朗, flourished about A. D. 477. Author of the 洞極眞經. He retired from the world and "investigated reality." Miura (p. 255) classes him as a Confucian, because he was greatly influenced by Yang Hsiung. He taught that Confucianism is concerned with external things, and is useful to the statesman, but that Taoism is concerned with internal or subjective reality,

and is therefore more fundamental. See also Ryukichi Endo, Bk. 2, chap. 3, sect. 3.

Both Ko Hung and Kuan Lang were influenced by Confucianism.

[5] The Seven Sages of the Bamboo Grove, a group of convivial philosophers who took their name from their meeting place. They flourished about the middle of the third century. They were largely influenced by Taoist thought (Doré, Vol. XIV, p. 332, and Miura, p. 257). The character translated as "sage" is not the one applied to Confucius, but is 賢 hsien ("illustrious"). See also Wilhelm, pp. 208-211.

[6] Chu-k'o Liang, 諸葛亮 , or K'ung Ming, 孔明 ; A. D. 181-234. This "darling hero of the Chinese people," famous in fiction and the drama as well as in history, was the great figure of the period of the Three Kingdoms, statesman, strategist, and author. His tablet was placed in the Confucian temple in 1724 because of some of his writings, and he is also claimed by the Taoists. For a brief notice of him, see Giles, Chin. Biog. Dict., pp. 180-182. He can hardly be called a philosopher. For a full account of his doings, see Brewitt-Taylor's translation of the San Kuo, or Romance of the Three Kingdoms, in which he is the principal character. Wang Pi 王弼, A. D. 226-249, wrote commentaries on both Confucian and Taoist classics. See Wilhelm, p. 209, and Giles, p. 834.

[7] Wang T'ung, 王通 (A. D. 583-616). A brilliant scholar, at the age of nineteen he proposed twelve plans for the government of the empire; and when these were not accepted, he retired to the country and taught his disciples. He produced a number of works, of which only one survives. He was influenced by the Taoist doctrine of change, and even advised a disciple not to read his book on government, because conditions had already altered. He was also influenced by Kuan Lang, holding that the doctrine of the mean is the common ground of Confucianism, Buddhism, and Taoism. Yet he was essentially a Confucian and a political philosopher, and in 1530 his tablet was placed in the Confucian temple, probably because of his commentaries on the classics (Giles, pp. 846, 847; Miura, p. 264; Ryukichi Endo, Vol. I, p. 35 R).

[8] Chavannes, T'oung Pao (1905), pp. 546 f.

[9] Cordier, pp. 262, 263; De Mailla, Vol. III, pp. 357 f. In A. D. 147, the Amitabha Sutra was brought to China by way of the Yüeh-chi, and the emperor Hüan not only patronized Buddhism, but built a temple to Lao Tzu. The Hou Han shu says that this emperor also received an embassy from An-tun, identified with Marcus Aurelius (Chavannes, T'oung Pao [1907], p. 185). See also Wilhelm, Chin. Civ., pp. 196-200. For the development of Buddhism and Taoism, see Wieger, Croyances rel., pp. 343-656.

[10] There are notices of Kumarajiva and Bodhidharma in Eitel, Handbook of Chinese Buddhism, pp. 59 and 24. The former lived at the court of the Wei from 397 to 415. He was an author and translator, is said to have invented an alphabet for Chinese, and is known as one of the "four suns" of Buddhism. The latter, the last of the Buddhist patriarchs of India, came to China and was received at the court of Liang Wu Ti about 520. He became dissatisfied and journeyed northward, where he is said to have died in 529. He was the founder of the Meditative School (Dhyana) of Chinese Buddhism.

[11] Fa Hsien 法顯 left for India in 399 and returned to China in 414, being the first of the famous Chinese pilgrims to India. There are translations of the account of his journey by Beal (Travels of Buddhist Pilgrims) and Legge (Travels of Fa-H'ien), as well as in Giles. For a brief account of the Chinese pilgrims to India, see Cordier, Vol. I, pp. 551-569.

[12] M. Tchang, *Tombeau des Liang,* pp. 23, 24, cited by Cordier, Vol. I, pp. 345, 346. The career of Buddhism was not one of uninterrupted progress during the medieval period. There were persecutions of Buddhism in the years 423, 446, and 458. In spite of this there were nearly 14,000 Buddhists in the monasteries between the years 512 and 516 (De Groot, *Sectarianism,* p. 33, cited by Cordier, Vol. I, p. 558).

[13] Fa Hsien accepts many fabulous tales as historical. Tchang (*ibid.*) says, "(Liang Wu Ti) perdit dans ses égarements le sens du pouvoir; les gouverneurs de province, mal surveillés, tyrannisèrent le peuple, semant le mécontentement et la désaffection."

[14] Some idea of the general conditions may be gained from the fact that between 452 and 618, twenty-eight emperors were killed and four dethroned, while thirteen ruled only one year or less. There are nine different dynasties listed for the period, only one of which, the Sui, can be said to have ruled the entire country.

[15] For a full account of the persecutions of Buddhism and the antagonistic attitude of the scholars, see De Groot, *Sectarianism and Religious Persecution in China.*

[16] *San chiao* 三教. *Chiao* means "to teach, train, and educate." It is used with other words to mean "master," "teacher," and "professor." *Tsung chiao* 宗教 is now used in the sense of "religion," while phrases containing the word are used for "the Pope," and for "convert," "doctrine," and "church." However, this is modern terminology, and it is certainly a mistake to take a Chinese term and use it for our idea of religion, and then to argue backward and say that when the word is used by the Chinese, it means what we understand by religion. It is possible to question whether Confucius, Lao Tzu, or the Buddha were what we mean by the expression "a religious man." We ourselves find it hard to define what we mean by religion. A man can be a genuine follower of any one of the three, and not believe in a personal God.

[17] Kuan Ti 關帝 or Kuan Yü 關羽; died in A.D. 219. One of the heroes of the Three Kingdoms period, and one of the most popular names in Chinese history. For a brief notice see Giles, pp. 383, 384. While the develpment of his cult is later, he received posthumous honors in 260, 583, 676, and at later times. Eventually he developed into the patron divinity of the military administration of the government, and his cult paralleled that of Confucius, the patron of the civil administration (Doré, Vol. VI, p. 79, and Shryock, *Temples of Anking,* sect. on the Kuan Yo Miao and Appendix 5). The present official title of Kuan Ti is Kuan sheng ti chün. 關聖帝君.

[18] The cult of T'ai Shan is the only Chinese cult which has been thoroughly studied. This was done by Chavannes, in *Le T'ai Chan.* The mountain has been sacred from the dawn of history.

[19] Kuan-yin has been more carefully studied than any Buddhist divinity except the Buddha himself. Many references might be given to European works. A résumé of the labors of modern scholars will be found in Doré, Vol. VI, pp. 200 f. The main problem is how this Bodhisattva changed from a man to a woman and became the Goddess of Mercy who is besought chiefly for sons. In addition to the various theories summarized in Doré, Dr. Hu Shih thinks that the cult was connected with the empress Wu of the T'ang dynasty.

Ti Tsang has not been given as much attention. He is the Bodhisattva who saves souls from the Buddhist purgatory. He is not even mentioned by Eitel. For what is known about him, see Johnston, *Buddhist China,* pp. 170 f.; Doré, Vol. VII, pp. 235 f.; Getty, *Gods of Northern Buddhism,* p. 90; Reichelt, pp.

77-126; and Shryock, *Temples of Anking,* sect. on Buddhist Temples. The best study of the cult is by De Visser in the *Ostasiatische Zeitschrift.*

Both these gods have mountains sacred to them, which is probably owing to the influence of the indigenous nature worship. Both have been modified so as to appeal to Chinese family sentiment, Ti Tsang as the savior of the souls of the dead, and Kuan-yin as the giver of sons.

20 *Lung Wang* 龍王 ("dragon kings"). Dragons are mentioned in the canon frequently and in Ssu-ma Ch'ien, etc. Buddhism brought with it the Naga worship of India. The first instance of the use of dragons in rain cults is the case of Tung Chung-shu, already mentioned, which antedates Buddhism in China. Since the T'ang period these gods have been officially recognized as rain deities. The fullest treatment of the subject so far is by M. W. De Visser, *The Dragon in China and Japan,* but there is still no adequate study.

21 The Ch'en Huang 城隍 ("city gods") are probably a development from the political features of the ancient gods of the Land and Grain. These older deities, originally nature gods, became the gods of the feudal states. When feudalism was abolished and the people were no longer allowed to sacrifice to them as local patrons—the Han rulers having their officials do this—the cults of the city gods arose in the medieval period. The city god is a patron deity, not of independent towns, but of cities which are subsidiary parts of a larger whole, the state. In this they resemble the Tyche of such cities as Alexandria, Antioch, and Constantinople. They are first mentioned by name in A. D. 230. Officials of the past are appointed to this position, and correspond in the spirit world to the magistrates in this. The representation of purgatory in their temples reflects Buddhism, and the services are usually performed by Taoists. The cult has several unique features (see Grube, *Religion und Kultus der Chinesen,* pp. 119 f.; De Groot, *Les Fêtes annuelles à Emoui,* Vol. II, pp. 586 f.; Doré, Vol. XI, pp. 875-893; and Shryock, *Temples of Anking,* sect. on the City God). There are short accounts by E. T. C. Werner (*Chinese Mythology*) and F. Ayscough (*Chinese Mirror*).

22 The trade deities connected with Chinese gilds have not been adequately studied. Morse ignores them in his book, *The Gilds of China. The China Review,* Vol. IX, p. 188, contains a brief article by De Groot on "Two Gods of Literature and a God of Barbers." Doré, Vols. XI and XII, contains references to a number of such gods, but no accounts of the cults. Lu Pan, the god of carpenters, is a good illustration of such divinities.

The development of the cults mentioned in this paragraph of the text often came later than the medieval period, but the roots of the system began then, and under the T'ang.

23 The account of Chang Yung 張融 is taken from Ryukichi Endo, Vol. I, p. 31 L. See also Miura, p. 262 His lifetime was A. D. 443-497.

24 Ku Huan 顧歡 about A. D. 500. Ryukichi Endo, Vol. I, p. 33 R: Miura, p. 263.

25 Li Shih-ch'ien 李士謙, about A. D. 590. He said that Buddhism was the sun, Taoism the moon, and Confucianism the five planets (Ryukichi Endo, *ibid.*).

The Chinese expression for this school is *San chiao yi chih* 三教一致 ("Three Doctrines, One End").

26 T'an Ch'iao 譚峭. He devoted himself to magic and Taoism. He may have had some disease, for he is said to have often lain insensible in the snow and rain, which would have been enough to have given him a reputation for

magical and supernatural power. Primarily a Taoist, he sought to reconcile the three doctrines by means of Tao, as an underlying principle something like the Christian principle of the Logos, but he differs from pure Taoism in working the Confucian virtues into his system. Giles (p. 710), has a very unsatisfactory account of him, and gives his date as the tenth century, but the sixth century is a more likely period, following Ryukichi Endo, Vol. 1, p. 34 R.

The Japanese scholar also places Wang T'ung in this group, although he is sufficiently Confucian to have his tablet in the temples. All the thinkers of this period were consciously syncretistic.

Probably the reason this school of thought has been so much neglected is because practically all the general books on the history of Chinese thought were written by orthodox scholars after the revival under the Sung, and as a school which saw no essential difference between Confucianism and the other two doctrines must have been very distasteful to the orthodox scholars, these men seem to have been largely ignored. Many European writers have assumed that there was no mental activity in China during the medieval period, which is absurd. There are enormous gaps in our knowledge of the history of Chinese thought, one of which is the medieval period, but there is no excuse for the statement frequently made that there was no real philosophic development in China from Hsün Tzu to Chou Tun-yi, a leap of about 1,200 years.

[27] Parker (*Studies in Chinese Religion*, p. 292 f.) describes the origin of the cult about 1050, and its eventual suppression in 1837. In Shryock, *Temples of Anking* (the section on the *San Shen An*, or "Temple of the Three Holy Ones"), there is a translation of an official document favorable to this cult. Although it was suppressed nearly a hundred years ago, the author has seen the three images on an altar.

[28] *Chin chi*, or *History of the Chin dynasty*, chap. 19, p. 3 R.

[29] Ma Tuan-lin, chap. 43, p. 38 L.

[30] *Ibid.*

[31] *Chin chi*, chap. 19, p. 3 R.

[32] Ma Tuan-lin, chap. 43, p. 38 L.

[33] *Chin chi*, chap. 19, p. 3 R.

[34] Parker, p. 221. The author has been unable to find any reference in the *Po Wei chi* verifying this statement. Parker gives no authority.

[35] Cordier, Vol. I, pp. 364-375.

[36] There is a notice of Sung Yun in Cordier, Vol. I, p. 349. Beal (*Buddhist Pilgrims*, pp. 175-208) translates the account of his journey.

[37] Eitel, p. 24. Bodhidharma is said to have been disgusted with Liang Wu Ti, and to have crossed the Yangtse standing on a reed. He held study to be useless, and is said to have sat facing a blank wall for nine years. He is a favorite with Chinese painters. See also the *Enc. Sin.*, p. 52. Pelliot has written an illuminating article on Bodhidharma in *T'oung Pao*, Vol. XII, pp. 671 f.

[38] *Enc. Sin.*, p. 304. Liang Wu Ti seems to have begun as a patron of the classics, education, and the Confucians, and to have become more and more immersed in Buddhism toward the close of his reign.

[39] De Mailla, Vol. V, p. 219.

[40] Hsien sheng 先聖 ("Sage of Former Times"); Hsien shih 先師 ("Teacher of Former Times"). The "city of Lu," (Ch'ü-fu), was ordered to repair the temple of Ch'ü-fu, and 100 families were assigned to maintain the worship. *History of Po Ch'i*, chap. 4, p. 7.

[41] *Sui shih*, or *History of the Sui dynasty*, chap. 9, p. 22 R. There is no

support, either here or in the *History of Northern Ch'i,* for the statement in Forke, *Geschichte Chin. Phil.,* p. 109, that in 555 an edict ordered the erection of Confucian temples in every city.

[42] *Kuo tzu ssu* 國子寺. The word 寺 signified an official residence. There is a tradition that when the Buddhist monks first reached China, they stopped in such a place, and afterwards used the term for their first monastery, the *Po ma ssu* 白馬寺, or White Horse Temple. At present the term is used almost exclusively by Buddhists. This is the older meaning. Cf. Wilhelm, p. 198.

[43] *Sui chi,* chap. 2, p. 8 R. Yang Chien probably was not attacking the Confucians so much as the aristocracy which controlled the system of education.

[44] *Sui chi,* Chap. 3, pp. 9 L and 10 R.

The title given Confucius was 先師尼父, "the Master and Teacher of Former Times, Ni." Ni was Confucius' personal name.

That given his descendant was 紹聖侯, "successful and Holy Marquis."

Legge (*Chinese Classics,* Vol. 1, Prolegomena, p. 92, in the passage already referred to several times) cites the Temple Record to the effect that Yang Ti built separate temples for Confucius and the Duke of Chou. This passage in the Sui history, which is the primary authority, does not say so.

[45] L. Giles, *Taoist Teachings,* p. 51.

[46] Legge, *S. B. E.,* Vol. XXXIX, p. 203, 252, 255.

[47] Forke, *Lun Hêng,* chap. 26, "Exaggerations of the Literati." *Mitt. des Sem.,* Vol. XI, pp. 103-117.

[48] A. B. Hutchinson, "Family Sayings of Confucius," *Chinese Recorder,* Vol. X, pp. 17, 96, 175, 253, 329, 428. Few scholars would disagree with the statement of Hutchinson (in his introduction, *Recorder,* Vol. IX, p. 445 f.) that the book is a compilation of the third century. Forke, (*Chin. Phil.,* p. 119), while agreeing with Hutchinson that the work was compiled by Wang Su 王肅 in A. D. 225, and that many anecdotes are apocryphal, does make some use of the book. Hutchinson's translation, on which my statement is based, and also that of De Harlez (*Babylonian and Oriental Record,* Vols. VI and VII, 1893-1894) are only partial.

[49] These stories are found in Doré, Vol. XIII, pp. 10, 11, 12, 13, 50, 69, 73, 78, 83, 92, 94, and 95. Doré sometimes gives his sources, usually modern works of little historical value. Unfortunately his interest is in collecting Chinese superstitions, and he makes no distinction between historical and legendary material. All these stories are found in the *Sheng chi t'u* 聖蹟圖. The stories of the arrow and of the buried image are found in the *Kuo Yü* and reappear in Ssu-ma Ch'ien's account of Confucius (*Mém. hist.,* Vol. V, pp. 340-343).

CHAPTER IX

THE T'ANG PERIOD, A. D. 618–907

With the accession of T'ang Kao Tsu in 618 began one of the most glorious periods in the history of China. Until 751 the country enjoyed relative peace at home, while abroad Chinese armies invaded Corea, Mongolia, Tibet, and Turkestan, one expedition even crossing the Pamirs. Civilization flourished, while the greatest poets and painters in Chinese history produced their art. The power of the country can be seen from the fact that in 780, when the dynasty was already past its prime, the standing army numbered 768,000 men.

The world was smaller than it had been. Harūn al-Rashīd was in communication with the T'ang emperor on the one hand, and with Charlemagne on the other. Harsha, the last great native ruler of India, had relations with T'ai Tsung. There was regular communication between China and India, Central Asia, Japan, and Indo-China. Buddhists were not the only religious travelers. The Nestorian monument, erected in 781, shows that this branch of Christianity had arrived in China even earlier. The Manicheans were there in 805. The Arabs were in touch with the Chinese, but it is uncertain at what date Islam secured a real foothold in China. Zoroastrianism reached China, and the Jews probably came during the ninth century.

It has not yet been shown that any of these foreign religions had an appreciable effect on the development of Chinese religion, with, of course, the exception of Buddhism, although it is conceivable that research may show that Buddhism itself was affected by the others. There was no lack of foreign ideas and foreign influence, but strangers arriving in China found more to take away than they brought.[1]

Taoist influence reached its highest point. The T'ang emperors bore the surname Li, which was also the name of Lao Tzu, from whom they claimed descent. Kao Tsu, the first T'ang ruler, built his ancestral temple at what he believed to be the birth-place of Lao Tzu, Kao Tsung gave to Lao Tzu the title of *Hsien yüan huang ti,* which is, incidentally, a much higher title than the one he gave to Confucius.[2] Taoist adepts were advisers of the emperors, and several of the later rulers of the dynasty died from the effects of drugs by which they hoped to attain immortality.[3] For three years at the beginning of the T'ang period, both Buddhism and Taoism were prohibited, but then the edict was withdrawn. Although there were temporary suppressions in 820 and 847, after the deaths of emperors caused by Taoist drugs, Taoism generally flourished during the period. In 741, Hsüan Tsung opened colleges for the study of the Taoist philosophers, and instituted examinations which resembled those in the classics. He gave Lao Tzu's book the name *Tao teh ching,* by which it is still called, and ordered that it should be substituted for the *Analects* and the *Chou li* in the provincial examinations, though it was replaced by the *Book of Changes* in 753.[4]

The career of Buddhism was somewhat checkered during the T'ang period. Shortly after the dynasty was established, Hsüan Tsang began his journey to India, and on his return in 645, was received in Ch'ang-an with a triumphal procession. There were persecutions of Buddhism under Hsüan Tsung (713–756), who later changed his views, and Wu Tsung (841–847), both of whom were addicted to Taoism, but on the whole Buddhism flourished. The empress Wu (684–705) was a Buddhist nun before she was taken into the emperor's seraglio.[5] At the height of her power, in 693, a delegation of Buddhists, led by Fa Ming, presented the empress with a book which contained a divine revelation that the empress was an incarnation of a daughter of Buddha.[6] She was delighted, and Buddhism made rapid progress, but this prosperity was followed by the persecution of Hsüan Tsung in 714. Later this emperor allowed the Buddhist scriptures to be published under his auspices in 730. Su Tsung (756–763) had a Buddhist chapel in his palace, and Tai Tsung (763–780) himself expounded the scriptures.[7] This emperor also established the Buddhist festival *Yü lan hui,* or Masses for the Dead, which seems to have originated in China with the Indian monk Amoghavajra, but which may have been based on an old Chinese custom.[8] These masses were adopted by the Taoists, and eventually became the chief source of revenue for the monks of both religions. In 819, Hsien Tsung, hearing that a monastery in Shensi had a bone of the Buddha which performed miracles, brought it in state to the capital. This caused the famous protest of Han T'ui-chih, which may be taken as the beginning of the Confucian revival. Although the T'ang period was one of prosperity for both Buddhism and Taoism, it also marks the beginning of their decay. The period gives ample justification for the unfavorable judgment of the Confucians upon both religions.[9]

Under the conditions which existed during the T'ang rule, two things would naturally be expected of the cult of Confucius. Under a strong government which followed in general the principles of the Han rulers, and with peace and wealth generally existing throughout the country, the cult would flourish. The scholar class always proved too useful to the emperor politically to lose its power or its patronage. They furnished him with a group of potential officials who usually did not have military, and never hereditary, power, and who as a class were always loyal to the emperor because they owed everything to him. This loyalty, and a knowledge of history so minute and thorough as to constitute the best possible scholastic training for administrative work, were inculcated in the scholars from the time they were children. Consequently, the scholar class was an invaluable tool in the hands òf the ruler, and was secure as long as the emperor himself was an educated and intelligent man. The rulers who did not patronize the scholars were of two kinds. There was the ignorant soldier who had conquered the empire with his sword and who thought he could govern it that way. Even such men usually realized the value of the scholars once they were firmly on the throne. On the other hand, there were the weaklings who were governed by eunuchs and other unworthy favorites, and who preferred flattery to loyal advice. These were the men whom the scholars had to fear most. There was usually a succession of them toward the close of a dynasty. Under a strong man the scholars flourished, even though his personal predilections were for Taoism or Buddhism.

In the second place, one would expect that while the cult of Confucius would flourish, it would also undergo considerable change. It was a period filled with new ideas, which created as well as followed precedents. With the possible exception of T'ai Tsung, none of the T'ang emperors could be called Confucian. Consequently they would care little for the conservatism that was an essential part of the equipment of the Confucian scholar, and would not be partial to scholars who took their canonical ideal too seriously. All these emperors were grossly credulous; and whatever faults the Confucians may have, they have always formed the most rational and least superstitious section of Chinese society. As a result, there would be a certain amount of conflict and a considerable amount of readjustment.

In 619, the year after the founding of the dynasty, T'ang Kao Tsu ordered that a temple should be built and dedicated jointly to the Duke of Chou and Confucius. The temple was in the capital, and in 624 Kao Tsu sacrificed there himself. Legge, again citing the Temple Record, says that this was done in 609 by Sui Yang Ti, but the passage in the Sui history, which has already been cited, does not say so, and the step seems to have been initiated by Kao Tsu.[10] It was a distinct retrogression for the cult of Confucius, since the Duke of Chou was given the title of *Hsien sheng,* which had formerly belonged to Confucius, who was ranked as the correlate.[11]

Apparently this policy caused dissatisfaction, and it was reversed by the next emperor, the great T'ai Tsung. Before he mounted the throne, Li Shih-min had already cultivated the Confucian scholars, and gathered a group of them around him as supporters.[12] After his triumph over the intrigues of his brothers and the abdication of Kao Tsu, T'ai Tsung at once proceeded to found schools. The *T'ai hsioh* in the capital became so famous that students came from foreign countries to attend it. In connection with the school, the emperor gathered a library of 200,000 volumes.[13]

In 628, an official named Fang Hsüan-ling [14] petitioned the emperor to the following effect. Although Chou Kung and Ni Fu (Confucius) were both sages,[15] Confucius was the more important for education. Before this [i.e., the T'ang] dynasty, the title of Confucius was *Hsien sheng,* and that of Yen Hui, *Hsien shih.* The petition was worded in such a way as to suggest that the older custom should be followed. The emperor adopted the advice, stopped [16] the sacrifices to Chou Kung, whose tablet was placed in the temple of Wu Wang, raised Confucius to the main altar with the title of *Hsien sheng,* and made Yen Hui his correlate with the title of *Hsien shih.* In 640, T'ai Tsung sacrificed there himself, after which scholars were ordered to lecture on the *Book of Filial Piety.*[17]

Two other changes were made by T'ai Tsung which were of so sweeping a nature as to revolutionize the cult. The first was a decree, issued in 630, commanding that all Chou and Hsien districts [18] throughout the empire should establish temples to Confucius, while the title of the sage was changed to *Hsüan fu.*[19]

In ancient China (that is, the China of the Chou period) the shrines or altars of nature deities were placed in the spots sacred to them, while each family had its ancestral temple. Each god had his one sacred place, and there did not exist a number of temples or shrines scattered over the country, all dedicated to the same divinity. The earliest instance in Chinese history of a number of temples dedicated to the same person occurred when Han Hui Ti ordered that temples be erected throughout the country to his father, Han Kao Tsu, in 195 B. c.[20] This was a political device similar to the deification of the Roman emperors. In the Eastern Han and the medieval periods, the government schools had shrines to Confucius, which meant that the sage received offerings in many places, but this decree of T'ai Tsung meant that in every city state temples to Confucius were erected. The sacrifices were still offered by the scholars, but in their capacity of government officials.

The second change was made in 647, when the emperor placed the tablets of twenty-two men in the temple for the first time. The record of the reign of Han Ming Ti shows that in the middle of the first century A. D. the temple at Ch'ü-fu was already known as belonging to Confucius and his seventy-two disciples. These men were all immediate pupils of the sage, mentioned in the *Analects* and the other sources dealing with Confucius. The references in the dynastic histories to the Ch'ü-fu temple mention only Yen Hui by name, but imply that the others received sacrifices also. The shrines in the schools appear to have contained the tablets of Confucius and Yen Hui only. The Temple Records which give the date when the sacrifices were first offered to each man in the state temples, say that only Yen Hui received sacrifices before 647. The temples constructed at the order of T'ai Tsung, it is evident from the Temple Records, as well as from the record in the T'ang history, contained these twenty-two added tablets.[21]

Most of these men were not immediate disciples, nor did they belong to the seventy-two,[22] since they were scholars of the Han period. It is curious that their tablets should have been put in the temples before the tablets of the seventy-two. All of the men are famous for their classical scholarship and their writings, and all rendered service to the Confucian cause.

This action of T'ai Tsung made the temples of Confucius into national halls of fame, where the great men of literary attainments were remembered. It set a precedent which was followed by all succeeding dynasties and by the Chinese republic, though it is not yet certain what the attitude of the Nationalist Government will be. The highest honor—always a posthumous one—which could come to a literary man, was to have his tablet placed in that select group. The roll of names suggests all that is best in the history of China. It was not enough to have produced good literature or first-class philosophy in order to enter: Chuang Tzu was one of the most brilliant minds China ever produced, and is regarded as a master of prose, but he was a Taoist; Hsün Tzu made great contributions to Confucianism, but his doctrine is unorthodox, and he criticized some of the earlier Confucians; Wang Ch'ung was profound and learned, but he criticized Confucius himself; Yang Hsiung was a great man, and his tablet, like Hsün Tzu's, has been in the temples, but was removed because he was an official of the usurper Wang Mang. The temples were more than halls of fame; they were standards of Confucian orthodoxy. Let a single blot be discovered in a man's record, and his tablet was removed. The requirements were that a man must have been a personal disciple of the sage, or else a great scholar, of unquestioned orthodoxy and blameless morals. All this did not come at once, but followed as a natural development to the precedent set by T'ai Tsung.

Tablets were added or removed, officially by an imperial decree, but practically by the Board of Rites.[23] Only thirteen of the twenty-two names added by T'ai Tsung are still in the temples, the others having been removed by imperial decree at various times and for various reasons. No attempt will be made to follow the fortunes of individual tablets, though they are sometimes very interesting, or the different order and arrangement of the names, which have changed from time to time, and on which the Board of Rites must have spent an enormous amount of time and study.

The creation of these temples should be considered in connection with the general policy of T'ai Tsung. He developed a strong government and reformed the civil and military services. In the capital were six colleges. The *Kuo tzu hsioh* was open to the sons and grandsons of officials of a certain rank. The *T'ai hsioh* was also for the sons of officials, and contained 500 students. The "College of Four Gates" contained 1,300 students, of whom a large number came from the common people, and there were also schools of law, calligraphy, and mathematics, which were limited to a few tens of students. Schools of various grades existed in the provinces, reaching down even to the villages. The most promising pupils in the provincial schools were sent to the colleges in the.capital, and there were also competitive examinations open to all by which one might enter.

Under the T'ang, candidates were selected for office in three ways. There were the graduates of the six colleges, of two other schools in the capital for the sons of nobles, and of the provincial schools. There were also the graduates of the open examinations. Finally, there were those selected by a special examination given by the emperor himself. There were numerous literary degrees, besides the possibility of appointment to official position. After 736, the appointment of officials was made by the Ministry of Civil Offices, while the examinations were controlled by the Ministry of Rites. There was constant conflict between the two, and a scholar might pass a brilliant examination without securing an appointment, while the sons of officials and others having influence might slip into the best positions. This abuse was fostered by the court eunuchs. In spite of it, the schools and the system of examinations were an efficient instrument in training men for government service, especially during the first century of the T'ang period.[24]

It is evident that the acts of T'ai Tsung in erecting temples to Confucius all over the country and in making them halls of fame for men of literary distinction were a part of a more general policy for the development of an effective civil service. It added a religious element to the ideal of education, and made Confucius much more than the patron saint of scholars. The sage now became the patron deity of the civil administration of the government, and as such, an important feature in the state religion. The emperor sacrificed to him whenever he visited the schools, which were located near the temples. He received regular offerings from the chief official of the district in which the temple was situated, as well as from the literati who constituted the past, present, and expectant officials of the state.

Under Kao Tsung (650–684) an attempt was made to restore the Duke of Chou to the position held by Confucius, but it was only temporary, and Confucius was soon replaced.[25] In 664, this emperor, to escape the dominance of the empress Wu, visited the grave of Confucius, and gave the sage the title of *T'ai shih*.[26]

In 739, Hsüan Tsung gave Confucius the title of *Wang,* or Prince, and the ceremonies in the Confucian temples were changed to conform with the increase in rank. Confucius was still one degree lower than Lao Tzu, and there were others on an equality with him. The

T'ang emperors began the practice of arranging their pantheon in regular grades and of advancing or degrading its members. Later dynasties continued the precedent, and the proceedings of the Board of Rites contain long investigations into the merits and services rendered by certain gods.[27] Confucius also has been subject to this imperial control.

Other important changes were also made in the reign of Hsüan Tsung. This was the emperor who first persecuted and then patronized the Buddhists, and in particular, the Indian monk Amoghavajra. Hsüan Tsung himself was a devotee of Taoism. It cannot be definitely shown that these facts had anything to do with his decrees concerning the Confucian temples, but one suspects that he may have been influenced by his own background.

In 719, when the heir-apparent entered school, the emperor himself sacrificed in the Confucian temple, after which scholars lectured on classic books, including the *Book of Filial Piety* and the *Book of Rites*.

The following year, Li Yüan-kuan [28] petitioned the emperor that in the Confucian temple [29] there should be ten images seated, while the seventy disciples and the twenty-two Hsien should have their pictures painted on the walls. Tseng Tzu should be placed among the ten because of his filial piety. The suggestion was adopted.

There can be only one interpretation of these terms, especially as the character for "image" is contrasted with that for "picture." [30] The passage implies that Confucius and Yen Hui were already represented by images, but no previous record said this.[31] In fact, nothing was said as to what the objects of worship in the shrines and later, the temples, of Confucius actually were. From that time onward there is no doubt about the facts. From 720 until 1530, the objects of worship were images, while from 1530 until the present they have been tablets with the name and a few other characters written on them.

The new class of ten were called *Cheh,*[32] and appeared in the main hall of the temple with Confucius and Yen Hui. There are at present twelve of them. The temple was now approximately in the form in which it has survived until the present, and may be described briefly. There was a main hall, oblong, with the long side running east and west. Against the north wall was the image, later only the tablet, of Confucius,[33] with Yen Hui at one side. Against the east and west walls were the ten *Cheh*. Before the main hall was a terrace, and below it a court, while on both sides of the court, east and west, ran cloisters. In these cloisters, against the east and west walls, were the portraits, probably mural paintings in the T'ang temples, of two groups of men. At the north end were the seventy-two disciples, now called *Hsien hsien*,[34] while toward the south were the group of later Confucians represented by T'ai Tsung's twenty-two names, now called *Hsien jü*.[35] In 739, sixty-seven more names were added.

At present the absence of images makes the Confucian temples strikingly different from Buddhist and most Taoist temples; but when the images were there, the similarity to Buddhist temples, particularly those of the meditative school founded by Bodhidharma, must have been striking. In place of Confucius, put the three Buddhas; instead of Yen Hui, and of three others who were placed with him as correlates in the Sung period, put the four great Bodhisattvas, and in place of the ten *Cheh,* put the Lo-han or the twenty-four deva kings.[36] The arrangements are so similar that it is difficult to assume it as a coincidence. Very little is known of the images in Taoist temples of that period, but in more recent times the same general arrangement has been followed. As the Confucian temple took this form in 739, when the remainder of the seventy-two were added, it seems likely that there was direct Buddhist influence, or indirect influence through Taoism. When Hsüan Tsung made the first change in 720, most of the immediate disciples of the sage were not in the temple, but they were added with the sixty-seven names placed there in 739.

One statement can be made with assurance. From that time until 1530, the whole cult of Confucius was so similar to those of unquestioned divinities, such as the city-gods, that he can be regarded only as a god himself. The cult has changed, swinging like a pendulum between the nature cults and the worship of ancestors. This period represents the extreme swing toward the nature cults, which was probably due to external influences.

The sacrifices were more elaborate in the capital than in the provincial cities. In the former, the sacrifice was the *T'ai lao,* including the offering of a bull, pig, and sheep. A prayer was offered, which followed the ancient precedents of the Sacrificial Odes of the *Book of Poetry.* There were music and a dance or pantomime called the Six Ranks.[37] The sacrificial ritual appears to have been an attempt to reproduce the customs of the Chou period. In the provinces, the *Hsiao lao* was used, and there was neither music nor pantomime.

In 740, it was decreed that there should be two celebrations a year, on the first *ting* day [38] of spring and autumn, and this continued to be the custom until 1927. The sacrifice was offered by the Three Dukes.[39] In the provinces, the sacrifice was held on the middle *ting* day.

Hsüan Tsung did one other thing which was of importance for Confucianism, though hardly for the cult. In 754 he founded what is known as the Han-lin Academy. This was a group of the finest scholars of the empire, who had charge of literary and historical works, the composition of the eulogies of great men which were given as posthumous honors, the sacrificial prayers, and the honors given to the empress and the members of the imperial family.[40] The Han-lin Academy was of great influence in strengthening Confucianism, and existed as long as the Chinese empire. One of the greatest blows Chinese scholarship has received in recent years was the burning of the library of the academy by ignorant fanatics during the Boxer rebellion.

The rebellion of An Lu-shan, which began in 751, was a disaster from which the T'ang dynasty never recovered, though it continued to exist for 150 years. One or two emperors made genuine attempts to reform the government, but the tide was too strong. The excesses of the Buddhists and Taoists resulted in acts that are amazing in a country with the culture of China, and even at the height of their influence the reaction against them had begun, a reaction which reached its full power under the Sung.

Han T'ui-chih, or Han Yü (767–824), is the leading Confucian of the T'ang period, and marks the beginning of the renaissance of Confucianism.[41] At twenty-four he obtained a literary degree and entered upon his official career. In 805, he was banished for the first time as the result of a dissertation on the abuses existing in the palace. His career was a succession of recalls and disgraces as a result of his zeal and probity. In 819, he issued his request on the subject of the bone of Buddha, and was promptly banished for the last time. He was recalled once more, but soon died as a result of the hardships of his exile. His name is one of the most famous in Chinese literature, and his style became the model for succeeding writers. An ardent Confucianist, largely influenced by Mencius, he was unflagging in his zeal for the classic ideal and bitter in his attacks upon Taoism and Buddhism.[42]

In his "Essay on the Origin of *Tao*," he pointed out the difference between the Confucian use of the term as the way of virtue which men ought to follow, and the Taoist use, as a mysterious something which can only be reached by the abandonment of all rational processes. Against this he held up the Confucian ideal of benevolence and justice, which the Taoists despised. He described how the Han scholars were influenced by Taoist thought, and the introduction of Buddhism in the medieval period; Confucianism was even forced out of the schools. He attacked the stories which made Confucius inferior to Lao Tzu, and the development of the monasteries, which had created a class, the monks, who performed no useful function in society. After reviewing the development of civilization and the difficulties overcome in each advance of culture, the duties which a man owed to his superiors and to his family, and the necessity for productive work, he showed how both Buddhism and Taoism would destroy the results of progress in civilization. They denied all obligations to society and were destructive of the fundamental relationships of the family. He compared the absorption in *Tao* and the passivity of Nirvana with the labors of the Confucian heroes from Yü to Confucius himself. He recognized Confucius and Mencius as the genuine and authoritative teachers, and accused Hsün Tzu and Yang Hsiung of impure doctrine. In a final malediction, he urged that the Taoist and Buddhist books should be burnt and their temples made into homes, in order that the *Tao* of the ancient rulers might be followed once more.

His petition on the "Bone of Buddha" began with historical comparisons between the great ancient rulers and the later emperors who patronized Buddhism. In particular he pointed out the disasters which came to the state as a result of the abandonment in Buddhism of Liang Wu Ti. After reminding the emperor of the efforts of the founder of the T'ang line to suppress Buddhism, whose failure was due to inefficient ministers, he appealed to him to carry out the intention of his ancestor. The Buddha was a barbarian, wearing different clothes and speaking a different language from the Chinese, a man who did not know the proper relationship between ruler and subject, or father and son. He went on to say that he was sure that the emperor had not been deceived by this superstition, but was merely providing a theatrical spectacle for the amusement of the people of the capital. He besought the emperor to throw the bone into the fire, because the people, being ignorant and obtuse, would misunderstand his majesty's intention and become more superstitious. After quoting the remark of Confucius that one should remain aloof from the spirits, he concluded by saying that if the Buddha had any supernatural power, he was willing to take the entire blame upon himself, if the emperor would only stop his project of bringing the bone to the capital.

It is not surprising that this man was persecuted and degraded, nor is it surprising that he began a new Confucian movement, and was known to later generations as the "Duke of Literature."

NOTES

[1] For a several survey of the T'ang period, see Cordier, Vol. I, pp. 407-572, and Wilhelm, pp. 223-227. Besides De Mailla, Gaubil's history of the T'ang dynasty, *Memoires concernant les Chinoise,* Vols. XV, XVI, is the most detailed study.

[2] 軒轅黃帝 . This title, which gives Lao Tzu the rank of emperor, was given in 667, and is still used in Taoist temples and by the tailors' gild, which worships Lao Tzu as its patron divinity.

[3] Clennell (*Historical Development of Chinese Religion,* p. 120) says that six of the T'ang emperors died from the effects of Taoist drugs. Cordier mentions three: Hsien Tsung, d. 820; Wu Tsung, d. 846; and Hsüan Tsung, d. 859. Cinnabar was commonly used in the preparation of these "pills of immortality."

[4] *Enc. Sin.,* art. "Taoism," p. 545.

[5] *Ibid.,* art. "Buddhism," p. 69.

[6] De Mailla, Vol. VI, p. 168.

[7] *Enc. Sin.,* p. 69.

[8] The *Book of Rites* (Legge, S. B. E., Vol. XXVII, p. 280, in the supplementary section on Earth, in Book IV, the *Monthly Proceedings*) mentions sacrifices to wandering spirits at the same time of the year as the Buddhist festival of Feeding the Hungry Ghosts, or the *Yü-lan hui,* is now held. Clennell (p. 105) says that the custom is indigenous, and was adopted by the Buddhists. Reichelt (*Truth and Tardition in Chinese Buddhism,* pp. 88 f.) thinks that the Buddhists began the custom in imitation of the Nestorian Christians, but offers no convincing evidence. Reichelt's theory rests ultimately on the collaboration of a Nestorian and a Buddhist in translating the Satparamita-sutra. There is no evidence that the Nestorians had developed masses for the dead, or the doctrine of purgatory.

Buddhists claim that the custom began with Buddha himself, but there is little question that in China the custom was developed by Amoghavajra and later patronized by the emperor. The festival is connected with the cult of Ti Tsang. Amoghavajra was a Tantrist, and developed this school of thought in China, thereby contributing largely to the decay of Chinese Buddhism.

[9] The Confucians say that both religions foster superstitious practices; that they are at variance with the doctrines of the canon; and that they are destructive of civilization, and especially of the family relationships, including

the duty of providing descendants, and that of worshiping the ancestors. In addition, Buddhism is a foreign faith. In 845, more than eight centuries after Buddhism was first introduced into China, the Buddhists were placed under the control of the bureau which was concerned with foreigners, because Buddhism came from India (Cordier, p. 512). At that time all foreign religions were persecuted (Wilhelm, pp. 224-225).

[10] Legge, *Chinese Classics*, Vol. I, Prolegomena, p. 92.

[11] *Hsin T'ang shu*, chap. 15, p. 40 L. Unless otherwise stated, the other statements in this chapter are taken from the same passage, which deals with the decrees concerning the Confucian temples.

[12] De Mailla, Vol. VI, p. 19. "Li-chi-min persuadé que les habiles gens sont l'âme du bon gouvernement, fit venir à la cour . . . tous lettrés célèbres, dont les ouvrages sont encore l'admiration des savans, et il en composa une académie qui subsiste de nos jours dans le tribunal des ministres de l'empire." Eighteen scholars are mentioned by name. Doré (Vol. XIV, pp. 343-346) gives a brief account of these men.

[13] Gaubil, *T'ang*, p. 453, cited by Cordier, Vol. I, p. 410.

[14] 房玄齡.

[15] 聖人 *shen jen*, usually translated "sage." The first word means "holy." The expression is a technical term. The Taoists use it to designate the third and highest state to which man may attain, the others being *hsien* 仙 ("immortal"), and *chen jen* 眞人 ("true man"). *Enc. Sin.*, p. 494. The Taoist use implies divinity, but the Confucian does not, and is used of the ideal men of antiquity, like Confucius and the Duke of Chou. The term might also be translated "saint."

[16] 罷 *pa*. This word, when used in a religious context, means that sacrifices were no longer offered in that particular temple, and that the tablet was removed. They might be continued in some other place, however.

[17] *Hsin T'ang shu*, chap. 15, p. 40 L.

[18] In ancient China, the country was divided among the feudal estates, but Ch'in Shih Huang redivided the land into districts of various sizes. The smallest was called 縣 *hsien*, and corresponds to the county in the United States. *Chou* 州 is a later term. A *chou* included half a dozen or so *hsien*.

[19] 宣父.

[20] Ssu-ma Ch'ien, chap. 8; Chavannes, *Mém. hist.*, Vol. II, p. 403.

[21] The following names were added by T'ai Tsung:

Tso-ch'iu Ming 左邱明	Chia Kuei 賈逵
P'u Tzu-hsia 卜子夏	Tu Tzu-ch'un 杜子春
Kung-yang Kao 公羊高	Ma Yung 馬融
Ku-liang Ch'ih 穀梁赤	Lu Chih 盧植
Fu Sheng 伏勝	Cheng K'ang-ch'eng 鄭康成
Kao Ch'ang-sheng 高常生	Fu Ch'uen 服虔
Tai Sheng 戴聖	Ho Hsiu 何休
Mao Ch'ang 毛長	Wang Su 王肅
K'ung An-kuo 孔安國	Wang Pi 王弼
Liu Hsiang 劉向	Tu Yü 杜預
Cheng Chung 鄭衆	Fan Ning 范寧

[22] It is not likely that the Tso-ch'iu Ming mentioned in the *Analects* is the author of the commentary on the *Spring and Autumn Annals*. Probably the original work was not a commentary on the *Annals,* but was connected with them later. There are a number of instances of different men having the same characters for their names. P'u Tzu-hsia was a personal disciple.

[23] The *Li pu* 禮部, or *Li kuan* 禮官, usually translated "Board of Rites." though "Ministry" would probably be a better term. One of the divisions of the central administration of the government. The organization has varied from time to time. Under the Manchus there were six boards or ministries; those of Civil Office, Revenue, Rites, War, Punishments, and Works (*Enc. Sin.,* p. 518). For a more detailed study, see Pao Chao-hsieh, *Government of China,* chap. V, pp. 99-184.

[24] P. W. Kuo, *Chinese System of Public Education,* pp. 42, 43. See also Wilhelm, pp. 219-220.

[25] *Tsu yüan,* sect. 子, p. 250; Doré, Vol. XIII, p. 101. Doré says that in this reign the sacrifice offered Confucius was the *Hsiao lao.*

[26] Cordier, Vol. I, p. 432. 太師 *T'ai shih* is translated "Great Master of the Doctrine."

[27] Chavannes, *Le T'ai Chan,* p. 385. In Shryock, *The Temples of Anking,* (the section on the City-God), there is a translation of such an investigation by the Board of Rites.

De Mailla (Vol. VI, pp. 226-227) says, "Jusqu'ici on n'avoit honoré Confucius que du titre de sage et de maître, et les cérémonies qu'on lui faisoit n'étoient relatives qu'à cette qualité; l'empereur ordonna qu'à l'avenir on lui donneroit le titre de prince, et les cérémonies qu'on lui feroit feroient conformes à ce titre d'honneur."

[28] 李元矐.

[29] The Confucian temples have had various titles. The T'ang designation used here is *Hsien sheng miao* 先聖廟. They have also been called *Wen-miao* 文廟, "Temples of Literature"; *K'ung Tzu miao* 孔子廟, literally "Confucian Temple"; *Hsioh kung,* 學宮, "Temple of the Scholars," or "Temple of Education"; and lastly, *P'an kung,* 泮宮, a name which goes back to the Chou dynasty, and has already been mentioned. It refers to the semicircular pools found before the temples, in imitation of the Chou buildings.

[30] *Hsiang* 象 ("image") is contrasted with *t'u* 圖 ("picture").

[31] The earliest known image of Confucius is among the sculptured reliefs found in the tombs of the Wu family, of the Eastern Han period, and represents the visit of the sage to Lao Tzu. See Cordier, Vol. I, p. 364 f., for a discussion of these finds and the various Sinologues who have worked on them. Mr. B. March, Curator of Asiatic Art in the Detroit Institute of Arts, possesses a picture of Confucius which is said to be a reproduction of the painting, done from the imagination of course, by the famous T'ang artist, Wu Tao-tzu, in the eighth century. Whoever did it, it is a magnificent piece of work, and does justice to the sage. Considering that we have to-day a stone relief of Confucius dating from the Eastern Han period, when the sage was first worshiped in the schools, it is quite possible that images were used from the beginning, but probably the fully sculptured images date from the Wei period. Laufer ("Confucius and His Portraits," *Open Court,* 1912) has figured and discussed the existing portraits of Confucius.

[32] The word *cheh* 哲 means "philosopher," but here it is an honorary title.

Detailed accounts of the *Cheh* are found in Doré, Vol. XIII, pp. 135-150. He translates the term "paragon."

[33] Cordier (p. 468) cites Watters, *Tablets in a Temple of Confucius*, p. ix, as saying that Hsüan Tsung placed the image of Confucius on the east. It was later moved to the north.

Doré (Vol. XIII, p. 102) says that in 712 Jui Tsung gave titles to Yen Hui and Tseng Tzu, and gave both the right to receive sacrifices in the temple. He neglects to say that Yen Hui already had that right. Moreover, this is in disagreement with the Temple Record, according to which Tseng Tzu first received sacrifices in 720. The Temple Record is probably accurate on this point.

[34] *Hsien hsien* 先賢 may be translated "Illustrious men of ancient times." It is a title given to these men.

[35] *Hsien jü* 先儒 "Scholar of ancient times." Like the other phrase, it is an honorary title.

[36] The deva kings are sometimes found in Buddhist temples in place of the Lo-han. There were usually only sixteen Lo-han in the T'ang period. Now there are eighteen.

[37] Some of the music used in the nineteenth century at the sacrifices to Confucius has been treated by Van Aalst in a small volume called *Chinese Music,* and also by Biallas, *Konfuzius und sein Kult.* This music, and the words which it accompanies, are given in full in the Temple Record. The statement in the *Enc. Sin.* (art. "Ritual Music," p. 487), that this music "was introduced from Bactria in the second century B. C. and bears traces of Greek origin," is more than doubtful. See Chavannes, *Mém. hist.,* Vol. III, Appendice 2, pp. 630 f. It is probable that the Pythagorean tubes giving the twelve notes in an octave were introduced from Turkestan or Bactria at that time, but more than this is not known. The notes symbolize the months.

The pantomime or dance existed in ancient China. One famous dance enacted the victory of Wu Wang at Mu. The rank of the person presiding at the ceremony was shown by the number of ranks of dancers. The ruler had eight, and in later times Confucius was given this number. The words are *Lu Yi* 六佾, "Six Ranks." The *Enc. Sin.* (p. 487) states that the dance was first used in the sacrifices to Confucius by Yung Ming of the southern Ch'i dynasty in A. D. 485. There is no such statement in the dynastic annals of the reign.

Both the music and the pantomime are grave, slow, and dignified. The dancers wear ancient dress and carry wands tipped with feathers. The music is confined to a small compass, and is said to symbolize the doctrine of the mean. Each tone of the octave is used as a key-note during one month of the year.

[38] *Ting* 丁 is one of a cycle of "the ten stems," which, in combination with another cycle, "the twelve branches,' has been used by the Chinese from ancient times for numbering the days. *Ting* is the fourth of the series. These cycles are also used in other ways, for instance in divination, and in numbering the years. The Chinese ascribe this last use to Wang Mang (Mayers, p. 368).

[39] The *San Kung* 三公 ("Three Dukes"), who were advisers of the emperor and three of his highest dignitaries, go back to the founding of the Chou dynasty and are mentioned in the *Book of History.* This was the collective name, and each had a special designation, which varied under different dynasties until the Eastern Han, whose names were used as long as the empire lasted (*Tsu yüan,* sect. 子, p. 22). The most distinguished man who occupied one of these positions was the Duke of Chou.

[40] De Mailla, Vol. VI, p. 239, and P. Huang, *Mélanges sur l'administration*, p. 22, cited by Cordier, p. 475. An account of the Han-lin, is found in Pao Chao-hsieh, pp. 275-280.

[41] Han T'ui-chih 韓退之, also called Han Yü, 韓愈, and Han Wen-kung, 韓文公.

[42] This account of Han T'ui-chih is taken from Margoulies, *Le Kou-Wen Chinois*, pp. 176-219. The abstracts of the two essays are based on Margoulies' French translation. The same author says in his introduction, p. lxxv, "Han Yü s'est adonné avec toute l'impétuosité et aussi toute la fermeté et le courage de son caractère à la propagation de la morale confucéenne dont il se fit l'apôtre et le régénérateur."

CHAPTER X

THE SUNG PERIOD, A.D. 960–1279

T'ang T'ai Tsung, although he destroyed the power of the feudal aristocracy which had grown up during the medieval period, had allowed the governors of the frontier provinces a large amount of initiative and power, somewhat after the manner of the Margraves of Charlemagne. The weakness of this system became apparent with the rebellion of An Lu-shan in 751, but it was not changed. Disorders continued, terminating with the equally disastrous rebellion of Huang Ch'ao, which really caused the fall of the dynasty. The fifty years which followed are politely called the period of the Five Dynasties by the Chinese, but there was no real dynasty. The country was divided among rival military leaders without any constructive policies. There were two items of interest during the period. One was a persecution of Buddhists in 955. The other was the development of printing, first in the province of Szechuan, and later for the whole country under the patronage of the politician Feng Tao.[1]

In 960, Chao Kuan-yin founded the Sung dynasty, which ushered in a new period of national greatness. Sung T'ai Tsu, which is the name by which the new emperor is generally known, endeavored to correct the mistakes of the T'ang by making the frontier commanders more directly responsible to the central administration, but later it was discovered that this system also had its defects, since energetic generals were at the mercy of court intrigues. The T'ang empire was powerful abroad, but at the mercy of its own generals, while the Sung enjoyed relative peace within their own territories, but have a most inglorious record in their dealings with foreign enemies, not because there was a lack of able men, but because these men were never allowed to exercise their abilities for long unhindered.

The situation outside China had changed. India was now in a state of disorder and anarchy about which relatively little is known, except through the medium of Moslem invaders. On the north and northwest of China strong states had arisen which cut off intercourse with central Asia and the west. During the Sung period, the chief foreign communications were with countries to the south, like Champa. China was more shut in on her own resources than she had been since the period before Han Wu Ti.

Shortly before the Sung dynasty began, a military lord had granted to a northern tribe certain territories. This resulted in a constant struggle between the Sung rulers and succeeding northern tribes and dynasties, which generally went against the Chinese, and caused the abandonment of North China to the invaders in 1127. These invaders adopted Chinese culture, but the invasions resulted in the shifting of the center of Chinese civilization to the south. The division into north and south continued until both were absorbed by the Mongols in the thirteenth century.[2]

In contrast to a majority of the T'ang emperors, most of the Sung emperors followed the example of the founder of the line in being genuine Confucians, though Cheng Tsung (998–1022) and Hui Tsung (1101–1125) were influenced by Taoist adventurers whose careers make an unsavory page in Chinese history. In general, the policies of the government were in the hands of Confucians when the rulers were able. Even when weaklings were on the throne the supremacy of Confucian doctrines was not seriously questioned. Matters of policy were disputed between different groups of literati, rather than between the scholars and outside groups, and the period is marked by a renewed and greatly increased interest in Confucianism.

A number of factors contributed to this end. Buddhism and Taoism had had their chance, and had been found wanting in the matter of giving an adequate policy to the state. Han Yü had discredited them, and his zeal had caused a revival among the Confucians. The Sung emperors patronized the Confucians, and more than this, the period was one of foreign humiliations which must have tended to make foreign influences within China unpopular. The country was largely shut off from foreign intercourse, and fell back upon its own past. Lastly, the development of printing made the accession of classical learning much easier than it had ever been before. These causes working together resulted in the development of what is sometimes called Neo-Confucianism.

While the great names of this movement belong to the Sung period, with the exception of Wang Yang-ming, its growth can hardly be said to have begun before the middle of the eleventh century. Its full force was not felt until the Ming period, due to the intervening Mongol dynasty. Religious habits are slow to change, and so the cult of Confucius continued along the general lines laid down by the T'ang. The chief change was in the increased prestige of Mencius and in the elaboration of the cult under the emperor Cheng Tsung, who was notoriously Taoist in his sympathies.

Like the T'ang, the Sung period is remarkable for its achievements in literature and art. Poetry flourished, excellent porcelain was produced, landscape painting reached probably the greatest heights it has ever attained in any country, and philosophers arose who can be compared on equal terms with the great thinkers of Europe. For the first time there was a critical study of history. Ssuma Kuang wrote the first general history since Ssu-ma Ch'ien. This was used by the school of Chu Hsi as the basis for the *T'ung chien kang mu,* which has been translated by De Mailla. Ma Tuanlin, although he actually wrote during the Mongol period, belongs to the Sung group. Attention was focused upon the literature and history of China, and the old books were examined in a critical manner.

It is not possible to attempt an adequate account of the Sung philosophy, nor is it necessary in this study. Beginning with Chou Tun-yi (1017–1073), there was a line of thinkers which reached its culmination in Chu Hsi (1130–1200). These men, and those of later times who were influenced by them, were unquestioned Confucians. Their interpretation of the classics has dominated Chinese thought, with few exceptions, until the present generation of scholars. Without entering into the details of their system, it will be enough to sketch the problem which they faced, and the way they tried to solve it.[3]

Their task was to rehabilitate the ancient ideal which was the essence of Confucianism so that it could include the intellectual problems which had been raised by Buddhism.[4] Many of these had not existed for the men who had written the canons, and so the Sung thinkers were obliged to interpret the canons in such a way as to answer questions which had never occurred to the original authors. The result was a new Confucianism which would have surprised Confucius himself.

It is not accurate to say that these men as a group borrowed from Buddhism and Taoism. The school was unfavorable to both, and most of its members would never have deliberately taken anything from either. That they were influenced by both is true, but not in the sense that they deliberately incorporated Buddhist and Taoist elements into their system.[5] They were influenced in the same way that Kant was influenced by Hume, one being obliged to answer problems which the other had raised.

In every case the Confucians answered these problems by developing some passage in the ancient literature. They found their chief inspiration in the *Book of Changes,* whose abbreviated nature lends itself to new interpretations, but it is hardly fair to say that this in itself shows the influence of Taoism, since the *Book of Changes* is not peculiarly Taoist. From the time of Confucius himself it had always been revered by the Confucians, and in the third century, Wang Pi had treated the *Book of Changes* rationally. In order to meet some of the problems raised by Taoist and Buddhist thinkers, particularly those connected with the evil nature of all sensuous desire, the futility of civilization and of progress in its development, and the nature of knowledge, the Sung Confucians were led to emphasize Mencius, who had combated these very notions, and two sections of the *Book of Rites,* known as the *Great Learning* and the *Doctrine of the Mean.* In the former occurs the phrase, "the investigation of things." [6] The Confucians eventually split into two schools on the interpretation of this passage, Chu Hsi holding for an objective examination of the universe, not unlike what we mean by science, while Lu Hsiang-shan and, later, Wang Yang-ming, interpreted it as meaning introspection. But the fact that this latter school was largely subjective does not in itself prove that it was borrowing from Buddhism, for introspection and subjectivity are found everywhere. The distinction in emphasis placed upon the subjective or the objective aspect of reality arises whenever epistemology is discussed, and cannot be patented by any one group, so that when the statement is made that Wang Yang-ming was influenced by Buddhism, it is necessary to prove something more than that his philosophy was largely subjective. Two more definite charges of borrowing may be mentioned.

Chou Tun-yi is credited with having introduced into respectable philosophy the diagram known as the *Plan of the Great Ultimate.*[7] It is said that "this conception . . . was originally used in connection with the secret devices for prolonging human life. . . . It seems likewise to have been of other than Chinese origin." [8] The actual source of Chou Tzu's diagram was a similar plan by a man of the Five Dynasties.[9] It is an attempt to visualize the account of the universe found in the *Book of Changes,* and even though it has been shown that the diagram had been used by Taoists and possibly had a foreign source, it is used by Chou Tzu only as a shorthand representation of the account in the *Book of Changes,* which is certainly indigenous and long precedes the activities of the adepts. There have been more than a few such plans or diagrams in the history of Chinese thought, beginning with one mentioned in the *Book of History.*[10] The *Book of Changes* occupies such a prominent place in Sung philosophy because the great task of these thinkers was to present the ancient Chinese thought in connection with a reasonable theory of the universe, and this book was the only one that permitted the development of such a theory. That there were many points in common between Taoism and Confucianism is true, and goes back to Confucius and Lao Tzu themselves, but it is less true of the Sung thinkers than of any Confucians since Mencius, with the possible exception of Han T'ui-chih.[11]

The other man who is accused of direct borrowing is Shao Yung (1011-1077), who stands somewhat aloof from the great Five. He refused to take office and eventually became a hermit, but on the other hand, he took an active interest in politics until his last illness, and kept up his friendship with leading Confucians until the end. His theory of numbers as an explanation of the universe seems strange, but is based on the *Book of Changes,* which is itself numerical. His idea of Heaven as an ideal world, corresponding to the actual or phenomenal world, can be developed from the Confucian doctrine of the "Rectification of Names." [12]

The matter of borrowing has been emphasized because the whole Sung school claimed to be rediscovering the classics and returning to the original meaning of Confucianism. Earlier Confucians, beginning with Hsün Tzu, were criticized because their doctrine was tainted with Taoism. A number of tablets placed in the Confucian temple were eventually removed because of this. The T'ang period, when Taoism and Buddhism were powerful, is represented by only two names. Hitherto, the Han commentators on the classics had been recognized as the final authority, but now a new interpretation was offered and became the standard. In more modern times the school of Chu Hsi has been accused of misinterpretation, and there has been a tendency to go back to the Han. The point to be made here is that the Han scholars borrowed more than those of the Sung period, beginning with Tung Chung-shu, who incorporated in his work the speculations of the magicians or adepts, and thereby changed the whole aspect of Confucianism.[13] The Sung philosophers made a deliberate attempt to free themselves from Buddhist and Taoist thought. Although their system is necessarily different from anything found in the canon, it is a system which is built upon an ancient Confucian foundation, and one in which all questions are eventually settled by the quotation of some ancient authority. In spite of the new development, the Sung Confucians are nearer to the spirit of Confucius himself than the scholars of the Han period were.

The results of this movement did not at once become apparent in the cult of Confucius, but under the Ming it caused a swing back toward the worship of ancestors and away from the nature cults. The effect seemed irreligious, and the Sung thinkers have been called materialists.[14] Bruce has effectually cleared Chu Hsi of this charge,[15] which has also been made against Confucius himself. Hsün Tzu was a monistic Confucian, because he made Heaven impersonal, but this is not true of Chu Hsi, nor of Confucius, who believed in a Heaven which had clearly personal attributes. In this they were conforming to the tradition of the early Chou period.

The return to the spirit of antiquity was manifested in another way. Confucius and the men of the Chou period had handed down their doctrines to a group of personal disciples who sought out their teacher and learned by conversation with him. This method had been largely abandoned in the formal system of schools which had developed under the Han, and was even less used during the T'ang period. The Sung thinkers resorted again to this system. The great men of the period were not developed in the government institutions so much as in the little groups which surrounded the philosophers. Large school systems may raise the average level of education and imprint a uniform culture, but they are bad incubators for independent thought. The periods of least originality in Chinese thought coincide with the periods of the most thorough development of the government system of education, and when profoundly original minds did break through the circle, as in the case of Wang Ch'ung, it was in spite of their education, and not because of it. On the other hand, the intimate daily contact with a great and illuminating mind brings to flower any possibilities in the character of the few pupils, as has been demonstrated many times since the days of Confucius, Buddha, and Socrates. The invention of printing made it possible to acquire the knowledge of the canon outside the government schools. This fact, combined with the presence of able teachers who were themselves independent thinkers, produced the remarkable achievements of Sung scholarship.

Turning to the actual cult of Confucius, it may be noticed that after a collapse during the period of the Five Dynasties, the worship was resumed even before the beginning of the Sung dynasty, in 931, and schools were reopened in 955.[16]

With the advent of the Sung there came an immediate revival of interest due to the emperor himself. In the first year of his reign (960) T'ai Tsu repaired the images of the *Hsien sheng* (Confucius), of the *Ya sheng* (Yen Hui),[17] and of the ten *Cheh*. He made pictures [18] of the seventy-two disciples, and of the twenty-one *Hsien jü*. The emperor himself sacrificed to Confucius, Yen Hui, and the ten *Cheh,* while his officials sacrificed to the others.[19] Between 960 and 963 the emperor visited the Confucian temple and the *Kuo tzu chien* three times.[20]

T'ai Tsung (976–998) also visited the same school and the temple three times, and had representations of the three *li* [21] painted on the walls. The city of Ho-nan fu was ordered to establish a *Kuo tzu chien* and a Confucian temple, while officials were appointed to take charge of them and to lecture on the sage. The emperor presented copies of the canon to the schools.[22]

The third Sung emperor, Cheng Tsung, was obsessed by Taoism. One of his ministers, Wang Ching-yü, after betraying the emperor in his relations with the Kitans and the state of Hsia,[23] persuaded him to plunge into a maze of Taoist superstition and fraud, which included letters addressed to the emperor from Heaven. Cheng Tsung also conferred a title upon Chang Tao-lin, founder of the Taoist society, and his descendants.[24] The same minister persuaded the emperor to make a religious pilgrimage in 1008, in the course of which he made the *feng* sacrifice on T'ai-shan,[25] and afterwards visited the temple of Confucius at Ch'ü-fu. The passage in the Sung history describing this event is interesting enough to be given in full.[26]

"In the period K'ai-yüan (713–742), the worship of the *Chih sheng wen hsüan wang* [Confucius] was made of the grade *Chung ssu,*[27] while rites were established for his disciples called *Tsung ssu.*[28] The three dukes were ordered to offer the sacrifice. The *Tsung ssu* was discontinued in 904 because of the rebellion of Liang Chu (Chu Wen, of the Later Liang dynasty), but in 931 it was revived. In 955, the *Kuo tzu chien* was rebuilt, and later, the Sung repaired it and added to it. Images of Confucius, Yen Hui, and the ten *Cheh* were made, and pictures of the seventy-two disciples and of the twenty-one *Hsien jü* were painted on the walls of the cloisters.[29] Sung T'ai Tsu wrote odes to Confucius and Yen Hui, and asked his ministers to compose odes for the rest. . . . T'ai Tsung ordered the officials to make drawings of the instruments [used at the sacrifices] and of the ritual of the three *li,* which were placed on the walls of the lecture hall.

. . . "In 1008, the emperor Cheng Tsung deified T'ai-shan, and announced that on the first day of the eleventh month he would visit Ch'ü-fu. Gifts were prepared for the sacrifice. The temple was decorated with yellow banners and hangings, and the clan of Confucius assisted at the sacrifice. The emperor wore the robes and boots of state, and offered the *Chou hsien li*.[30] He also visited the hall of the father of Confucius,[31] and asked members of his suite to pour a libation to the seventy-two disciples and to the *Hsien jü*. In former times the officials prepared the sacrifice, and the emperor merely bowed [before the altar], raising his folded hands, but on this occasion the emperor performed the kowtow [32] as an expression of his reverence for Confucius and the canonical learning. He wrote an ode, which was engraved on a stone monument placed in the temple. After this he visited the grave, riding on a horse, not in his palanquin, where he offered a libation of wine, and kowtowed twice. He issued an edict conferring on Confucius the title of *Hsüan sheng wen hsüan wang*.[33] At the sacrifice a prayer was read,[34] and the victims were those of the *T'ai lao*. The temple was repaired, and ten local families of the K'ung clan were appointed to look after the grave and the temple.

"The emperor gave titles to the parents of Confucius, and to the mother of Po Yü.[35] In 1009, the ten *Cheh* were given the title of duke, the seventy-two disciples were made marquis, and the *Hsien jü* were made barons. The instruments and vessels used in the imperial sacrifice were allowed to remain in the temple, and a stele was erected with the names of the officials who had accompanied the emperor engraved on it. The character *hsüan* was changed to *chih* in the title of Confucius, because *hsüan* was the personal name of the emperor.[36] The emperor presented money and cloth to the family of Confucius and gave to five members the privilege of being eligible to office. He also presented to the temple 150 volumes made under the patronage of his predecessor, T'ai Tsung, and 800 *liang* of silver vessels. An edict commanded the *T'ai ch'ang li yüan* [37] to fix the number of vessels used in the sacrifices [to Confucius] in *chou* and *hsien* cities.

"The seat [altar] of the *Hsien sheng* and those of the *Hsien shih* should be furnished with the following articles; a wine-pot; eight vessels for fruit and meats; four other vessels, two of which were round on the outside and square on the inside, while two were square on the outside and round on the inside; three boxes with compartments for containing the animals used as victims; another wine-pot, engraved with designs of clouds and lightning; a metal vessel for holding water; a round, covered, bamboo box. The wine-pots were furnished with spoons and square veils. These were placed on a tray, which was provided with cloth purificators, and after the sacrifice the cups and vessels were inverted and placed upon it. There were also two candles, two wine-cups, and four trays for them."

The lesser altars were not so elaborately furnished.[38]

"Jen Tsung (1023–1064) visited the school and the temple, and performed the kowtow twice."

It was not until the reign of Jen Tsung that the Neo-Confucian movement began to make itself felt. This emperor persecuted the Taoists and executed Wang Ching-yü, the notorious minister of Cheng Tsung, in 1025.[39] The representative of the K'ung clan was made a duke in 1055. Fan Chung-yen and Ou-yang Hsiu, the first of the great Neo-Confucian officials, reformed the examination system and founded schools.[40] The record of the Sung history continues with the reign of Shen Tsung (1068–86).

"In 1074, an official of the *Kuo tzu chien,* named Chang Tseh,[41] together with others, asked that images of Mencius and Yang Hsiung be placed in the temple [42] and that Confucius should be given the title of *ti.*[43] This was referred to the authority on titles and ritual, the *Liang tzu li kuan* [composed of members of the Han-lin Academy and the Board of Rites], and was rejected."

The official reason for the rejection of the title of *ti* for Confucius was that this term was not used as a title of nobility during the Chou period, when Confucius lived, but it is probable that the real reason was the idea of divinity associated with the word, which would have been obnoxious to the Neo-Confucians. The tendency to deify Confucius struggled continually with the tendency to rationalize him and keep him human, even into the period of the Republic.

"An official named Chiang K'uei [44] petitioned that Yen Hui should be given the title *Yen kuo kung,*[45] while his mother should be given the title *Hsien ssu.* There should be sacrifices to Yen Hui and the other *Cheh,* the victims killed before they were presented, but no prayer. However, the Board of Rites decided that the historic titles of Confucius and Yen Hui should not be changed, and that as the *Cheh* were already included in the worship, the former practice should be continued. The

Board petitioned that in the sacrifices the precedent set in 1074 should be followed. An edict conferred on Mencius the title *Tsou kuo kung*.[46] Another official, Lu Ch'ang-yü,[47] petitioned that in the spring and autumn sacrifices, Mencius should be honored as the correlate, or *p'ei*, of Confucius, but others thought that the correlates should be contemporaries of the sage."

Shen Tsung was the patron of the reformer Wang An-shih. The bitter conflict between Wang and his opponents need not be mentioned, since all the parties were Confucian, except that the struggle was reflected in the placing of Wang's tablet in the temple next to that of Mencius by the emperor Hui Tsung in 1102, and its removal by the emperor Ch'in Tsung in 1126 at the instance of Yang Shih, after Wang's party had fallen from power.

A little later (1084) the Board of Rites did make Mencius a duke, and placed his image on the *P'ei* altar, in spite of the objection that he was not a contemporary of Confucius. All Confucian temples were ordered to make the change. Apparently to show its complete impartiality with regard to the various doctrines of the Nature, the Board of Rites at the same time placed the tablets of Hsün Tzu, Yang Hsiung, and Han T'ui-chih among the *Hsien jü*, thus including all the Confucian versions of the long-drawn argument. Hsün Tzu and Yang Hsiung have since been removed.

In 1091, Cheh Tsung visited the schools and the temple in the capital, K'ai-feng, and sacrificed. Hui Tsung made a member of the K'ung family a marquis in 1102. The same year, an official of the *Kuo tzu chien* named Chao Tzu-lieh [48] petitioned that as the T'ang had given Confucius the title of *wang*, his image should wear the costume of that rank. Until this time, the dress of the Han period had been used. Thereafter that of the Chou period was adopted, because Confucius had been a man of the Chou dynasty. A similar change was made with the correlates. In 1108, the tablet of Tzu Ssu was added to the *Hsien jü*, and sixteen columns, indicating an official of the highest rank, were placed before the gate of the temple.

Chapter 105 of the Sung history also discusses the number of the immediate disciples, and after admitting that both Ssu-ma Ch'ien and the *Family Sayings* give the number as seventy-seven, decides for the number seventy-two because that had been generally accepted since the reign of T'ang K'ai-Yüan.

The same passage tells that in Tsou,[49] the native place of Mencius, there was a temple dedicated to him, and that at that time the disciples of Mencius were placed as correlates in his temple. Mencius thus appeared in his own temple in the place of honor, and in the temples of Confucius in a secondary position.

In 1007, it had been ordered that in the cities of the empire, the chief celebrant at the sacrifice should fast for the three preceding days and that the officials of the district, not simple scholars who had passed the examinations but had not received official appointments, should offer the sacrifice. In 1072, it was decreed that at the sacrifices the officials should wear their state robes. These steps mark the final change of the status of Confucius from the patron of scholars and education to the patron of the civil administration of the government.

This ends the important items of the Sung period. In 1127, after the capture of the emperor, the capital was moved to the south, and from that time the Sung history is a record of imbecile emperors and court politicians foiling the efforts of heroic generals in a losing struggle with northern invaders. Already the star of Genghiz Khan was rising in the north, and it was not long before Kubilai and Bayan completed the debacle of the unfortunate Sung. In 1233, the head of the K'ung was made a duke. When the dynasty was in its last throes in 1241, six of the great Sung philosophers were honored by having their tablets placed in the temple.[50] It was a fine gesture, but it did not keep back the Mongol armies.

NOTES

[1] For a general survey of the period of the Five Dynasties, see Cordier, Vol. II, pp. 5-54; Wilhelm, pp. 227-232. For the development of printing, see Carter, *Invention of Printing in China.*

[2] For a general account of the Sung period, see Cordier, Vol. II, pp. 57-183; Wilhelm, pp. 233-252.

[3] The best account of the Sung philosophy is in the two books of Bruce, *Chu Hsi and His Masters* and *The Philosophy of Human Nature,* the latter being a translation from Chu Hsi. See also *Le Philosophe Tchou Hi, sa doctrine, son influence,* by P. Stanislas Le Gall; T. McClatchie, *Confucian Cosmogony;* and De Harlez, *L'Ecole philosophique moderne de la Chine.* Wieger (*Hist. des croyances réligieuses,* pp. 659-671) contains a brief account of the Sung school.

[4] Wieger (p. 658) gives a list of twenty philosophic works, some of which were accounts of Milesian Greek thought, but in the main Indian, which had been translated into Chinese by A. D. 443. By the Sung period, Chinese scholars had at their disposal the thought of India up to the tenth century, and to some

extent that of Greece. This subject does not seem to have been thoroughly investigated. Thales, Anaximander, Anaximenes, Asangha, Vasubandu, and Nagarjuna were known in China. See also Winternitz, *Geschichte ind. Lit.,* pp. 243, 244.

[5] See Wieger (p. 665) for a translation of the unfavorable judgment of Ou-yang Hsiu on Buddhism.

[6] *Ko wu* 格物.

[7] 太極圖. For the way in which this diagram was used, see Bruce, *Chu Hsi and His Masters,* pp. 126-160.

[8] Wilhelm, p. 249.

[9] The Sung system of philosophy, particularly as found in Chu Hsi, became the orthodox standard in China, and under the Ming and Ch'ing dynasties grew so rigid as to hinder thought. There was naturally a reaction, led by Yen Jo-chu (1636-1704) and Hu Wei (1633-114). Yen made an attack upon the Sung text of the *Book of History,* though it is only fair to say that some of his criticisms had been anticipated by Chu Hsi himself. Hu Wei centered his attack upon the *T'ai chi t'u,* which he showed had originated with a Taoist named Ch'en T'uan (d. 989). The result of the work of these men was a school of the seventeenth and eighteenth centuries which insisted on using the Han texts of the canon. The present generation of Chinese scholars, represented by K'ang Yu-wei and Hu Shih, have turned their attention on these Han texts with destructive effect. It is hardly fair to say that "the Sung philosophy was a structure reared more on speculation than upon the classics." The Sung thinkers were obliged to develop a system which would be as inclusive as the western systems which had been brought to China, and they conscientiously tried to use the canon as the basis for it. The *T'ai chi t'u* could be eliminated from Sung thought without injuring its essentials. See Ryukichi Endo, Vol. II; p. 4, for an account of Ch'en T'uan 陳博. For Yen Jo-chu and Hu Wei, see the *Chung kuo jen ming ta tsu tien,* pp. 1624 and 696. There is an account of them in the report of the Library of Congress, 1928-29, Division of Chinese Literature, App. 2, pp. 303-306.

[10] Mayers (art. "Ho t'u lou shu," pp. 60-63) gives a summary of various schemes of this kind.

[11] It is recognized that Confucianism and Taoism have always had many points in common. Terms like *tao* are translated in Confucian books, but left untranslated in Taoist. In the *Analects,* for instance, some striking Taoist statements are put in the mouth of Confucius. Therefore from the very beginning the two doctrines have had many things in common, and some points of difference, the chief of these latter being on questions of ethics and politics. On one of the most important ethical problems, the nature of man, there is no doubt in the author's mind that the Sung thinkers were not only more sound than the Han, but closer to the mind of Confucius, because they followed Mencius, while Tung Chung-shu and his school were under the influence of Hsün Tzu. The present tendency among scholars is to exalt Hsün Tzu, as a practical man who recognized realities, and to decry Mencius as a mere idealist. It seems to the author that the position of Mencius is much more sound and practical. Moreover, the Sung school made genuine efforts to be critical and rational, in which they followed Confucius and Mencius, while Tung Chung-shu can hardly be said to be either. For this side of Tung Chung-shu, his superstition, from which Confucius and the Sung school were singularly free, and his uncritical acceptance of the theories of the adepts or magicians, see Franke's *Studien zur Geschichte des Konfuzianischen Dogmas.*

¹² Shao Yung 邵雍 is more Taoist than any of the other Sung thinkers. Wilhelm (p. 249) says that his doctrine of a "former Heaven" is derived from Taoist sources. However, Hu Shih, in his *Logical Method in Ancient China* (pp. 37, 46-52), points out that the Platonic concept of an ideal world corresponding to the actual is a corollary of the genuinely Confucian doctrine of the "Rectification of Names." Bruce (*Chu Hsi and His Masters*, pp. 30-38), in his account of Shao Yung, stresses the real contribution this man made to the development of Confucian thought. For Shao Yung's interpretation of the *Book of Changes* by a theory of numbers, see Mayers, pp. 62, 63.

¹³ Compare Wilhelm, pp. 177, 178. "Justification was found for a form of monarchy which inclined more and more toward absolutism, and used for its tool bureaucratic officialdom. Of course no amount of interpretative art could discover in the straightforward ancient writings a warrant for the innovations; hence the creation of accessory tradition. Thus arose a coherent cosmogeny embodying equally the magical ideas of the *fang shi* and the echoes of the genuine Confucian doctrines." This is Wilhelm's judgment on the Han Confucianism. No one has accused the Sung philosophers of forging the classics they quoted. The recent publication of T'ang texts discovered in Japan shows considerable difference between the T'ang and Sung texts.

¹⁴ For instance, Wieger (p. 657) says, of the Sung period, "les Lettrés devenus athées et matérialistes, ne peuvent plus faire fond sur l'ancien théisme."

¹⁵ Bruce, *Chu Hsi and His Masters*, pp. 281-314. Bruce's argument is careful and detailed, and seems to the author conclusive. In this argument, it is not enough to show that Chu Hsi sometimes used the term *Heaven* as if it were a non-personal law of the universe. It is necessary, if he is to be classed as a materialist, to show that he never used the term as signifying a person, or as having personal attributes, and that he held that Heaven could not be a person. Bruce has shown that this is not so.

¹⁶ Unless otherwise stated, the references to the cult of Confucius under the Sung are taken from chap. 105 of the Sung shih.

¹⁷ The title *Ya sheng* here refers to Yen Hui, although it was later given to Mencius. Mencius was not included in the ten *Cheh* of the T'ang period, and was not placed in the temple until 1084.

¹⁸ *Hua* 畫.

¹⁹ According to the *Wen hsien t'ung k'ao*, the title *Ya sheng* was given to Yen Hui in 720, and he is mentioned under this title under the years 739 and 952. Mencius was given the title in 1330. This information was furnished by Prof. Mei and Dr. H. G. Creel, of Harvard University. The *Enc. Sin.* (p. 128) says that in 979 T'ai Tsung bestowed posthumous honors on forty-four generations of the descendants of Confucius. This has not been checked.

²⁰ The name used for the Confucian temple here is *Wen hsüen wang miao* 文宣王廟. The *Kuo tzu chien* 國子監 was a government school in the capital. It originated in the Han period.

²¹ The *San li* 三禮 is held to mean the *li*, or ritual, appropriate to Heaven, Earth, and Man. However, the *Sui history*, in the chapter on *li*, says that it refers to Heaven, Earth, and the ancestors. *Tsu yüan*, sect. 子, p. 33.

²² Possibly these were among the first printed books. The Sung list of the canons, which has been used ever since, had not yet been made, and this is probably the list of thirteen made by T'ang T'ai Tsung, which included the *Book of Changes*, the *History*, the *Odes*, three editions of the *Spring and Autumn Annals* with the commentaries by Tso, Kung-yang, and Ku-liang, the *Book of Rites* and two other ritual books, the *Chou li* and the *I li*, the

Analects, an ancient dictionary called the *Erh ya,* the *Book of Filial Piety,* and Mencius (*Enc. Sin.,* p. 122). The Han list is usually five, but sometimes the *Record of Music* is added to make a sixth. The present arrangement, said to have originated with the Sung, is divided into two groups, the Five Canons, or *ching* 經, which include the *Book of Changes,* the *Odes,* the *History,* the *Rites,* and the *Spring and Autumn Annals,* and the Four Books, or *shu* 書, the *Analects, Great Learning, Doctrine of the Mean,* and *Mencius.* In view of the later criticism of the Sung school, it may be noticed that the *Chou li,* the *I li* and the *Book of Filial Piety,* all of which the Sung eliminated from the list, are now viewed with very great suspicion, and the first two may have been largely the work of Han scholars. The Five Canons of the time of Han Wu Ti did not include the *Book of Rites,* which had not yet been compiled, but did include the *Record of Music,* which is now a section of the *Book of Rites,* as are also the *Great Learning* and the *Doctrine of the Mean.*

[23] Cordier, Vol. II, pp. 88, 89.

[24] *Enc. Sin.,* art. "Master of Heaven," p. 340, and art. "Chang Tao-lin," p. 89. Besides the title, the emperor also gave large estates in Kiangsi which remained in the hands of the Chang family until the fall of 1926, when they were confiscated by the Nationalist Government. No adequate study has yet been made of the Taoist society founded by Chang Tao-lin. With the exception of a lapse during the medieval period, the head of this society has always been a member of the Chang family, who is called the *T'ien shih* 天師 and resided at Lung hu shan 龍虎山 in Kiangsi. The organization was loose, but extended over the country. Dr. Hu Shih says that the T'ien shih fled in 1926 before the Nationalist troops and during the winter of 1927 a meeting of Taoists was held in Shanghai to discover what had become of him.

[25] The passage in the Sung history dealing with the sacrifice of Cheng Tsung on T'ai-shan has been translated by Chavannes, *Le T'ai Chan,* pp. 235-261.

[26] This passage occurs in the *Sung shih,* chap. 105, pp. 47 R f.

[27] *Chih sheng wen hsüan wang* 至聖文宣王 is the title finally given by Cheng Tsung. It had not, of course, been given in the reign K'ai-yüan 開元, which is one of the reign titles of T'ang Hsüan Tsung.

According to the *Chou li,* there were three grades of offerings. The *Ta ssu* 大祀 includes jade, silk, and animal victims. The *Chung ssu* 中祀 included animals and metals. The *Hsiao ssu* 小祀 consisted only of animals. In the time of the Ch'ing, or Manchu, dynasty, the *Ta ssu* was offered to Heaven, Earth, Shang Ti, T'ai-shan, the gods of the Land, and Confucius. The *Chung ssu* was offered to the sun, moon, the gods of agriculture and of silk culture, the former emperors, Wen Ch'ang, and Kuan Ti. The term *Hsiao ssu* was changed to *Ch'ün ssu* 羣祀, and was offered in ordinary temples. The term *ssu* is here equivalent to "rite" (*Tsu yüan,* sect. 丑, p. 199).

[28] *Tsung ssu* 從祀. The name means "added rite," and was used for the sacrifices to the *Hsien jü.* It dates from the time of T'ang T'ai Tsung (*Tsu yüan,* sect. 寅, p. 254).

[29] The word *wu* 廡 is used for the covered halls which run down the eastern and western sides of the court before the main hall in Confucian temples. It is translated "cloister."

[30] *Chou hsien li* 酌獻禮. This ritual is now used in the worship of shen 神, or gods of lesser rank. It implies the pouring of a libation (*Tsu yüan,* sect. 酉, p. 253).

[31] A note or comment at the beginning of chap. 47 of Ssu-ma Ch'ien, presumably made by one of the Ch'ien-lung editors, says that in ancient times, in Lu, there was a temple to the father of Confucius on the Chung-ni Mountain 仲尼山. However that may be, this is the first reference to the cult of the father in the text of the dynastic histories. It appears as if this, and other changes, developed at the Ch'ü-fu temple, and were not mentioned in the official histories until imperial notice was taken of them. The hall is now situated to the rear of the main hall of the temple, and is a separate building. Chavannes evidently did not think the note to Ssu-ma Ch'ien of historic value, since he made no reference to it.

[32] The K'o-t'ou 磕頭 has become anglicized as "kowtow." It consists of falling on the knees and bending forward until the head touches, or almost touches, the pavement. It is considered a mark of greater respect than the chu kung 鞠躬 ("bow"). The kowtow may be performed a number of times, depending on the degree of the ceremony. The greatest number used is nine. A more literary term for the kowtow is k'ou shou 叩首.

[33] 玄聖文宣王, the first title given to Confucius by Cheng Tsung. A literal translation of the characters would be awkward. The emperor left his palanquin because the trees were so thick. Under the Manchus, visitors were obliged to proceed on foot to the grave.

[34] The terms used here for prayer are chu wen 祝文, which is the phrase now used in translating the Anglican word "collect," a prayer appropriate to a special occasion.

[35] The father of Confucius was given the title Ch'i Kuo Kung 齊國公, and his mother the title Lu Kuo fu-jen 魯國夫人. The other lady was not honored because she was the wife of Confucius, which would have been opposed to Chinese propriety, but because she was the mother of his son, Po Yü. Her title was Tan Kuo fu-jen 鄆國夫人.

[36] This custom, apparently a case of royal taboo, is at least as old as the Western Han period, when the surname of Hsün Tzu was changed because it was the personal name of the Han emperor Hsüan (73-48 B.C.). Under the Ch'ing dynasty, a stroke was omitted in writing the character ch'iu 丘, the personal name of Confucius, and the character was deliberately mispronounced as Mo. This also was a royal prerogative.

The new title, like the older one except for the first character, begins with the characters Chih Sheng 至聖, quoted from the Doctrine of the Mean and Ssu-ma Ch'ien's eulogy of Confucius. Every subsequent title has included these two characters, generally translated "perfectly holy."

[37] The Board of Rites presided over by the T'ai ch'ang, a high official whose title goes back to the Northern Ch'i dynasty, but whose office existed as early as the Ch'in period. The title was abolished by the Ch'ing dynasty (Tsu yüan, sect. 丑, p. 233).

[38] The following list gives the Chinese terms. The use of the various utensils is taken in each case from the Tsu yüan.

One ts'un 尊, a wine-pot.

Eight pien tou 籩豆; two kinds of vessels, one used for fruits, and the other for pickled or dried meats, vegetables, etc.

Two kuei 簋, round outside, square inside.

Two fu 簠, square outside, round inside. These vessels are represented and described in Laufer's Chinese Pottery of the Han Dynasty.

Three *chu* 俎, boxes with compartments for the animal victims.

One *lei* 罍, a wine-pot with designs of clouds and lightning.

One *hsi* 洗, a metal vessel for holding water.

One *fei* 篚, a round bamboo box. The box is called *ch'ang* 筐, when it is rectangular.

The wine-pots were furnished with *cho* 勺 ("spoons") and *mi* 幂 ("square veils").

They were placed on the *tien chin* 坫巾, a pottery sacrificial tray or rest, on which were the *chin* 巾, cloth purificators or coverings. The libations were poured onto the tray.

Two *chu* 燭, candles.

Two *chiao* 爵, wine-cups.

Four *tien* 坫, trays or rests for the candles and cups.

The lesser altars were furnished with two *pien,* two *tou,* one *kuei,* one *fu,* one *chu* ("box"), one *chu* ("candle"), and one *chiao.*

[39] Cordier, Vol. II, p. 94.

[40] De Mailla, Vol. VIII, pp. 228-230.

[41] Ch'ang Tseh 常秩.

[42] This reference would make it appear that there had been no image of Mencius in the temple before 1084. The list of the ten *Cheh,* which was not given in the T'ang history, is as follows:

Yen Hui 顏回	Tzu Kung 子貢
Min-tzu Ch'i 閔子騫	Jen Yiu 冉有
Jen Po-niu 冉伯牛	Chi Lu 季路
Chung Kung 仲弓	Tzu Yiu 子遊
Tsai Wo 宰我	Tzu Hsia 子夏

Later in the Sung period Tseng Tzu was advanced to the position of *Cheh.* When Tseng Tzu became a correlate, Tzu Chang was added. Still later, Yiu Lo and Chu Hsi brought the number up to twelve. Yen Hui had always been prominent as the favorite disciple of the sage. Tseng Tzu, Tzu Ssu, and Mencius were presumably made correlates because of their authorship of three of the *Four Books* emphasized by the Neo-Confucians.

[43] The character *ti* 帝 was originally used as the title of deceased emperors who received sacrifices from the living ruler. It also appears in the term *Shang Ti* 上帝, the equivalent of Heaven, which Chavannes translates "the emperor on high" and which in the early Chou period was a supreme, monotheistic deity. Later, in the theory of the Five Emperors, the term *Shang Ti* was used in the plural. Since Ch'in Shih Huang, the word *ti* has been used as the title of the emperor. In modern usage the term has two meanings—"emperor," and "god." As in this instance the purpose was obviously to give Confucius an increase in rank above his title of *wang,* or "prince," the word should be translated as "emperor." The idea of divinity is associated with the word, however. Certainly the intention was to change the title of Confucius, and not to change the substance of his personality. That the title was refused indicates that the Neo-Confucians, always rationalistic, did not wish Confucius to approach the status of a nature god. The title had already been given to Lao Tzu, and was later conferred on Kuan Yü. Ct. Hopkins' *Pictographic Reconnaissances, Jour. J. A. S.,* 1926, p. 465.

⁴⁴ 蔣夔.

⁴⁵ 袞國公.

⁴⁶ 鄒國公.

⁴⁷ 陸長愈.

⁴⁸ 趙子櫟.

⁴⁹ 鄒.

⁵⁰ The *Enc. Sin.* (p. 128) translates the title 衍聖公 as "Widely Holy Duke." This was the highest title the representative of the K'ung family attained. As such he took rank at court with the Grand Secretaries and immediately below the imperial princes.

The six were Chou Tun-yi 周敦頤, Shao Yung 邵雍, Chang Tsai 張載, Ch'eng Yi 程頤, Ch'eng Hao 程灝, and Chu Hsi 朱熹.

CHAPTER XI

The Yüan, or Mongol, Period, a. d. 1280–1368

The Yüan, or Mongol, dynasty was foreign, and marks both an interlude and a commencement in Chinese history. The Mongols took China as they found it, and did not attempt the sweeping "reforms" that have marked European conquests. On the other hand, the period is characterized by a freedom of intercourse with other countries and civilizations which had profound results in China as well as elsewhere. The modern spoken language, Mandarin, took its form, and a new literature was born, though it was to be centuries before the medium would be recognized by scholars. The cult of Confucius was elaborated still further, but no fundamental changes were made in the practice of the Sung.

The Mongols had been the dominating influence in Chinese affairs long before Kubilai became the *de jure* emperor of China in 1280. The development of this obscure and uncivilized tribe, and the power which was wielded by the family of its first leader for 150 years, remain among the enigmas of history, and among the best arguments for the importance of individual variation as an historical factor.

Early in their career of conquests, a descendant of the Kitan royal family, which had ruled northern China during a part of the Sung period, was appointed to high office, and Yeh-lu Ch'u Tsai was of great influence in changing the Mongols from a savage tribe of nomads into one of the greatest instruments for the spread of culture which has ever existed. Under his guidance, the Mongols learned from every people with whom they came in contact, and the policy of borrowing from anywhere whatever seemed to be of value was continued for three generations. Besides this, the necessities of their enormous empire resulted in an amount of intercourse which is amazing, even outside their actual domain. Marco Polo was not an isolated case, he was a commonplace of Mongol rule, and the flow was in both directions. A king of England received the sacrament at the hands of a Nestorian Christian from the north of China who was then a prelate of that church in Baghdad. The Vatican Library contains a considerable correspondence between the Popes and the Mongol rulers. Some of the Mongols were allies of the crusaders in Palestine. The court at Karakorum or Khanbalik was graced by dignitaries and ambassadors from all the known world. Ibn Batūta, sitting in a tea-house in Hangchow, met a man from a village in Morocco which adjoined his own, and saw the same man several years later in the Sudan. Printing passed across to Persia with the Mongols, and possibly gunpowder, which had been used in China in 1232 as a device of warfare. The Mongols habitually employed men of other nations, but in positions far from their native lands, so that Marco Polo became the magistrate of Yangchow, and a man who may have been Chinese commanded under Hulagu in Persia.[1]

This general policy of the Mongols was applied to religion as well. They were interested in all religions, permitted great freedom after their empire had been established, patronized several creeds, and delighted in debates between the representatives of different faiths. Originally the Mongol religion seems to have been a crude shamanism, but like the other features of their culture, it soon changed. Genghiz carried with him on his campaigns in Central Asia a venerable Taoist hermit, Ch'ang Ch'ün, with whom he discussed the nature of reality and similar subjects in his spare moments between battles.[2] Nayan is said to have been a Christian and to have carried the Cross on his banners.[3] The later Ilkhans of Persia became Moslems. Debates were held at court between Taoists and Buddhists until, in 1256, Mangu definitely decided in favor of the latter. In 1269, the Lama P'ags-pa reduced the Mongol language to writing, and thereafter the Tibetan form of Buddhism was in great favor.[4] Kubilai was strongly in favor of the Buddhists in their recurring struggles with the Taoists, and edicts were issued in 1258, 1261, and 1280 which restricted the latter. In 1284, nine scholars of the Han-lin Academy were ordered to commemorate the Buddhist triumph in this dispute in an essay which was engraved on stone.[5]

A number of the features of modern Chinese culture developed at that time, and among them were two which affected religion in particular. The novel, while its beginnings can be traced to the professional story-tellers of an earlier date, is essentially a product of the Mongol period. Much religious folk-lore and belief have been preserved by the novels. It is singular that this source has been neglected in the study of modern Chinese religion. The language used was not the literary style of the classics, but the spoken language. Under the republic this style of writing has become generally accepted, but for 600 years it was ignored by scholars.[6]

The other influence was the drama. Here again the beginnings reach back into earlier periods. There are two types of drama, the civil and the military. Wang Kuo-wei, the leading modern scholar in this field, thought that the theater originated in the religious pantomimes of the ancient period. But there is little question that the development of the Chinese theater as it is to-day began in the Mongol period, and there are no extant dramas of an earlier date. Although gods often appear in them, the plays are not primarily religious, but from Mongol times they have been connected with the temples of certain gods, which have stages built for such dramas, and theatrical performances have been a part of religious festivals "in order to amuse the god." Such plays have not been allowed in Confucian temples, nor is divination permitted in them.[7]

Under such a dynasty and such conditions, the cult of Confucius would continue, but hardly develop. The emperors patronized the cult in much the same way that they patronized other religions, gave a new title to the sage, and added names to the temple. In 1294, Kubilai gave two estates to the K'ung family.[8]

The characteristic doctrines of the Sung school, especially those of the two Ch'eng and Chu Hsi, were spread throughout the north by Chao Fu, who is known as the leading scholar of the Mongol period.[9] Other Confucians, such as Ma Tuan-lin and Ching Li-ch'ang, refused to take office under a foreign dynasty, retiring into private life, where they taught and wrote.[10]

At the instance of Yeh-lu Ch'u Tsai, Ogotai reëstablished the *Kuo tzu chien*. Kubilai placed it under the direction of Hsü Heng, a noted essayist and scholar of the school of Chu Hsi.[11] Another college was established at Ch'ang-an. It was due to the existence of this institution that the steles on which the canons had been engraved in 837 have been preserved to the present day.[12]

In 1273, Kubilai ordered that a Confucian temple be built in his new capital, the modern Peiping, and that sacrifices be offered in the spring and autumn. The sacrificial officers were directed to wear their state robes according to their rank, while scholars not in office were to wear the costume of the T'ang period. The temple was not finished until 1306, in the reign of Ch'eng Tsung.[13]

In 1308, Wu Tsung gave to Confucius a new title, *Ta ch'eng chih sheng wen hsüan wang*,[14] an analysis of which shows the Chinese custom in conferring successive posthumous honors. *Wen hsüan wang* was the title given by T'ang Hsüan Tsung in 739. *Chih sheng* was prefixed to this in 1012 by Sung Cheng Tsung. To these five words two more were now added—*Ta ch'eng*. A translation would seem redundant to us. This custom of prefixing new characters to an already existing title as an additional honor was pursued not only in the case of Confucius, but with various other deities, like the city-gods, and forms another link between the cults of the nature gods and that of Confucius.

The Mongol decline began shortly after the death of Kubilai in 1295, with quarrels among the Mongols themselves and inefficient government. No men of the caliber of their earlier leaders appeared. Being aliens, their position in China became more and more precarious. Everywhere the Mongols had assimilated the culture of the peoples they governed, and Kubilai had become a patron of Chinese civilization and art as soon as he was firmly on the throne. In their growing weakness, his successors threw sops to an increasingly hostile public opinion in the form of honors which would please the Confucians. In 1316, Jen Tung sacrificed to Confucius, and to Yen Hui, Tseng Tzu, Tzu Ssu, and Mencius who were placed on the *P'ei* altar. The father of Confucius was made a duke and a title was given to his mother. A number of the great Sung Confucians were added to the tablets.[15] Some had been placed there in the last days of the Sung period but as most of China had been controlled by the Mongols at the time, the change was probably not effective. In 1330, Tung Chung-shu was added to the list, the father of Confucius was made a prince, and further honors were given to his mother, while the four correlates were made dukes. Later, the Manchus were to adopt the same ineffective devices.

While no fundamental changes were made in the cult, the sacrifices were more elaborate than ever before, or since. The Mongol rulers were trying to show that they were greater than any dynasty that had existed before them, and to make their rule popular with the Chinese. For the first time there was an account of the details of the sacrificial ritual in the dynastic history,[16] and as it gave the description of the central act of the cult at its height of splendor, the ceremony may be described in full.

The list of sacrificial vessels was given in detail, and was much larger than that of the time of Sung Cheng Tsung.[17] The temple was furnished with 686 vessels of bronze, 384 vessels of bamboo and other kinds of wood, three vessels of porcelain, and 632 pieces of cloth, probably silk, used as veils or covers. This was the equipment of the temple in the Mongol capital,[18] and the arrangements in provincial cities were less elaborate. Included in the list was an incense-burner. Chinese scholars differ in their views of the beginnings of the use of incense in religious ceremonies, but all agree that its religious use was not earlier than the Han period.[19]

The names of the different pieces of music, or chants, were given, but no further detail. When the term *music* was used in connection with the sacrifice, it included not only the notes played on the various musical instruments, but the poetry chanted by the choir made up of scholars from the neighboring *Kuo tzu chien,* and the pantomime or posturing, performed with wands tipped with feathers. The notes, chant, and posturing were carefully coördinated and took place at the same time.

The times of sacrifice were fixed as the first *ting* days of spring and autumn, but if there were some reason for postponing the ceremony, it might take place on the second *ting* day.

The victims were an ox, five sheep, and five pigs, which were placed in a box with compartments facing the altar, and they were not moved during the ceremony, but were consecrated by the official, who laid his hand upon them.[20] Two kinds of wine were offered, as well as dishes of prepared food of various sorts.

There were three sacrifices during the ceremony, each made by a different celebrant, of which the first was the most important. At the first sacrifice, a piece of silk and a screen were offered. The silk bore on it the full title of Confucius. The screen consisted of a tablet set in an upright frame, and was inscribed with a prayer, or praise ode. Following the ceremony, the piece of silk and the screen were ceremonially buried in the court of the temple.[21] The following prayer, while not taken from the Mongol ceremony, may illustrate the type. It was actually used in the Manchu period.

"O great teacher, thy virtue surpasses that of a thousand sages,
And thy way excels that of a hundred kings.
Rivaling the sun and moon,
Thy light shines forever.
Truly there is none
Like thee among us.

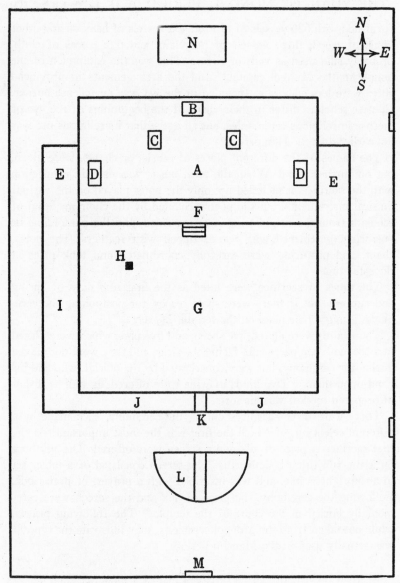

PLAN OF A CONFUCIAN TEMPLE

This is slightly different from the temples of the Mongol period, when the *Tsung Sheng Tsu,* as it is now called, was at one side of the Great Hall.
A. The Great Hall. B. Altar of Confucius. C. *P'ei* altars. D. *Cheh* altars. E. Side rooms. F. Terrace. G. Court. H. Pit. I. Cloisters. J. Store rooms. K. Sacred Gate. L. Pond. M. Main entrance, not built until a man of the district had taken the degree of *Chuan Yüan.* N. *Tsung Sheng Tsu.*

"The time is here for us to observe the rules of propriety and to make music. Beating the bells and drums of the *P'i Yung* college,[22] we offer thee sweet incense. We present the water of the *P'an*[23] to thee in the *pien* and *tou* sacrificial vessels.

"Now it is spring (or autumn), wherefore we respectfully offer thee this sacrifice according to the ancient rites. The reverent and constant observance of thy moral teaching is the expression of our gratitude to thee. Mayest thou enjoy this sacrifice."[24]

It does not seem worth while to enumerate the titles and number of the various sacrificial officials, but the description of the ceremony itself will indicate the chief officers and their duties. The three celebrants remained silent throughout the service. They were guided in all that they did, and were directed when to perform their acts by one of the attendants in a sort of recitative.

On the day before the ceremony, at about three o'clock in the afternoon, the ceremonial inspection of the victims took place, although the exact moment when the animals were killed, which was always before the actual sacrifice, was not specified. The inspecting officials vested in their robes and went to the hall where the victims were prepared,[25] standing in lines on either side of the entrance, facing east and west. The master of ceremonies [26] conducted the inspectors into the hall, where they stood facing north.

An attendant [27] was waiting beside the victims, and after bowing, announced, "It is completed."

The master of ceremonies, addressing the inspectors, repeated, "It is completed."

"They are fat," continued the attendant, and this also was repeated by the master of ceremonies. Then he conducted the inspectors to the sacred kitchen, where they observed the washing of the victims. The ceremony of inspection was then ended, and the inspectors left.

On the night of the sacrifice, at a quarter of an hour before one,[28] the first celebrant [29] and his two assistants who were to sacrifice in the two cloisters [30] vested in their robes and waited in a side apartment. Those taking part in the sacrifice belonged to two groups, the officials who came to offer the sacrifice, and the temple attendants. The celebrant belonged to the first group, while the master of ceremonies belonged to the second. The visiting officials, with the exception of the celebrant and his two assistants just mentioned, dressed in their scholar's gowns and stood outside the sacred gate on the west side, facing east.

The herald [31] and his assistant [32] then entered the court. The former stood at the southeast corner of the terrace before the great hall, and faced west, while his assistant stood at the southeast corner of the court, by the steps leading to the sacred gate, and also faced west.

This was followed by an inspection of the arrangements for the sacrifice. The inspection was made by the first celebrant and his two assistants, already mentioned. The master of ceremonies conducted the inspectors into the temple enclosure, and at the same time the attendants were reviewed by a director.[33] When the first celebrant, who was to inspect the great hall, and performed his duty first, entered the hall, the master of ceremonies said, "I beg you to inspect the arrangements which have been prepared," and when they reached the steps leading from the court to the terrace before the great hall, he said, "Ascend the steps." When the inspector was under the eaves of the great hall, the master of ceremonies said, "Approach the sacred seat of the *Ta ch'eng chih shen wen hsüan wang* [Confucius]." On reaching the altar, they counted and inspected the offerings, facing north. Then the master of ceremonies said, "Approach the sacred seat of *Yen kuo kung* (Yen Hui)." On reaching the *P'ei,* or correlate, altar, they faced east, and inspected the offerings. This was repeated for the other *P'ei* and the *Cheh* altars; and the other two inspectors, the assistants to the celebrant, inspected the preparations in the cloisters. After this, the rooms where the cleansing of the hands took place, and those where the wine was kept, which were beside the great hall, were also inspected. The inspector of the western cloister examined the pit where the silk banner and the screen-tablet were to be buried,[34] which was on the western side of the court. The inspection being completed, the celebrant and his two assistants retired to a side room and removed their robes.

The sacrifice was now ready to begin. This was announced by striking the great bell, which reverberated through the silence of the night for several minutes. The attendants vested in their robes and were reviewed once more in a side room by their director, who reported to the master of ceremonies when they were ready. An usher [35] conducted the supervisor of sacrifice [36] and the supervisor of ritual [37] to their places, where they stood facing west.

The herald cried, "Let the officers of music take their places, with their instruments." This was repeated by his assistant. The following commands were then given by the herald, and repeated by his assistant, who stood by the gate, 100 yards away.

"Let the sacrificial attendants takes their places."
"Let the students take their places."
"Let the assistants to the celebrant [38] take their places."
"Let the celebrant take his place."

These commands were obeyed by those to whom they were addressed, the celebrant, his assistants, and the students being conducted by ushers to their places on the terrace or in the court before the great hall. The celebrant was directed, "Stand facing west."

The herald, chanting in a high-pitched, quavering voice, commanded that the music of "Welcoming the Spirits" [39] be played. This music was repeated eight times.

All officers of lesser rank than the first celebrant then kowtowed twice, directed by the assistant herald, who cried, "Bow and kowtow," and "Rise." They were standing in the court.

The assistant herald added, "Every officer will attend to his service."

Then the first celebrant was directed, "Proceed to the place of cleansing," and meanwhile the music of "Cleansing the Hands" was played. The celebrant stood facing north, holding with both hands a tablet. These tablets were originally memoranda of business to be conducted at interviews with the emperor, but later they lost their practical, and acquired a symbolic and ceremonial use, being borne by officials on important occasions.[40] The tablets were made of jade, ivory, or bamboo, and were unlike the memorial tablets bearing the name of the spirit, in that they tapered toward the bottom and were pointed at the top. On reaching the place of cleansing, the celebrant put the tablet in the ceremonial belt or girdle which was a part of his costume, washed his hands, dried them on a towel which was handed to him by an attendant, and took the tablet again, after which the music stopped. He was directed in every action, being guided by ushers and accompanied by attendants, but he himself remained silent throughout the entire service.

Then the celebrant went to the great hall, and as he mounted the steps, the music of "Entering the Hall" was played until he was before the altar. He was directed to prepare himself, and faced north, putting the tablet in his belt. He knelt, and three times offered incense before the image of Confucius. The incense was burning in a metal vessel, which was presented toward the altar with both hands.

The music of "Presenting the Banner" was then played. The acolyte holding the silk banner inscribed with the title of Confucius [41] handed it to the celebrant, who presented it before the altar with both hands and returned it to the acolyte. The celebrant took the tablet in his hands again and performed the kowtow, rose, retired a few steps walking backward, knelt, and performed the kowtow twice more. He was then directed to the *P'ei* altar, and the ceremony was repeated. When the offering to the correlates had been completed, the celebrant retired to the music of "Descending the Hall," and resumed his original position outside, standing with his face toward the west.

It was then announced that the officer in charge of the food [42] should present the victims, and later, that the celebrant should perform the rites.[43] This presentation of the food and the victims was the oldest feature of the sacrifice, going back to prehistoric times, and the Yüan history apparently considered that the rite was so well known that it was unnecessary to say more than that it occurred. The victims were consecrated by laying the hand upon them, while the dishes of food were offered with both hands toward the altar, and then returned to the acolyte. The food was not supposed to be actually on the altar, but on a side table. The victims were not killed during the sacrifice, and there was no statement that blood was offered. There was no trace of the idea of eating the flesh of the god, nor was the food burned or destroyed at the altar.

This was followed by the libation. The ceremony of cleansing was again performed. The celebrant went to the room where the libation cups, or chalices, were kept, faced north, put his tablet in his girdle, and washed and dried three chalices, which were carried by an acolyte. Then he proceeded to the apartment, to the side of the great hall, where the wine was kept, while the music of "Ascending the Steps" was played. With appropriate ceremony he removed the veil from the wine vessel, and held a chalice while an acolyte filled it with wine from an ox-shaped vessel. Three chalices were filled and borne on a tray by an acolyte. The celebrant approached the altar to the music of "The Libation," put his tablet in his girdle, knelt, and thrice offered incense. The acolyte gave him a chalice, which he presented before the altar, and poured a libation into the tray. This was repeated with the two other chalices. He took his tablet again, and the music ceased.

An acolyte then knelt on the left of the celebrant, facing east, and chanted the ode, reading from the screen-tablet which he held. After the ceremony had been repeated at the *P'ei* altars, the celebrant retired backward and performed the kowtow. Following this, the celebrant and the officer of prayer retired to appropriate music, and the first sacrifice was ended.

The ceremonies for the second and third sacrifices were so similar to the first that it does not seem worth while to repeat the details. While the temple assistants remained the same, the celebrants were different for each sacrifice. The silk banner, the prayer, the victims, and the dishes of food were omitted from the last two offerings, and the only presentation was the libation. The wine was of a different kind, and was taken from a vessel shaped like an elephant.

When the last celebrant entered the hall, the lesser celebrants were commanded to offer the sacrifices at the two *Cheh* altars in the great hall, and the altars in the cloisters, of which there were several in each cloister, how many, the Yüan history does not say. Three offerings were made, the *Cheh* sacrifices taking precedence.

After the last offerings were presented, it was announced that the officer in charge of the food should remove the *pien* and *tou* vessels, which contained various prepared foods. The music of "Removing the *Tou*" was played, and the officer knelt before the sacred seat, removed the vessels, and retired. Following this, the music of "Sending Away the Spirits" was played, and all the officials below the rank of the first celebrant kowtowed twice.

Then the silk banner and the prayer-screen were carried to the pit in the courtyard, to the "Music of Burying." The three celebrants went to the pit and faced north.

"Let them be buried," chanted the herald. After this was done, the celebrants seated themselves in the courtyard. The musicians with their instruments, the choir, and the dancers then withdrew, and the doors of the temple were closed.

The officials retired to a side apartment, where they stood in a circle, the first celebrant on the west and the other two on the east, and bowed to each other, after which they retired to the vesting room and resumed their ordinary clothes.

The victims were removed, and portions sent to those whom the emperor wished to honor, following an ancient custom at least as old as the Chou dynasty.

This account of the rubrics of the service as it existed under the Mongols is largely devoid of color, whereas it is in reality one of the most impressive rituals that has ever been devised. The silence of the dark hour, the magnificent sweep of the temple lines, with eaves curving up toward the stars, the aged trees standing in the courtyard, and the deep note of the bell, make the scene unforgettable to one who has seen it even in its decay.[44] In the days of Kubilai the magnificence and solemnity of the sacrifice would have required the pen of a Coleridge to do it justice. The great drum boomed upon the night, the twisted torches of the attendants threw uncertain shadows across the lattice scrolls, and the silk embroideries on the robes of the officials gleamed from the darkness.

The flutes sounded, and the chant rose and fell in strange, longdrawn quavers.

"Pai," and the officials fell to their knees, bending forward till their heads touched the ground.

"Hsin," and they were erect again.

Within the hall, the ox lay with his head toward the image of Confucius. The altar was ablaze with dancing lights, which were reflected from the gilded carving of the enormous canopy above. Figures moved slowly through the hall, the celebrant entered, and the vessels were presented toward the silent statue of the sage, the "Teacher of Ten Thousand Generations." The music was grave and dignified, and the sound of the harsh Mongolian violin was absent. The dancers struck their attitudes, moving their wands tipped with pheasant feathers in unison as the chant rose and fell.

It would be hard to imagine a more solemn and beautiful ritual, or one set in more impressive surroundings, and yet the thought forces itself forward, How would this sacrifice have affected Confucius himself?

In the light of what he said and did, there can be little question about the answer. He would have been horrified and displeased. He can be quoted against the making of human images, and against the worship of the dead by any except their own descendants. He opposed innovations, and there is no precedent for such a sacrifice to a private man in the ancient writings, or for many of the details of the worship, such as the use of incense. He was not only a profoundly humble man himself, conscious of his own failings, but he refused to admit that any man of the past deserved the sort of titles that had now been given to him. He shared the tragic fate, not of failure, but of success, with other great men who have endeavored to serve their fellows, and have been rewarded by their followers in ways that would have revolted them.

"Acts of the greatest reverence," says the Book of Rites,[45] "admit of no ornament." [46]

NOTES

[1] For a general study of the Mongol period, or for special accounts of some of its features, there is more material available in European languages than for any other period of equal length in Chinese history. The statements in this brief summary are to be found in Cordier, Vol. II, pp. 188–432, Cordier's edition of Yule's *Marco Polo*, Defrémery and Sanguinetti's translation of *Ibn Batuta*, Howarth's *History of the Mongols*, Montgomery's *Yaballaha III*, Carter's *Invention of Printing in China*, Bretschneider's *Medieval Researches*, and Schlegel's article, "On the Invention and Use of Firearms," in *T'oung Pao* (1902).

Bretschneider (Vol. I, p. 4) says that Hulagu's lieutenant, Ko K'an 郭伉, was a Chinese. He is honored by having his tablet in the temple of the god of War. His Chinese nationality is doubtful, because he has a Mongol name, Kuka Ilka, and was a relative of Subutai. Ko K'an seems to be a transliteration of the Mongol name.

[2] Bretschneider (Vol. I) has translated the account of Ch'ang Ch'ün and his relations with Genghiz Khan. It is interesting not only as showing the great Mongol in a very favorable light, but as evidence for the existence of a high type of Taoism during the Mongol period.

[3] Cordier, Vol. II p. 311.

[4] *Ibid.*, pp. 337, 338.

[5] Chavannes, *Chancellerie mongole*, cited by Cordier, p. 336.

[6] The *Liao Chai*, translated by Giles as *Strange Stories from a Chinese Studio*, contains much material concerning Chinese views of the future life, the world of spirits, etc. *The Three Kingdoms* has a great deal of religious material, for instance, K'ung Ming's sacrifice to the winds. The list might be continued indefinitely. It is evident that there is a large amount of colorful material awaiting investigation. Our knowledge of Chinese folk-lore is slight, and unless investigated soon, many sources will be unavailable. A dozen or more novels or volumes of stories have been translated into English.

[7] The greatest scholar in this field is Wang Kuo-wei 王國維, whose recent death is a blow to Sinology. He had collected many hundreds of references to pantomimes, dancing, masks, and other subjects connected with the theater, all earlier than the Mongol period. The best English book on the subject is Zucker's *Chinese Theater*. There is no satisfactory account of the relation of the theater with certain temples, particularly those which show Taoist influences, like the temples of the city-gods, the *Tung Yo*, and the *Ho Shen*.

[8] *Enc. Sin.*, p. 128. It is reported that the nationalist government has recently confiscated these estates.

[9] For a brief account of Chao Fu, see Appendix I, or Giles, *Chin. Biog. Dict.*, p. 59.

[10] For Ching Li-ch'ang, see Appendix I, or Giles, p. 148. There is a short notice of Ma Tuan-lin in Giles, p. 570.

[11] De Mailla, Vol. IX, pp. 430, 431. For Hsü Heng, see Appendix I, or Giles, p. 303.

[12] Chavannes, *Chancellerie mongole*, cited by Cordier, Vol. II, p. 339.

[13] This, and other quotations from the dynastic history, are from the *Yüan shih*, chap. 76, p. 55 L.

[14] 大成至聖文宣王.

[15] The following Sung thinkers were honored by the Mongols in 1313.

Chou Tun-yi.   Chu Hsi.
Ch'eng Hao.   Ssu-ma Kuang.
Ch'eng Yi.   Chang Ch'ih.
Chang Tsai.   Lu Tsu-ch'ien.
Shao Yung.

[16] *Yüan shih,* chap. 76, p. 55 L f.

[17] The following is the list of sacrificial vessels.

A. 686 *Vessels of Bronze*

1 *chiao tien* 爵坫, a tray.
248 *tou* 豆
115 *fu* 簠
115 *kuei* 簋
6 *teng* 登, originally a pottery dish for food, later made of bronze
6 *hsi tsun* 犧尊, wine vessels shaped like oxen
6 *hsiang tsun* 象尊, wine vessels shaped like elephants
2 *shan tsun* 山尊, wine vessels with a mountain design
6 *hu tsun* 壺尊, wine vessels with round mouths and square bodies
2 *chu tsun* 著尊, wine vessels with lightning designs
2 *t'ai tsun* 太尊, undecorated wine vessels
2 *lei* 罍, wine vessels with clouds and lightning designs
2 *hsi* 洗, flat, round bowls for the water used in washing
27 *chu* 枓, spoons
28 *tien* 坫, trays
118 *chiao* 爵, wine cups

B. 384 *Vessels of Bamboo and Other Woods*

248 *pien* 籩
3 *fei* 篚
133 *tsu* 俎

C. 3 *Vessels of Porcelain or Pottery*

2 *p'ing* 瓶, vases
1 *hsiang lu* 香爐, incense-burner

D. 632 *Cloths, Probably of Silk*

241 *pien chin* 籩巾, veils or covers for the *pien*
248 *fu kuei chin* 簠簋巾, veils for the *fu* and *kuei*
133 *tsu chin* 俎巾, veils for the tsu
10 *huang chin meng tan* 黃巾蒙單, yellow silk cloths

The authority for the explanation of these things is the *Tsu yüan.* Pictures of many of the vessels are found in the Temple Plans. Explanations given for the list in chapter X are not repeated.

[18] Kubilai built his new capital on the site of an ancient city, the capital of the Chou state of Yen. The Mongol name was Khanbalik. From the time of Ming Yung Lo, the name was Pei Ching 北京, familiar to us as Peking. The name was recently changed to Peiping 北平. For descriptions of the various cities on the site, see Bredon's *Peking.*

[19] There are three views of the origin of the use of incense in China: (a) It was introduced from abroad by the Buddhists. (b) Its use was indigenous, and began in the Han period. This was probably an aromatic plant, not incense.

(c) It was used in the Chou period, not in worship, but in order to eliminate bad smells. See *Tsu yüan,* sect. 巳 , p. 190. Laufer (*Chinese Pottery of the Han Dynasty*) has discussed this question.

[20] The victims used in Chinese sacrifices are treated in various ways. The organs are sometimes inflated with air. Sometimes the hair is shaved, sometimes parts of the hair are allowed to remain, etc.

[21] At the services seen by the author, the prayer was written on paper and burned in an iron stand at the close of the service. This may be the provincial use, or an innovation of the Manchus.

[22] The *P'i Yung,* already mentioned, was an educational institution supposed to have existed in the early days of the Chou period.

[23] The *P'an* were semicircular pools, said to have been placed before buildings belonging to the nobles of the Chou period. They are copied in the Confucian temples.

[24] This is taken from *A Collection of Chinese Prayers,* Huang and Shryock, *Jour. Am. Oriental So.,* Vol. XLIX, No. 2, pp. 129, 130.

[25] 省牲所．

[26] 引贊者．

[27] 禮牲者．

[28] Seventy-five minutes before *Tsu*丑 , the period from 2 to 4 **A. M.**

[29] 初獻官．

[30] 分獻官．

[31] 明贊．

[32] 承傳贊．

[33] 糾儀．

[34] 望瘞．

[35] 引禮者．

[36] 監祭官．

[37] 監禮官．

[38] 陪位官．

[39] This music has been translated into western notation by Van Aalst, *Chinese Music,* under the title of the "Guiding March," but the score of Van Aalst is not the same as that used by the Mongols.

[40] The name of this tablet is *hu* 笏．

[41] The banner is called *pei* 幣, and the ceremony of presenting it, *tien pei* 奠幣．

[42] 禮饌官．

[43] 行禮．

[44] The author was present at the ceremony of inspecting the victims in Nanking in the spring of 1917; at the sacrifice of the *K'ung chiao hui* on the birthday of Confucius at Anking in 1920, when he took part in the service as an assistant to the celebrant; and at the state sacrifice in Anking in the spring of 1921; and he also witnessed the similar state sacrifice to Kuan Ti in Anking in the fall of 1923.

[45] Legge, *S. B. E.,* Vol. XXVII, p. 400.

[46] The ceremony of the sacrifice to Confucius may be compared with another

great ceremony of the state religion of China, the sacrifice to Heaven by the emperor at the winter solstice. See Blodget, "The Worship of Heaven and Earth by the Emperor of China," *Jour. Am. Oriental So.,* Vol. XX, pp. 58-68, and Hodous, *Folkways in China,* chap. 37, pp. 220-235. No adequate study has been made by European scholars of the sacrifices to Kuan Ti, which parallel those to Confucius.

Biallas (*Konfuzius und sein Kult,* pp. 100-106), in his description of the cult at Chü-fu, gives a number of details of the sacrifice not mentioned in the dynastic history, including a translation of the odes used, and the arrangement of the vessels on the altar. Edkins has translated a different set of odes, in the *Jour. N. China Branch of the R. A. S.* Vol. VIII. Biallas also gives the music of two of the melodies. Van Aalst gives the music for welcoming the spirit.

CHAPTER XII

THE MING PERIOD, A. D. 1368–1643

The collapse of the vast Mongol empire is almost as mysterious as its formation. The enormous distances, bankruptcy due to an inflated paper currency, the civil wars, and the relatively small numbers of the ruling race all contributed to the result. The empire came into being because of the appearance of genius in one family, and disappeared when that genius died out. The career of Tamerlane a few decades later showed what a single man could still accomplish in Central Asia.

In China the Mongols were disliked as foreigners, and as soon as their feeble leadership became apparent, rebellion began. The progress of the Chinese was aided by the fact that during the aggressive days of the Mongols they had destroyed the city walls throughout China, or allowed them to fall into disrepair, so that they were not able to offer much resistance after they lost the initiative. Native leaders sprang up over the country who warred among themselves as well as with the Mongols, and the country eventually fell into the hands of Chu Yüan-chang, who set up the Ming dynasty.

The first and third emperors of the Ming dynasty were great men, but the remaining fourteen rulers of the line were mediocre or degenerate. The power was wielded by eunuchs and unworthy favorites, and the administration was so corrupt that long before the final debacle it became apparent that China would fall an easy prey to the first formidable opponent.[1]

During the reigns of Hung Wu (1368–1399) and Yung Lo [2] (1403–1425) there was still a considerable amount of intercourse with foreign countries. There were friendly communications with Tamerlane, in spite of the fact that Tamerlane was on the point of invading China when he died. The second Ming emperor was dethroned by Yung Lo and disappeared as a Buddhist monk. Alive, he was a constant menace to the new ruler, and Yung Lo made strenuous efforts to locate him, which included the establishment of a separate department of the government created for this purpose, and a number of embassies to foreign countries where it was thought the deposed emperor might be hiding.[3] This caused a continuance of the intercourse with other countries, but it soon stopped. The last great Chinese voyage, which reached Ormuz in the Persian Gulf,[4] was in 1431.

After this the policy of the Chinese changed, and even commercial relations with foreign countries were discouraged. China was closed to foreigners, so that when the Europeans again reached China in the next century, the earlier intercourse was forgotten, and the tradition grew up that China had always been isolated. The progress of the Ottoman Turks in Western Asia completed the separation of Europe and China.[5]

China was shut in on itself. For the first century of Ming rule the school of Chu Hsi dominated thought, although no great thinkers appeared. In 1415, Yung Lo collected the writings of 120 scholars of this school.[6] This emperor was also responsible for the greatest encyclopedia which has ever appeared in any language, but which, unfortunately, has been almost entirely lost.[7] After this, intellectual achievement lapsed, with one brilliant exception. This was the philosopher Wang Shou-jen, or Wang Yang-ming (1472–1528).[8] He was not only a thinker, but a great administrator and general, who suppressed a dangerous rebellion in south China. In philosophy he differed on important points from Chu Hsi, and derived his thought from Chu Hsi's opponent Lu Hsiang-shan. Yet all these men are considered legitimate Confucians, and their tablets are in the Confucian temple.

Lu Hsiang-shan (1139–1192) was a contemporary of Chu Hsi, with whom he held friendly debates. Both derived their thought from the Ch'eng brothers, but emphasized different sides, Chu Hsi teaching what we would call a scientific investigation of the universe, while Lu Hsiang-shan held that all things are subjective, existing only in the mind, and that education should consist largely in reflection. The essence of his philosophy is expressed by his sentence, "The mind is law."[9] He held that the distinction between the external and the internal or subjective is only that between movement and quietness, while to investigate things is to investigate oneself. On the conception of the two principles of law and matter[10] he is not otherwise different from the prevailing Sung philosophy, and uses both terms.[11]

The keynote of the thought of Wang Shou-jen is the phrase, "Knowledge and action are one."[12] While this has led to Wang's being called a pragmatist, it is really a statement of philosophic idealism, since it is a development of Lu Hsiang-shan's position that the difference between the subjective and the objective is only that between movement and quietness, or non-action, and that reality is subjective. Action is to know the reality of that which is concerned, while knowledge is to act in a complete way. To seek law outside the mind is to make knowledge and action two things, but to seek law within the mind is what the sages taught concerning the One. Wang recognizes intuition, and, like Plato, seems to base his argument on the a priori certainty with which certain propositions are received. Intuition [13] is the foundation of virtue, and the mind, when clear, is heavenly law.[14] The will [15] is the response to intuition, or the intuition in action. External objects, or things,[16] are the objects of will, and are caused or created by will, for without will there is no object.[17]

Wang Shou-jen was unquestionably a great thinker, and had a considerable number of followers. In Japan his greatness was recognized, and his writings are more studied in China to-day than they have been in the past, but on the whole, Chu Hsi continued to dominate Chinese thought during the Ming and Manchu periods.

It has been said that Wang Shou-jen was largely influenced by Buddhism, but while this is quite possible, and there are similarities between him and such thinkers as Vasubandu, no adequate study has yet been made which would enable us to make positive statements.[18] At least the development of his thought can be traced through Lu Hsiang-shan to Ch'eng Ming-tao. Too much emphasis has been laid on his differences from Chu Hsi, and not enough on the points which they have in common. These two thinkers illustrate the large latitude which exists within what may be called orthodox Confucian thought.

Wang Shou-jen had disciples after the manner of the Sung thinkers, but he was not a teacher in the government school system, and his ideas do not seem to have affected official education, which had become more stereotyped than ever before.[19] The eight-legged essay, an artificial composition in which skill in balancing characters took the place of real literary merit, became a prominent feature of the examinations. The interpretations of Chu Hsi, who was a really great and liberal thinker, were hardened into a system which prevented further development. Nevertheless, the government schools were never more thorough and inclusive, nor the regulations for examinations and degrees more carefully worked out. Memorizing and cleverness in juggling characters took the place of vitality and strangled independent thought. The system produced the type of scholar who had no interests outside the interpretation of the canon, and who would ignore the new type of learning which was soon to be thrust upon China.

Hung Wu issued several decrees reorganizing the *Kuo tzu chien*. The titles of professors, the details of the provincial school system, the numbers of students, the subsidies for their support, the course of study, the daily program, and the examinations were all determined. Military arts and mathematics were added to the curricula at first, but were later removed. The military examinations, separate from the literary examinations, which had been abolished by the Mongols, were revived in 1506. From 1450 on, admission to official service was determined by the length of time spent in school, not on the results of the examinations. There were separate schools for the sons of nobles, and education was provided even for villages. Some students were subsidized, others not, but provision was made for support if the student did good work. The Ming emperors were fairly favorable to science, but educational thought throughout most of the period was dominated by the school of Chu Hsi, which was not partial to innovations.[20]

The division between north and south China, which has troubled the country before and since, caused difficulties in the educational system of the Ming. From the time of Yung Lo, there were two capitals, Nanking and Peking, south and north. The rivalry between scholars from the two sections, and the accusations that this or that part of the country was favored in granting degrees, finally led to a division of degrees, so many being arbitrarily awarded to scholars from northern districts, and so many to those from the southern.[21]

The school of Chu Hsi, which dominated intellectual life before 1500, and has continued to be the standard interpretation of Confucianism to the present, was hostile to Buddhism and Taoism. As a result, these religions entered upon a period of intellectual decadence, since scholars lost caste by having anything to do with them. This did not prevent them from continuing their hold on the people, especially through the masses for the dead and the worship of deities like Kuanyin for the birth of sons. In spite of the literati, even emperors patronized the monks, and there are many Buddhist works of art dating from this period, especially the long reigns of Chia Ching and Wan Li which filled the sixteenth century.

The literati, shut up in their past, and admitting the supremacy of the Confucian principles, turned their attention to the ways in which Confucius and his followers should be honored.

The first ruler of the dynasty, Hung Wu, had been a Buddhist monk as a young man, but on becoming emperor he was lavish in the honors he paid to Confucius. When he entered Nanking in 1368, the first year of his reign, he went at once to the Confucian temple, and in the second month he offered the *T'ai lao* sacrifice to Confucius in the *Kuo hsioh*, or government college.[22]

He also sent a representative to sacrifice in Ch'ü-fu, giving him the following directions. "The doctrines of Confucius are as broad and as great as Heaven and Earth. The whole world should sacrifice to him. As the ruler of all under Heaven, it is my duty to put his *Tao* into practice. I request you to sacrifice to Confucius at his home. Be reverent." [23] It is possible to take these words too seriously, but they certainly represent the nearest approach to a conception of Confucius as the deity of a missionary religion of which the emperor was the chief agent.

At the same time it was decreed that sacrifices be offered twice a year, spring and autumn. The emperor himself offered incense, and the prime minister was the first celebrant, while the second and third sacrifices were made by scholars from the Han-lin academy and the *Kuo tzu*.

In 1370, the emperor took away all titles from gods other than Confucius.[24] It is difficult to say whether this means that Hung Wu wished to honor Confucius by making his position unique, or whether it represents the rationalistic influence of Chu Hsi, from which Confucius was temporarily exempted. The latter is much more probable. The Neo-Confucians were opposed to the honors which the state had heaped on a multitude of divinities since the practice had been started by the T'ang. The pantheon was crowded with spiritual princes, dukes, earls, and barons, some of whom had come in the front door, some up the back stairs.[25] While the Confucians recognized that it might be politic for the state and its officials to accept these popular cults at times, they regarded them merely as superstitions which were useful in regulating the people. This edict of Hung Wu probably means that the emperor, under Confucian influence, had decided that the honor paid these hero and nature gods had grown too great, and should be curtailed. The exception of Confucius from this change was only temporary, and was probably due to the reluctance of the Confucians to apply their rationalism to their own patron saint.

In 1371, the Board of Rites made slight changes in the ritual of the Confucian sacrifice. The number of *pien* and *tou* vessels was changed from eight to ten, the *pien* were constructed of bamboo, and porcelain was used for the other vessels, while the victims were killed and prepared before being taken to the hall. There were sixty musicians, and forty-eight performers in the pantomime in six ranks with two leaders,[26] making 110 in all, which does not include the temple attendants and acolytes. The Board of Rites wished that the musicians and dancers should be chosen from the best professional performers in the capital, but this was vetoed by the emperor, on the ground that the sacrifice should not be a professional performance. He insisted the selection be made from among the scholars, and from the students in the government schools. This decision was in accordance with classical precedent, which had always been against anything that might tend toward the creation of a priestly caste.

Mencius was removed from the *P'ei* altar in 1372, but replaced the following year. In 1374, the time of the sacrifice was changed to the second *ting* day because of an eclipse, which would have made the regular time unfavorable. A new imperial academy was begun in 1382, on the west of the temple, and the emperor frequently went to inspect the construction. When it was finished, he sacrificed there himself, and issued an edict that sacrifices should be paid Confucius throughout the country, while the rites for the provincial districts were fixed in detail.

In 1384, it was decreed that all the temple officers and attendants below a certain rank [27] should offer a lesser ceremony called the *Shih tsai li* [28] to Confucius on the first and fifteenth of every month; that is to say, at the new and full moon. In 1393, the music at the sacrifices was established by decree. The details are not given in the Ming history, but the music, odes, and directions for the pantomime which were published under the Manchus [29] show that each dynasty used its own music and odes, and gave different names. One character indicated that the music was that of a certain dynasty, while a second identified the particular piece. This was in accordance with classical precedent, when not only the dynasties, but in the Chou period, the various feudal states, used different types of music called by different names.[30]

The ministry of works was ordered to enlarge the Confucian temple in 1397. Yang Hsiung had been removed from the temple in the previous year, probably because of his connection with Wang Mang. In 1425, the representative of the K'ung family was given an official residence in the capital. The next year, the rationalistic influence of Chu Hsi was again felt when the Board of Rites was requested in a petition to investigate and revise the titles given to the men honored in the temple, but nothing appears to have been done. In 1437, three more names were added.

The year 1438 marks an addition to the cult. A petition to the emperor pointed out that as Confucius received sacrifices because of his filial piety, the correct relation between father and son should be exemplified in the temple. The father of Confucius had a title, and was commemorated in a hall to the west of the temple, an inferior position. The fathers of Yen Hui and Mencius had the title of duke, but those of Tseng Tzu and Tzu Ssu had only that of marquis, and fathers should not be ranked below their sons. Therefore, the petition urged, the fathers of Tseng Tzu and Tzu Ssu should be given the title of duke, and the fathers of the four men, the correlates of Confucius, should be placed on the *P'ei* altar in the temple to the father of Confucius. The emperor approved, and issued a decree to this effect.

When the temple at Ch'üeh-li [31] burned, in 1476, the emperor rebuilt it, and the new temple was finished five years later. He erected a·stele with an inscription, and sent an official to sacrifice there. The ranks of the dancers were increased from six to eight, bringing the number of performers in the pantomime to sixty-four. In 1496, the number of musicians was increased to seventy-two. During the Chou period, eight ranks of dancers were allowed to the ruler, or *wang*, only.

In 1521, the emperor ordered that the ancestral temple of the K'ung clan at Ch'ü-chou, which was a different building from the memorial temple of Confucius and his disciples, should be rebuilt, and commanded K'ung Ch'eng-yi,[32] a descendant of the sage, to offer sacrifice on its completion.

The year 1530, the ninth year of the reign of Chia Ching, is very important in the history of the cult. This emperor, whose temple name was Shih Tsung, was a weak but interesting character. From the beginning of his reign he was infatuated with the Taoist adepts. In 1523 one of his ministers sent in a memorial on the subject, to which the emperor made no reply. Then in 1530, under the influence of a scholar named Chang Tsung, he sanctioned important changes in the cult of Confucius, and seems to have followed Confucian guidance for several years; for in 1536 he destroyed Buddhist temples in the capital. By 1539 he had reverted to his earlier views, and gave up most of his state duties in order to pursue Taoist researches. In 1546, he elevated a Taoist adept to high position in the hope that he would be able to secure from him the formula for the drug of immortality. Shortly after, the emperor instituted a search for books on immortality, and with the help of assiduous officials, secured 769 volumes. In 1566, the emperor fell ill, and one of the ministers memorialized the throne, blaming all the ills of the empire on the emperor's infatuation for the Taoists, and recalling the days, thirty years before, when the young emperor had been a model Confucian. The old ruler repented, and on his death-bed issued a decree admitting his faults.[33]

Chang Tsung, under whose influence the emperor made the reforms in the cult of Confucius, is also an interesting character. He was born in 1475 and died in 1539. After failing seven times, he finally took a degree in 1521. Chia Ching was not the son of the preceding emperor, and when urged by a majority of the officials to adopt his predecessor as his father, he declined, and instead canonized his actual father. Chang Tsung supported the emperor in this, and as a result was rapidly promoted and acquired great influence. He exercised this power for good, not only in the reforms of the cult of Confucius, but in putting down bribery and other evils, and in remaining clean-handed himself. On the other hand, he was proud and revengeful, and made many enemies, but the emperor always remained loyal to his friend. It was not until after Chang Tsung's death that Chia Ching turned again to his Taoist favorites. The conversations between Chang Tsung and the emperor have been published.[34]

The petition of Chang Tsung in 1530 may be summarized as follows. The sacrificial record [35] should be revised. Filial piety required that sons be honored after, and not before, their fathers, and therefore a hall dedicated to the father of Confucius and the fathers of Yen Hui and the others should be erected to the north of the great hall. This was the place of honor, while the west, where the hall had been placed previously, was an inferior position.

Confucius should no longer have the title of wang. During the Chou period, when Confucius lived, this title was held only by the ruler, and when the feudal lords usurped the title, Confucius protested. If Confucius were indignant that his own feudal superior should take the title of wang, how much more unfitting was it to give the title to Confucius himself.

The building should not be called a miao ("temple"), but rather a tien ("hall").[36]

The objects of worship within the temple should be tablets only, and the images should be destroyed. (Presumably the same reasoning applied here, that is, there had been no images in temples during the Chou period, and Confucius himself had spoken against them.)

There should be ten *pien* and *tou* vessels used in the sacrifice, and only six ranks of dancers. (This was because in the Chou period only the ruler might have eight ranks.)

The correlates and others commemorated in the temple should not have titles of nobility, but should be called simply *Hsien hsien* and *Hsien jü,* the illustrious and the scholars of antiquity.

The tablets of twelve men should be removed from the temple,[37] six of them to sacrifices in their native places rather than with Confucius. Five new names should be added.[38]

The emperor approved of the suggestions made in the petition, and ordered the Board of Rites to consult with the members of the Han-lin Academy and the ministers. Ch'u Cheh [39] protested that it was not right to destroy the images,[40] and other ministers supported him. The emperor was angry, degraded the protestants, and explained why he thought the suggestions of Chang Tsung were good. The sage should not be treated as if he were an emperor, and should have the titles in use before the T'ang period, which were *Hsien sheng* and *Hsien shih.*

Then one of the censors, named Li Kuan,[41] sent in a petition: It was the custom to honor Heaven and to reverence one's own father. The virtue of Confucius was supreme. No one could approach him, just as no one could climb to Heaven. If Confucius were regarded as Heaven, it would not be too much. The Sacred Ancestor (Hung Wu, the founder of the Ming line) took away the titles of other gods, but left those of Confucius.[42] Since the T'ang period, the music and rites of an emperor had been used in the worship of Confucius. Sung Cheng Tsung wished to give the title of *ti* to the sage, and did not do so only because this title was not used in the Chou period, during which Confucius lived. Chou Tun-yi spoke of the sage as "The prince of ten thousand generations without end." [43] The petition besought the emperor to change his decision.

The emperor was furious. In the allusion to the reverence paid to his father, he saw a veiled sarcasm referring to his own act of canonizing his actual father instead of the preceding emperor. Chia Ching removed Li Kuan from office and degraded him, ordering the Board of Rites to consider what titles should be given. They decided that Confucius should have the title *Chih sheng hsien shih K'ung Tzu,*[44]

"The Master K'ung, the Perfectly Holy Teacher of Antiquity." The great hall should be called the *Hsien shih miao,* or temple of the *Hsien shih,* while the central gateway should be called the *miao* gate. The four correlates received separate titles, ending with the word "Master," and each containing the word "Holy." The remaining disciples, including those on the *Cheh* altars, were divided into two classes. The first, consisting of the seventy-two and a few others, received the title *Hsien hsien,* while the second, containing the great Confucians of later ages, received the title *Hsien jü.* The *Kuo tzu chien* of Nanking was ordered to prepare the wooden tablets, and the images were destroyed. Some great works of art must have perished in this iconoclastic destruction. A rear, or north, hall was built, and sacrifices were offered there every spring and autumn just before the sacrifices in the great hall, the offerings being of the same grade. While the word *wang* was no longer used in the main temple, it remained in the titles of the ancestors of Confucius. This rear hall was called the *Ch'i sheng kung tsu.*[45]

There is no further material of importance during the Ming period, though a number of names were added to the temple during the reign of Wan Li. Corruption, incapacity for government, and rebellion were so weakening the administration that an unimportant tribe in Manchuria was soon to receive the country as a gift.

Most of the changes made in 1530 became permanent. The images, with a few exceptions in private temples, and earlier titles of nobility were never renewed, though the eight ranks of dancers were restored by the Manchus. The cult swung back from the nature and political cults toward the worship of ancestors. When the Jesuit missionaries reached China a few decades later, they were able to take the position that the rites paid to Confucius were reverential only, not religious. Had they arrived before 1530, there would have been no question, and they would have been obliged to condemn the cult as the worship of idols. It is somewhat ironical to find Catholic missionaries approving and taking advantage of a "reformation" in China which was similar in some of its effects to the movement they were organized to combat in Europe.

It is still more remarkable that both reformations should coincide in time. Personal reasons entered into both movements, though Chia Ching's anger at the veiled insult to his father seems more respectable than the amatory desire of Henry VIII. But in neither case can the personal element be considered the chief factor, since the permanence of the changes in China, as in England, demands greater causes than personal whims. In China, it is safe to assume that the cause was the rationalistic influence of Chu Hsi, and the historical sense awakened by him which led public opinion eventually to recognize the absurdity and impropriety of giving Confucius titles and worship which he would have abhorred.

Under Wan Li and the last Ming emperors, the Jesuits reached China by way of the sea, and soon rose to a surprising prominence, partly because their leaders were exceedingly able and liberal men, partly because of their superior scientific attainments. In the Mongol period, the civilization of China was more advanced than that of Europe, but during the intervening 150 years, the Chinese inventions of printing, gunpowder, and the compass, diffused to the other side of the continent, had resulted in the development of science in Europe. The Chinese rulers recognized the attainments of the Europeans, but the conservatism of the scholar class, the stereotyped and thorough system of education which culminated in the examinations for government positions, and the power which this placed in the hands of the literati prevented the Chinese from taking advantage of the new science. They were to suffer from the defects of their own intellectual achievements. At a time when they should have been looking toward the future, they were concerned only with commenting upon their past.

NOTES

[1] Cordier (Vol. III, pp. 5-89) gives a summary of the period, and De Mailla, (Vol. X) a more detailed account. Delamarre's *Histoire de la Dynastie des Ming* is a translation of a work by the Manchu emperor Ch'ien Lung, and is intended as a supplement to De Mailla. Unfortunately, only Vol. I, which brings the account to 1505, appears to have been published.

Cordier (Vol. III, p. 86) gives the following summary of the Ming period. "Le gouvernement des Ming marque une période d'effacement dans l'histoire de la Chine: le princes qui sont à la tête de l'empire sont ou faibles ou médiocres; la littérature et les arts sont en pleine décadence. Le seul intérêt de l'histoire de cette époque est la lutte sans cesse renouvelée contre les envahisseurs du nord, qui finirent par triompher, et l'arrivée des étrangers."

[2] The emperors of China are generally referred to by their temple names, or *miao hao* 廟號, given as posthumous titles by their successors. Since 163 B. C., in the time of Han Wen Ti, they have also had reign titles, or *nien hao* 年號 which are really the names of periods rather than of emperors, and are used in giving dates. For instance, the name K'ai-yüan signifies a period (713-742) in the reign of T'ang Hsüan Tsung. For periods preceding the

Ming dynasty, the *miao hao* have been used in referring to emperors. But it has long been the custom in European works to omit the *miao hao* when referring to the emperors of the Ming and Manchu dynasties, and to use the *nien hao* as if it were the name of the emperor. This has been so general that the temple names of Ming and Manchu rulers are almost unknown, while their reign names are familiar to those interested in Chinese history. Therefore the author has referred to these rulers by their reign titles, using Chia Ching instead of Shih Tsung, for example, and K'ang Hsi instead of Sheng Tsu Jen.

[3] The second Ming emperor, Chien Wen, ascended the throne in 1398 on the death of his grandfather, Hung Wu, and at once proceeded to deprive his uncles of all power. Five were degraded, but a sixth revolted successfully and in 1403 became the emperor Yung Lo. At the capture of Nanking, Chien Wen and some of his friends disappeared, and it was believed that they had disguised themselves as Buddhist monks. The efforts of Yung Lo to find him were unavailing, but the story goes that after nearly forty years he was recognized and returned to Peking, where he lived in seclusion until his death in 1440. Besides the accounts in Cordier, Delamarre, and De Mailla, there is a notice of him in Giles, p. 196, under his personal name, Chu Yün Wen.

[4] Cordier, Vol. III, p. 41.

[5] Catholic missions in China were founded by John of Monte Corvino, who reached Peking in 1294. They flourished for a time, and are mentioned by John de Marignolli (1342-1347). No one knows what became of these missions after the close of the Mongol period. The separation between Europe and China was so complete that, although the Pope made efforts to find out what had happened, and appointed a number of missionaries, no information has been discovered, from that day until now, as to what happened to the missions or the missionaries. When the Jesuits reached China in the latter half of the sixteenth century, they could find scarcely a trace of the earlier missionary work. The Nestorians seem to have vanished at about the same time (*Enc. Sin.*, p. 375).

[6] Cordier, p. 39.

[7] The *Yung lo ta tien* 永樂大典, 1408. There were 11,095 volumes, and the contents were grouped under four heads, (a) the Confucian canon, (b) history, (c) philosophy, and (d) general literature. There were three copies of this enormous work, the last of which was destroyed by the Boxers. Some volumes are to be found in museums and libraries.

[8] Henke's work on Wang Yang-ming translates his biography, some essays, and correspondence, but is not critical and makes little or no attempt at a serious account of his philosophy. Giles has a notice of him on p. 841. The brief account of Lu Hsiang-shan and Wang Yang-ming given here is taken from Ryukichi Endo, Vol. II, sect. 4, pp. 8 f., and pp. 20 f.

[9] *Hsin chi li* 心卽理.

[10] *Li* 理, ("law") and *ch'i* 氣, ("matter").

[11] Ryukichi Endo, Vol. II, sect. 4, p. 8 f.

[12] *Chih hsin ho yi* 知行合一.

[13] *Liang chih* 良知.

[14] For the way in which the terms translated as "law" and "matter" were used by the Neo-Confucians, see Bruce, *Chu Hsi and His Masters*, pp. 99-125.

[15] *Yi chih* 意志.

[16] *Wu* 物. The expression *ko wu*, or "the investigation of things," on which

the dispute between Chu Hsi and Wang Shou-jen hangs, is found in the *Great Learning*, verse 4. Legge (*Chinese Classics*, Vol. I, p. 222) translates this passage as follows; "The ancients . . . first ordered well their own states. Wishing to order well their states, they first regulated their families. Wishing to regulate their families, they first cultivated their persons. Wishing to cultivate their persons, they first rectified their hearts. Wishing to rectify their hearts, they first sought to be sincere in their thoughts. Wishing to be sincere in their thoughts, they first extended to the utmost their knowledge. Such extension of knowledge lay in the investigation of things."

Without entering into such questions as whether Legge has adequately rendered the Chinese text, it is fairly clear that the interpretations of both Chu Hsi and Wang Shou-jen can legitimately be put upon the text of Tseng Tzu.

The passage might be freely translated as follows: "Good government depends upon well-ordered families. The family depends upon the individuals composing it. An individual is good or bad as his will is bent. A good will depends upon accurate and sincere thinking, and this in turn upon knowledge and judgment. In order to acquire adequate knowledge and sound judgment, it is necessary to "investigate things!" From Mencius onward, the Confucians have insisted that the acquisition of knowledge or wisdom is an obligatory virtue.

[17] Ryukichi Endo, Vol. II, sect. 4, pp. 20 f.

[18] It is said that Wang Shou-jen uses technical Buddhist terms in developing his thought. If this is true, it would certainly show borrowing. Dr. C. H. Hamilton, of Oberlin, has recently translated from the Chinese text an essay of Vasubandu on the thesis that nothing exists except consciousness. This manuscript has not yet been published.

[19] Dr. Kuo (p. 57) says that the emphasis which Wang Shou-jen placed on introspection and the union of theory and practice did eventually affect Chinese education. It is hard to see how it could have had much effect during the Ming period. Wang's theories caused much dispute, and by the time his position was fixed, the dynasty was crumbling.

[20] These details of the Ming educational system are taken from Dr. Kuo (pp. 53-57).

[21] De Mailla, Vol. X, p. 186. Delamarre (pp. 209, 210) says the degrees were apportioned between three districts, the third, which received only ten degrees, including the provinces of Szechuan, Yünnan, Kuangsi, and Kueichou. The north received thirty-five degrees: and the south, fifty-five. It is obvious that by the Ming period, culture was much stronger in central and southern China, probably because of invasions in the north from the Sung period onward.

[22] *Ming shih*, chap. 2, p. 14 R.

[23] *Ming shih*, chap. 50, p. 51 R. Unless otherwise stated, the quotations from the Ming history are taken from this passage.

[24] The Chinese text of this passage is: 洪武三年詔革諸神封號惟孔子封爵仍舊.

[25] An instance will illustrate what is meant by the term "back stairs." A deity named Chang Hsien 張仙 was popular during the Ming and Manchu periods. One story of the origin of this cult is that a concubine of the last ruler of an independent state in Szechuan was taken into the harem of the founder of the Sung dynasty. The emperor found that she still kept a portrait of her former husband, but she cleverly said that it was a picture of a divinity worshipped by women desirous of offspring. Later the worship of this not too

respectable "god" spread, and he was ennobled (Giles, art. "Hua-jui Fu Jen," p. 323).

[26] The dancers stand in lines on both sides of the entrance to the great hall, with a lane between them up which the celebrant passes. There was therefore a leader provided for each group.

[27] The underlings of the officer called the *Chi chiu* 祭酒.

[28] 釋菜禮.

[29] The name of this work is the *Li yo yi ch'i t'u p'u* 禮樂彝器圖譜.

[30] One section of the *Odes* contains specimens of the poetry of fifteen different feudal states. The Chou rulers had an official whose duty was to collect the odes of the states. Confucius was deeply affected by hearing for the first time the music of Ch'i. It is obvious that the *Encyclopedia Sinica*, p. 487, is mistaken in saying that the music now used at sacrifices to Confucius "was introduced from Bactria in the second century B.C. and bears traces of Greek origin." The musical tubes were brought from Bactria, or Turkestan, but nothing is known as to what music was played on them. Van Aalst and Biallas give the music of one of the hymns to Confucius. The most detailed study of Chinese music is Amiot's *Mémoire sur la musique des Chinois,* which translates into European notation the music of a hymn to the ancestors, but does not treat the music of the sacrifice to Confucius. That music is given, however, in the Temple Records, as well as the postures used in the pantomime.

These records, so far as the author is aware, were issued only during the Manchu period. They are not always dated. Doré (Vol. XIII, p. 122) says that the second was issued under K'ang Hsi in 1714. They are therefore first-class authorities for the Manchu, and possibly the Ming, periods, but not for earlier periods. The plans contain pictures of the musical instruments and the sacrificial vessels, as well as the odes and music. Chinese musical notation consists of characters which stand for the notes given by pitch-pipes of a certain length. In these temple records, nothing indicates the length of time a note is held. Each word in the various odes has a note placed beside it.

Chinese musical instruments are divided into eight groups, according to the materials from which they are made (*Enc. Sin.,* pp. 387-390). Among the instruments used at the sacrifices to Confucius are the sonorous stone, stone chimes, bells, drums, stringed instruments like lutes plucked with the hands, flutes, wooden gongs of various sorts, clappers, reed organs, and clay ocarinas. The music is slow, reverent, and with a certain amount of orchestration, which resembles, at least to one not a trained musician, the more quiet compositions of moderns like Ravel and Schoenberg. M. Courant and L. Laloy have written treatises on Chinese music.

[31] The native place of Confucius was Ch'üeh-li 闕里, a village of Ch'ang-p'ing in Shantung. After the death of his father, his mother moved to Ch'ü-fu. The grave is located about a mile from the modern city.

[32] 孔承義.

[33] Cordier, Vol. III, p. 55; De Mailla, Vol. X, pp. 303-330.

[34] For Chang Tsung, see Giles, p. 46, and the *Chung kuo jen ming ta tsu tien,* p. 968. His biography is given in the *Ming shih,* chap. 196, p. 1 R.

[35] *Ssu tien* 祀典

[36] *Miao* 廟, the generic term for "temple," is commonly used by Buddhists and Taoists, and is not ordinarily applied to ancestral temples and buildings in memory of great men, which are usually called *Tsu t'ang* 祠堂. *Tien* 殿 means a "hall," not necessarily used for religious purposes.

[37] Of the twelve names removed from the temple in 1530, the *Ming shih* mentions three, Shen Tang 申黨, Kung Po-liao 公伯寮, and Ch'in Jen 秦冉 as being entirely eliminated, and mentions two, Ling Fang 林放 and Ch'u Yüan 遽瑗, as being transferred to temples in their native places. The last two were later restored to the Confucian temples.

[38] The five names added were Hou Tsang 后蒼, Wang T'ung 王通, Ou-yang Hsiu 歐陽修, Hu Yüan 胡瑗, and Tsai Yüan-ting 蔡元定.

[39] Ch'u Cheh 徐階.

[40] The Chinese text of this passage is as follows: 宜用木主其塑像宜毁.

[41] Li Kuan 黎貫.

[42] Doré (Vol. XIII, p. 105) and Du Halde (in his account of the reign of Hung Wu) say that Hung Wu issued a decree for the destruction of the images in the Confucian temple, which was later repealed. The author has been unable to find any such edict, or any statement referring to such an edict, in the passages of the *Ming shih* where one would expect to find it. One is obliged to conclude that the French scholars, or at any rate, Du Halde, followed some secondary and less reliable source.

Doré also records that in 1476 the number of *pien tou* was increased to twelve, which is probably correct, though it has not been checked by the author.

[43] *Wan Shih Wu Ch'ung Wang* 萬世無窮王. Since Chou Tun-yi was recognized as the founder of the Neo-Confucian school, and was revered by all followers of the school, this argument against the destruction of the images and the other changes of 1530 indicates that the changes were due to the influence of the Neo-Confucians, and that the conservative Li Kuan was quoting their own master against them.

[44] 至聖先師孔子, which has remained the title of Confucius until the present. There is no intimation of either divinity or imperial rank in this title.

[45] 啓聖公祠. This rear temple is now called the Tsung sheng tsu 祟聖祠 The list of tablets there is given in Appendix III.

CHAPTER XIII

THE MANCHU PERIOD, A. D. 1644–1912

Although the Manchus, a coalition of Tungusian tribes, descended from the Niuchi or Jurchi of the Sung period and living on the northernmost frontier in the district now named after them, had developed under pressure into a formidable opponent of the Chinese during the reign of Wan Li, they were still incapable of conquering China with their own power when they were actually invited into the country by the Chinese themselves. The Ming dynasty had disappeared in a rebellion which devastated provinces, and resulted in the sacking of the capital and the suicide of the emperor. In despair, the commander of the only effective Chinese force remaining, Wu San-kuei, invited the Manchus to aid him in restoring order. They came gladly, and remained to found a new dynasty, called the Ch'ing, which survived the rebellions of those Chinese who had requested the presence of the Manchus, and endured more than 250 years. A number of the rulers were able men and two of them, K'ang Hsi and Ch'ien Lung, must be numbered with the half-dozen greatest emperors of Chinese history.

The Manchu rule was consolidated by K'ang Hsi, maintained by Yung Cheng, and expanded by Ch'ien Lung until the Chinese empire extended from Siberia to Indo-China and from the Pacific to the Pamirs and India. The reigns of these three men extended from 1662 to 1796, and these 134 years represent the glorious period of the dynasty. Toward the end of the reign of Ch'ien Lung, cracks were already apparent in the Manchu edifice, and a steady decay set in after his death. The nineteenth century is the most humiliating in all their history to the Chinese. A succession of weak rulers refused to learn from the foreigners whose pressure upon China became increasingly urgent. The T'ai-p'ing and Moslem rebellions about the middle of the century cost more lives than the World War and swept bare the richest provinces of the empire. Some idea of the depopulation caused by these civil wars may be gained from a decree issued in the central province of Anhui at the close of the T'ai-p'ing rebellion, authorizing any one who came into the province to take out title deeds to the land he occupied. A China so injured, and ruled by a succession of alien weaklings, was in no position to resist foreign aggression.[1]

Among the first acts of the Manchus on securing the empire was the reorganization of the educational system. Shun Chih (1644–1662) restored the *Kuo tzu chien,* and at the same time founded schools for the Manchu bannermen, as the Manchus took every precaution to keep themselves separate from the conquered race, though they adopted Chinese civilization and patronized it. K'ang Hsi revived the examination system for degrees and the opportunity of entering the civil service. When K'ang Hsi took the throne in 1662, it was an open question whether the Manchu power was not about to collapse. Although hardly more than a boy, the new emperor was well advised until he himself had matured, and by his adoption of what might be called a Confucian program he secured the support of the influential Ming literati. This support was of inestimable value to the Manchus. It placed on their side the articulate portion of public opinion, gave them a trained and loyal body of civil officials, and after the collapse of the rebellion of Wu San-kuei, forced the opposition to Manchu rule into the underground channels of secret societies.[2] In justice to both K'ang Hsi and the literati it should be said that the emperor fully justified the confidence of the scholars. He became one of the greatest of patrons of Chinese scholarship, which produced under his leadership some of its most monumental works. He himself was not only a cultured and well-educated man, but an able author.[3] The group of maxims generally known as the *Sacred Edict,* which was elaborated by his son Yung Cheng, has been of great influence in molding Chinese opinion. Incidentally, this edict placed both Buddhism and Taoism outside the pale of intellectual respectability, and contributed to their degradation. The Manchu emperors were officially committed to the supremacy of Confucian principles, though some may have subsidized Buddhist and Taoist temples, continued the privileges of such personages as the Taoist "pope," and permitted the legitimate practices of the monks.

In many respects, the ideas of the Chinese throughout the Manchu period still corresponded to those current in Europe during the later middle ages. The industries were organized into gilds like those in medieval Europe. There was at first no feeling of a loss of national rights in the granting of either extraterritoriality or the treaty ports, both of which had existed at various times in Europe. There was, in fact, hardly any feeling of nationality at all, at least in the sense in which it existed in Europe at the time, and exists in China to-day, but this again was characteristic of the middle ages. The parallel holds true especially of the scholar class. The nationality of Thomas Aquinas or Duns Scotus or William of Occam had little or nothing to do with their life or work. The narrow-mindedness of the Chinese literati was not due to their patriotic fervor, for they had none and willingly served an alien, but to the exclusiveness of their culture. In their attitude toward education they were not unlike the scholars of Europe, who considered no man educated unless he had at least mastered Latin and was familiar with Latin literature. There is no cause for surprise in the attitude of the Chinese literati toward the science of the foreigner. Despite the triumphs of modern science, the academic faculties of western universities even to-day are inclined to patronize mere scientists, who are not always at home in Greek and Latin and may not be masters of an elegant style. That the Chinese scholars should despise any form of learning which departed from the study of the canon was in the best scholarly tradition of Europe as well as of China. The difference between Europe and China lies rather in the relative positions of the scholar class. In Europe and America scholars were only scholars, but in China they were also the official class. The great educational system of the Chinese, which had functioned so well from the time of the Han until the nineteenth century, furnishing the empire with loyal and trained officials, was now to be the principal reactionary force against the acquisition of the new knowledge. The early Manchu emperors patronized the scientific Jesuits and appreciated their achievements, but in general the literati were opposed to them. The battle between western science and the classical Confucian education ended only with the extinction of the older system.

All this did not happen at once. K'ang Hsi, Yung Cheng, and Ch'ien Lung encouraged schools, both at the capital and in the provinces. There were separate schools for the sons of nobles. Inspectors sent out by the central authorities conducted the examination for degrees, but while this acted as a check on the work done in the provincial schools, it was also a handicap because the students came to realize that their standing depended only upon the examinations conducted by a stranger, not upon their daily work. The vast examination grounds in the great cities, with their thousands of tiny cells, have been the marvels of foreign visitors. The strain of the examination was so great that men frequently went insane. It was no accident that spectacles were almost an essential part of the equipment of a scholar. The system produced wonderful memories and incredible powers of application, but discouraged analysis and independent thought.[4]

The achievements of Chinese scholarship grew under the great Ch'ien Lung,[5] but in the nineteenth century the schools degenerated. It became increasingly evident to the keener Chinese minds that the system was inadequate, but little was accomplished. The scholars would have opposed reform in any case, if one may judge from the general attitude of academicians everywhere. Had there been emperors of the caliber of K'ang Hsi in the nineteenth century, this opposition might have been overcome, but instead there were weaklings who could not even maintain order. From the middle of the century, the time of the T'ai-p'ings, till the end, China was dominated by the remarkable but sinister empress dowager, Tzu Hsi, who ranks with the empress Lu of the Han and the empress Wu of the T'ang period as one of the three most powerful women of Chinese history. These rulers owed their power not only to their own characters, but to the implicit obedience which a son owes to his mother. Their reigns were doomed to failure from the start because of their necessary reliance upon eunuchs, who are notoriously corrupt and unprincipled, depending for their power upon court intrigues. As a result, the periods in Chinese history which were dominated by women have been nearly everything they should not be.

But although the period ended in disaster, and the literati neglected scientific learning, it was a time of great scholarly activity. K'ang Hsi was successful in securing the support of the Ming literati, and they continued the disputes of the Ming into the Manchu period. Miura [6] considers that there were no philosophers during the Manchu period who can be considered to have made any advance in the development of Chinese thought. There were, however, thorough scholars, whom Miura somewhat arbitrarily divides into four groups. These are the school of Ch'eng Chu, or the followers of the Ch'eng brothers and Chu Hsi; the school of Lu Wang, or the followers of Lu Hsiang-shan and Wang Shou-jen; a group which attempted to harmonize these two schools, and which shows the influence of both; and the school of historical criticism. These groups overlap. Hsieh Wu-liang does not use this classification, but gives summaries of the leading scholars, most of whom belong to the earlier reigns. On the whole, the school of Chu Hsi predominated. Hsieh Wu-liang considers that what philosophic discussion there was existed in the debates between the followers of Chu and Wang, but that philosophy was at a low ebb, and that scholars tired of the metaphysical arguments, turning instead to historical criticism. In this field the Manchu scholars were more able than any who had preceded them.

At the beginning of the dynasty, Lu Fu-t'ing in general followed Chu Hsi, but identified the nature (of man) with matter. He also pointed out that in the Sung system, the *T'ai Chi,* or "Great Ultimate," must be outside the *Yin* and *Yang,* the dualistic principles of the universe, which would necessitate a new ultimate.[7] Lu Fu-t'ing's idea is not easy to follow, but it seems to resemble Fichte's.

T'ang Ch'ien-an (1627-1687) was a student of Shun Hsia-feng. At first he tried to reconcile Chu Hsi and Wang Shou-jen, but later went over to the school of the former, whom he held to be a more orthodox follower of Confucius and Mencius. To discuss philosophy without a knowledge of Chu Hsi, he said, was like sailing without a knowledge of navigation.[8] Lu Chia-shu (1630-1692) also upheld Chu Hsi and opposed Wang Shou-jen.[9]

Yen Yüan (1635-1704) at first followed Wang Shou-jen, then turned to Chu Hsi, and finally rejected both, founding the school of historical criticism. He differed from the Sung thinkers on the doctrine of the nature. The Sung, he claimed, were dualistic, using the two principles of law and matter. Yen Yüan was monistic, and denied that Heaven, Earth, and man had any nature other than matter. He appears to be somewhat inconsistent, because he follows Mencius in holding that the nature is good. However, the complex of ideas represented by any technical Chinese term cannot be translated by a single English word. As earlier remarked, it is a mistake to translate the Chinese, and then argue from the meaning of our own terminology. Yen accused the Sung thinkers, through the medium of Chou Tun-yi, of being influenced by Taoism and Buddhism, and he endeavored to restore the original canonical ideal, which he called the doctrine of Yao and Shun. In doing this, he rejected the Sung interpretations and texts of the canon, and returned to those of the Han.[10]

Tai Tung-yüan followed Yen Yüan in his preference for the Han texts of the canon, and also sought to avoid the dualism of Chu Hsi, but he identified the nature with law, in which he followed the idealistic school of Lu Wang.[11]

During the reign of Ch'ien Lung there was an interesting school which endeavored to combine and harmonize the Confucian doctrines with those of Buddhism. The leading men of this group were

P'eng Tseh-mo, Lu T'ai-shan, and Wang Ta-sun. This marked a return to the position of the medieval and T'ang thinkers before Han T'ui-chih and the Neo-Confucians. It is probable that the teachings of these scholars resulted in actual religious practices, for in the reign of Tao Kuang a little later it was necessary to issue several edicts suppressing cults which placed images of Confucius, Lao Tzu, and Buddha on the same altar.[12]

Among the other scholars of the Manchu period were Hu Wei, Yen Jo-chu, Ku Yen-wu, Huang Tsung-hsi, Wang Fu-chih, and Li Erh-ch'üeh. Toward the close of the nineteenth century there arose a reform party among the literati, several of whom inspired and assisted the ill-fated emperor Kuang Hsü in his attempt to adjust China to modern civilization. This attempt failed because Yüan Shih-k'ai revealed the plan to the dowager empress Tzu Hsi. T'ang Tzu-t'ung (died 1898) was the leader of this group. He was at first influenced by Christianity, but later devoted himself to the study of the Confucian and Buddhist classics, particularly the *Hua yen ching*. K'ang Yu-wei and Liang Ch'i-ch'iao lived on into the period of the republic, when they were of considerable influence. The men of this school, desiring to adopt the advances in civilization made by the west, all show in their thought the result of their western studies, even when they react against occidental influence.

The consequences of the conflict between western knowledge and Chinese culture did not directly affect the cult of Confucius as long as the Manchu rule continued. The causes of the eventual overthrow of the cult were forces which developed during the Manchu period, but they did not directly affect the cult until the republic. The published edicts of the various reigns give evidence that interest in the cult was never greater than under the Manchus, although no startling changes took place.

In 1645, the title of Confucius was slightly changed, but the older form was restored in 1657, and remained. In 1712, Chu Hsi was given additional honors and placed among the ten *Cheh*.[13]

In 1684, K'ang Hsi issued an edict commanding that in the services at the Ch'ü-fu temple, the celebrant should be required to kneel three times, each time performing the kowtow thrice, making nine kowtows in all. The music used was to be that of the government colleges.

In 1727, Yung Cheng decided that the twenty-seventh day of the eighth month should be observed as the birthday of Confucius. On that day no slaughtering of animals was allowed, and government employees were prohibited from using meat. It might be noted that the classics do not state on what day of the year Confucius was born. The prohibitions suggest Buddhist influence, although it was an ancient Chinese custom to fast before religious festivals.[14]

In 1723, the ancestors of Confucius commemorated in the Tsung sheng tsu, or rear temple, received the title of *wang,* or prince.[15] In 1724, considerable changes were made in the list of tablets. Five of the twenty-two tablets removed from the temple under the Ming were restored, and twenty new names were added. It seems a legitimate conclusion to draw that the Manchus, being non-Chinese, were not over-particular about the additions to the temple roster, and wished to win popular favor by adding names.[16] It is also possible that under the Manchus there may have been a reaction against the Ming reformation of the cult.

In 1729, an edict ordered the reconstruction of the temple at Ch'ü-fu. The decree ordered that the temple should be dignified and magnificent, and that the imperial treasurer should bear all the expense, in order that the temple might be perfect and exhibit the sincerity of the emperor in worshiping the sage. The tiles of the roof should be of imperial yellow.[17] Later, Ch'ien Lung changed the tiles of the Peking Confucian temple to the same color—an improvement which cost the government 200,000 taels.[18] This was in 1737, and at the same time, the tiles on the temple of Mencius were changed to green.

In 1747, a petition to the emperor requested that in order to show the proper respect to Confucius, the ceremony and music appropriate to the emperor should be used at the sacrifices. A decree replied that while the virtue of Confucius was as great as Heaven and Earth, so that even the ceremonies offered to an emperor could not express the proper respect, yet as Confucius himself disliked elaborate ceremonies, it would not be appropriate to worship him with rites which he would have disapproved. Moreover, there were already definite regulations establishing the form of the ceremony. For these reasons the petition was rejected.[19] It seems clear that the same forces were struggling for the control of the cult which had existed during the Ming period. On the one hand was the tendency to make Confucius into a nature god, which had been uppermost during the T'ang, Sung, and Mongol periods. On the other was the rationalistic influence of the Sung Confucians, which would have restricted the position of the sage to that of a great man only. It is probable that this latter force was strengthened by the historic sense of the scholars of the Manchu period, but a section of the scholar class continued to urge the exaltation of their patron saint.

In 1767, a petition requested that the birthday of Confucius should be added to the list of state sacrifices. A decree replied that as the birthday of Confucius was not recorded in the classics and as scholars had never agreed on any date, and as there were already two occasions, spring and autumn, when the highest respect was paid to the sage, another occasion for sacrifice would be unnecessary. This prohibition, however, did not apply to the scholars as private individuals, and it became the custom for groups of literati to form associations which were allowed to offer sacrifices in the Confucian temples on the birthday of the sage, a custom which was continued into the period of the republic.[20] The next year an edict ordered that several antiques of the Chou period, which had been kept in the imperial treasury, should be placed on exhibition in the Confucian temple in the capital.[21]

It was the custom of Ch'ien Lung to offer sacrifices himself to Confucius, but in his old age he was obliged to discontinue the practice. When he reached the sixtieth year of his reign an edict announced his purpose of sacrificing once more in person. After this the great emperor abdicated the throne.[22]

There is one interesting item for the reign of Chia' Ch'ing. In 1802 a petition requested a change of date in the autumn sacrifices to Confucius. The reason appears to have been that the customary date fell either on the birthday of Chia Ch'ing or the day of the death of Ch'ien Lung. It is not expressly stated. At any rate an edict set the precedent that when the state sacrifices fell on such a day, they should be held in spite of it, and no change was made.[23]

There are few records for the nineteenth century, beyond the names of various men who were honored by having their tablets placed in the temple, and the statements that at times the temples were repaired. In 1828, Tao Kuang ordered that a special sacrifice should be held in commemoration of the victory over the Moslem rebels.[24] In 1842, the same emperor instructed the governor of Shantung to revise the ritual of the sacrifice with a view to making it more dignified.[25] In 1861 the autumn sacrifice seems to have been neglected during the turmoil of the T'ai-p'ing rebellion, for an edict of Hsien Feng ordered the punishment of the officials in charge of the services.[26] The reign of T'ung Chih was a period of exhaustion following the rebellion. In 1864 a memorial called attention to the dilapidated condition of the temple at Ch'ü-fu, and the next year an edict ordered that proper protection be given to the temple, while all ceremonies should be properly performed. In 1868, at the suggestion of Li Hung-chang, who was just rising to power, the viceroys of the Liang-kiang (Kiangsu, Anhui, and Kiangsi) and Hu-Kuang (Hupeh, Hunan, Kuangtung, and Kuangsi) were ordered to contribute 20,000 taels to the governor of Shantung to be used in reconstructing the temple of Confucius at Ch'ü-fu.[27] The imperial treasury was clearly impoverished when it could not afford this relatively small sum, which may be compared with the ten times greater expenditure of Ch'ien Lung on the tiles of the roof alone.

Besides the imperial edicts, there are other sources for the cult of Confucius during the Manchu period. Encyclopedias and collections of reprints were issued. Reference has often been made to the Temple Records, of which there were a number during this period. The cities of the *hsien* rank and other political divisions, like the provinces, issued gazetteers which were in reality local encyclopedias. One *hsien* city issued editions of its gazetteer in the reigns of Shun Chih, three under K'ang Hsi, Tao Kuang, T'ung Chih, and Kuang Hsü. There was a great deal of this local literary activity during the Manchu period. These gazetteers always contain accounts of the local Confucian temple, and are valuable source-books giving, for instance, the inscriptions on monuments which have long been destroyed. The gazetteers of such places as Ch'ü-fu and Ch'üeh-li are of great value in the study of the cult, often giving details that are not found in the general histories. The following passage may be taken as an illustration.

"At the close of the Ming dynasty the ancient ritual and the musical instruments were no longer used. A few instruments were left, but they were broken and in poor condition, while the sacrifices were no longer carried on with the splendor of the old days. In 1684, some officials [the names are given] gave money for new instruments, but still the ceremonies lacked the old elaborateness. In 1742, an imperial decree commanded that certain sacrificial vessels be placed in the *Hsioh kung* [the Confucian temple], and the former glory was restored. The order of the sacrifice was arranged by the emperor Yung Cheng in 1731, and was as follows: the welcome of the spirit, the first sacrifice, the second sacrifice, the third sacrifice, the removal of the offerings, and the farewell to the spirit. In 1787, the music for the sacrifices was published, and in 1799, an edict commanded that a copy of the music be placed in each temple. This music continues to delight us. The number of attendants was fixed at thirty-six in 1698, but in 1786, four more were added so that there would be substitutes." [28]

No great developments took place during the reign of Kuang Hsü, though six tablets were added to the temple at various times. After the emperor, who was well-meaning but ineffectual, actually took a share in the affairs of state, there followed in rapid succession the Sino-Japanese war, the attempted reforms of the emperor under the inspiration of T'ang Tzu-t'ung, K'ang Yu-wei, and Liang Ch'i-ch'iao, the defeat of the reform movement, the death of T'ang Tzu-t'ung and the incarceration of the emperor, the Boxer uprising and the flight from Peking, and the Russo-Japanese war. It is not surprising that there was little time to elaborate the cult of Confucius.[29]

The Manchu rule was about to collapse, and even the Manchu princes saw the writing on the wall. In 1906, under the rule nominally of Kuang-Hsü, but actually of a regent, a final appeal was made to the Chinese literati. An edict announced that the sacrifices to Confucius would be placed on an equality with those to Heaven and Earth.[30] This had no effect on hostile public opinion. It was not the conservative, scholarly reformers who were to set the torch to the conflagration, but the revolutionary Sun Yat-sen. The attempt to change within the existing government had been postponed too long, and a more radical step was about to be taken.

NOTES

[1] The relations of the Chinese with western countries during the Manchu period are about the only feature of Chinese history which has been thoroughly studied by occidental scholars. Any general history of China will have more than half its space filled with this material. It seems enough to refer to Cordier, Vols. III and IV, for the general facts. In spite of this, western authors have had very little interest in the internal development of China during the period, the account of which must be sought in Chinese and Japanese sources. There is a good general history of the Manchu period in Chinese, the *Ch'ing tai t'ung shih* 清代通史. Two volumes have appeared.

[2] This is the view of Sun Yat-sen in the *San ming chu yi*, p. 58.

[3] See Cordier, Vol. III, p. 334. Among the scholarly works produced under

K'ang Hsi were the great dictionary which goes by his name, an encyclopedia of 1,628 volumes, and a geographic survey of the empire carried out by Europeans under the direction of the emperor. The *Sacred Edict* appeared in 1671, and was elaborated by Yung Cheng in 1724.

[4] These statements about the schools under the Manchus are taken from Dr. Kuo, pp. 58-60. Under Yung Cheng, Russian students were admitted to the *Kuo tzu chien*.

[5] Among the vast scholarly works produced under Ch'ien Lung were the edition of the twenty-four dynastic histories, used in this study, and the Catalogue of the Imperial Library, which appeared in 1772 (see Cordier, Vol. III, p. 406).

[6] Miura, p. 461.

[7] Hsieh Wu-liang, sect. 3, p. 29.

[8] *Ibid.*, p. 31.

[9] *Ibid.*, p. 32.

[10] *Ibid.*, p. 34.

[11] *Ibid.*, p. 37. There are accounts of the scholarly development under the Manchus in articles by Hu Shih and others in the 最近之五十年, a memorial volume issued in connection with the fiftieth anniversary of the Shanghai newspaper *Shen Pao* 申報.

[12] Hsieh Wu-liang, sect. 3, p. 39. See also the account of the similar school in chapter VIII of this study, and notes 23, 24, 25, and 26 to that chapter.

[13] *Ta Ch'ing hui tien shih lieh* 大清會典事例, chap. 436. This work has no pagination. In spite of the high standards of Chinese scholarship under the Manchus, the lack of exact references is a grave defect. Valuable works like the *Tsu yüan* and the *Chung kuo jen ming ta tsu tien*, as well as individual authors, seldom give the exact sources for their statements. The arrangement of such works is also so inconvenient that it is difficult to find material.

[14] *Ibid.*

[15] *Ta Ch'ing Shih Tsung Hsien Huang Ti sheng hsün* 大清世宗憲皇帝聖訓. *Edicts of the reign Yung Cheng*, in thirty-six volumes, published in 1740. Vol. 32, pp. 1 R - 2 R.

[16] *Ibid.*, pp. 3 L - 4 R. Of the tablets at present in the Confucian temples, twelve were added during the Sung period, two during the Mongol period, sixteen during the Ming period, and forty-five under the Manchus. See Appendix II.

[17] *Edicts of Yung Cheng*, Vol. XLIII, p. 6 L and R.

[18] *Ta Ch'ing hui tien shih lieh*, chap. 436. Also *Ta Ch'ing Kao Tsung Hsün Huang Ti sheng hsün* 大清高宗純皇帝聖訓. Published in 1807 in 300 volumes. The *Edicts of Ch'ien Lung*, Vol. CCXLV, p. 3 R and L.

[19] *Ibid.*, p. 17 R and L.

[20] The author took part in such a service of the *K'ung chiao hui* 孔教會. or Confucian Society, in the city of Anking, of the province of Anhui, in 1920. The society was composed of the officials and literati of the city. This service was held at about 11 A.M., not at night, like the state sacrifices. It was not so elaborate as the latter.

[21] *Edicts of Ch'ien Lung*, Vol. CCXLV, p. 18 R and L. There are few antique pieces which unquestionably date to the Chou period. Some bronzes and pieces of jade make up most of the collection. Probably this edict refers to the famous stone drums, which were formerly supposed to belong to the period of Confucius, but are now held to be several centuries later. See the *Enc. Sin.*.

p. 149. A French expedition in 1917 excavated the tombs of some feudal princes of about the time of Confucius, and further exploration may make valuable finds, but at present such work is not possible. See V. Segalen, *Le Tombeau du Fils du Roi de Wou, Bulletin de l'Ecole française de l'Extrême-Orient*, Vol. XXII, pp. 41 f., and S. W. Bushell, "The Stone Drums of the Chou dynasty," *Jour. N. China Branch of the R. A. S.*, Vol. VIII, pp. 133 f.

[22] *Edicts of Ch'ien Lung*, Vol. CCXLV, p. 17 R.

[23] *Ta Ch'ing Jen Tsung Sui Huang Ti sheng hsün* 大清仁宗睿皇帝聖訓 *Edicts of Chia Ch'ing*, published in 1824, in 110 volumes. Vol. LXI, pp. 6 L - 7 R.

[24] *Ta Ch'ing Hsün Tsung Ch'eng Huang Ti sheng hsün* 大清宣宗成皇帝聖訓 *Edicts of Tao Kuang*, published in 1856, in 130 volumes. Vol. LI, p. 8 L.

[25] *Edicts of Tao Kuang*, Vol. LI, p. 15 R and L.

[26] *Ta Ch'ing Mu Tsung Yi Huang Ti sheng hsün* 大清穆宗毅皇帝聖訓 *Edicts of T'ung Chih*, published in 1880, in 160 volumes. Vol. XXXVII, p. 1 R.

[27] *Edicts of T'ung Chih*, Vol. XXXVII, pp. 4 R - 6 R.

[28] This passage is taken from the article on the Confucian temple in the *Huai-ning hsien chih* 懷寧縣誌, or gazetteer of Huai-ning, sect. 9, on temples. Every gazetteer has articles of this sort. The earliest extant gazetteer was written about 347 A. D., but they did not become numerous until the Sung period. Twenty-five Sung gazetteers are known to be still in existence. Library of Congress, Div. of Chinese Literature, 1929-1930, p. 343.

[29] There is an interesting account of these events in E. T. Williams, *Hist. of China*, pp. 365, 366. Williams gives full accounts of the relations of the foreign powers with China during the Manchu period.

[30] Forke, *Geschichte Chin. Phil.* p. 109. The edict is to be found in the *Ch'ing shih kao*, which has not been used as a source-book in this study.

CHAPTER XIV

The Republic, from 1911 to 1927

The attack on the classic system of education began long before the close of the Manchu period. For convenience, it may be said to have started in 1842 with the establishment of five treaty ports. In these ports under foreign control, missionary schools teaching principally occidental curricula were set up almost at once. In 1860, the *Tsung li yamen,* or Ministry of Foreign Affairs, was established. Two years later the school of interpreters was organized by Sir Robert Hart and afterward administered by Dr. W. A. P. Martin. Auxiliary schools for interpreters were established at Shanghai and Canton.

Enlightened members of the literati were already advocating changes in the old system. In 1867, Tseng Kuo-fan, the conqueror of the T'ai-p'ings, established a school of mechanical engineering at the Kiangnan Arsenal near Shanghai. In 1875, Li Hung-chang attempted to modify the government examinations, but the conservative forces were too strong for him. However, in 1887, mathematics and science were introduced into the examinations. Educational commissions, appointed as early as 1868, traveled abroad, observed, reported, and were ignored, but the Sino-Japanese war proved to be a stimulus for the new education. An essay written by the viceroy Chang Chih-t'ung, called the "Exhortation to Learning," had a considerable effect in overcoming conservative resistance. A few years later, in 1898, came the unsuccessful attempt of the emperor Kuang Hsü to take the power out of the hands of the empress dowager and reform the government. A series of revolutionary decrees appeared under the influence of a group of young reformers, but success was only momentary, for the conservative forces rallied, and Yüan Shih-k'ai with his European-trained army went over to the side of the empress dowager. The emperor was secluded in what amounted to an imprisonment, and the reformers fled or were executed.

But the humiliations which followed the suppression of the Boxer

movement forced even the most conservative to realize the necessity
of reform. In 1901, attempts were made to modernize the old schools.
The eight-legged essay, which had been the principal feature of the
examinations since the Ming period, was eliminated the same year.
The Russo-Japanese war opened the eyes of the orient to the practical value of the new knowledge. At last, in 1905, Yüan Shih-k'ai
was instrumental in having the examination system abolished.[1]

It was too late to save the dynasty. The contact with the occident
had awakened a national consciousness among the Chinese. The missionaries had taught, and the armies and fleets of the foreign powers
had demonstrated, the effectiveness of science and the aggressive
function of nationalism. The failure of the Manchus to institute
reforms in time had created a situation in which the reformers were
arrayed against the Manchu government. The country was honeycombed with secret societies and public opinion was alienated from
the government. In 1911 the Manchu yoke was thrown aside, and
a republic established. One of the first acts of the new government
was to end all connection between the civil service examinations and
the government educational system.

Sun Yat-sen was inaugurated as provisional president at Nanking
on January 1, 1912, and on February 12 the Manchus abdicated at
Peking. It became evident at once that the young republic was going to be troubled by the gap between north and south, a gap which
had existed at least as far back as the medieval period. The great
business interests of China, both Chinese and foreign, represented
by such an organization as the Hongkong Shanghai Banking Cor-
poration, wanted a stable government. The foreign powers had to
have some one to whom they could present their demands. Both
these forces were accustomed to dealing with Yüan Shih-k'ai and
the group he represented. Sun Yat-sen realized the situation and
resigned, while Yüan became president of the Chinese Republic,
organizing a government at Peking.

In 1914, it became apparent that Yüan Shih-k'ai, under family
pressure, was trying to make himself the founder of a new dynasty.
He even went so far as to order a complete set of imperial dishes
from Ching-teh-chen. Public opinion was outraged, for democracy
was the catchword of the new movement. By the beginning of 1916,
Yüan found that he could not command the support even of his own
henchmen. His scheme collapsed, and he died of chagrin, but the
Peking government went on, ignoring Sun Yat-sen. Li Yüan-hung,

Feng Kuo-chang, Hsü Shih-ch'ang, Tsao Kun, Tuan Chi-jui, and Chang Tso-lin followed each other in a shifting scene which baffled foreign observers, while parliaments, armies, and leaders sprang into existence from nowhere and vanished as mysteriously. Great forces were struggling beneath the surface, but all that was visible was the froth caused by their movements.

In order to understand the developments of recent Chinese history it is necessary to go back a little. The victory over the T'ai-p'ings was due to the efforts of three Chinese, Tseng Kuo-fan, Tso Tsung-t'ang, and Li Hung-chang. The first two were not politicians, but Li Hung-chang fished in the muddy waters of court intrigue until he rose to be viceroy and a man of immense wealth and power despite the failure of the war with Japan, for which he was largely responsible. Gradually his protégés and the protégés of his protégés, rose to power, first Yüan Shih-k'ai, and then a group of men who had been educated for Yüan's modern army. Li Hung-chang had come from a small city in northern Anhui called Ho-fei, and many of the group of men who eventually became prominent came from this district, being allied with the Li family. When it became apparent that Yüan Shih-k'ai's attempt to restore the empire would fail, due to the public opinion created by Sun Yat-sen, these men deserted him. They formed an organization which took its name from the province to which most of them belonged, and was called the An-fu Club. The word *an* means "peace," and the club always stood for peace, at almost any price. It would probably have favored a restoration of the empire as the best means of securing order, and it represented the conservative forces of the country. But its leaders were clever enough to realize the strength of the republican sentiment, and were as liberal as they were forced to be. The club stood aloof from attempts to restore the empire until it could be seen whether such attempts had any chance of success, and therefore was not implicated in their failure. It was able to defeat the schemes of Sun Yat-sen and maneuver him into political impotence. The official leader of the An-fu group was Tuan Chi-jui, but the real force was Wang Yi-t'ang, who seldom took official position, but who held the club together and mediated between the various generals. It was this group of astute and unprincipled politicians, who did, however, stand for order and peace, with whom the foreign powers preferred to treat. Sun Yat-sen, baffled for the moment, retreated to Canton, where he set up a series of governments.

The twenty-one demands, made by Japan upon Yüan Shih-k'ai during the World War, caused an outbreak of national feeling led by the students of the schools created under the republic. The first real blow to the An-fu group came as a result of this wave of student patriotism, when in 1919 the students formed a union which extended over the entire country, aroused public opinion, and forced the resignation of several An-fu leaders who were accused of selling the resources of the country to foreigners. The students' union continued to exist, and became a real political force. The final blow to the northerners, which almost threw the country into the hands of the extreme radicals, was the shooting of unarmed students by the Shanghai police on May 30, 1925.

Sun Yat-sen, in desperation at the failure of the foreigners to recognize his government, had allied himself with the Russians, and his party, the Kuo-min-tang, combined with the Communists who had been created by Russian influence. The death of Sun Yat-sen a little later made him into a saint, a greater force than he had ever been during his life, and the affair of May 30 made his party the representative of all the Chinese nationalistic aspirations. His army, led by Chiang K'ai-shek, swept northward with hardly a serious struggle, and the country was apparently united once more, for how long no one can say. In this political struggle the conservatives wished to continue the state cults, while the radicals wished to abolish them.

Startling changes in Chinese culture, held back by Manchu conservatism, began as soon as the republic was declared, and since the Nationalists have come into power, the transformation has been amazingly rapid. No change in Europe or America can be compared with it in extent and velocity. The Chinese are reconstructing their social, economic, educational, military, and political systems almost over-night. Foreign observers are apt to see only the disorder, the battles, the inefficiency, and the corruption, but these phenomena are incidental. It is obvious that such conditions will frequently throw the worst elements of society into positions where they can do harm, and that in such a time of changing values the old moral sanctions will be weakened, and the political authorities ineffective. It is not remarkable that there has been disorder, but it is very remarkable that under such trying circumstances the Chinese people have, on the whole, exhibited such self-control.[2]

It appears that while the Chinese are violently reacting against the political interference and dominance of western imperialism, they have been completely subjugated by western ideas and inventions. Airplanes, automobiles, and poison gas are the order of the day. Returned students from abroad are in demand for every position, "science" has become a popular catchword, foreign clothes are a sign of progress, hideous foreign buildings are replacing the beautiful native architecture, and even the designs of porcelain are being copied from foreign models.

The old government system of schools is gone, with its memorizing of the Confucian classics, its noisy recitations, and the picturesque ceremonies of bowing and offering presents before the picture or tablet of Confucius on the opening day of school and on the birthday of the sage. Gone are the terrible strains of the government examinations, the honor of the old degrees, and the scholarly path up the civil service.

Yet much of the prestige of the scholar class continues, even though the methods and subject-matter of education have been changed. A degree is still the requisite for most government positions, but the degrees are those granted by western universities. *Po shih,* the old title for the scholars of Ch'in Shih Huang and the Han emperors, is now used for those who have become doctors of philosophy.

Under the republic, the attempt has been made to reconstruct the entire system of education for a nation of 400 million people, without adequate funds, without trained teachers, without proper textbooks, without buildings and suitable equipment. In this stupendous task, the leaders have been further handicapped by civil war and generally disturbed conditions, by the appropriation of their funds by warring generals, and most of all by the fact that since 1919 the students have found themselves possessed of great political power. To lead demonstrations against foreign aggression, to harangue the shopkeepers and country folk on the subject of patriotism and to burn Japanese goods has been much more exciting than studying for an examination. The students of China, boys in their teens, have not been content to study history; they have been making it.[3] Old-fashioned schools linger on in the country districts, but have vanished in the large cities. As the old scholars who grew up under the Manchus pass away, it is becoming increasingly difficult to find men with the old mastery of the canon and of the classical language.

Most of the leading scholars under the republic belonged to this older group, the young liberals of the days of Kuang Hsü. The supporters of the empire were silenced or ignored, and the conservatives of the republic were sometimes the very men who had advocated reform under the Manchus. This may be illustrated by K'ang Yu-wei, a distinguished scholar and historical critic, who was one of the advisors of Kuang Hsü in his attempt at reform. Under the republic, he was a respected but lonely and futile figure, combating the radical changes of the movement he had fostered. There were other great scholars who held over from the days of empire. Chang T'ai-yen, perhaps the most notable, continued to love the canonical books and to write the classical language. Wang Kuo-wei, the tutor of the last Manchu emperor, made investigations into the development of the Chinese drama, which is in itself a sign of the changes that had come over Chinese scholarship, for in the old days the drama was not thought worthy of serious research. Liang Ch'i-ch'iao, the most brilliant mind of modern China, was remarkable for his variety of interests, ranging from the organization of the British Parliament to the criticism of Chou literature. These older men have recently passed from the scene.

In their place are younger men still more under foreign influence and still more aggressive in their reaction against foreigners and foreign institutions. Liang Su-ming criticizes Buddhism and yet prefers it to Christianity. T'ai Hsü is leading a reformation within Buddhism, marked by summer conferences, similar to those conducted by the Y. M. C. A., and a Buddhist monthly magazine. The most remarkable figure in Chinese scholarship at present is Hu Shih. A doctor of philosophy of an American university and a student of John Dewey, he has published a history of ancient Chinese philosophy which has won him the respect of the most conservative scholars. This work was written, not in the classical style, but in the modern language which had been spoken in North China since the Mongol period and used in novels, but had been considered beneath the dignity of a scholar. Hu Shih's work was so successful and influential that he may be said to have revolutionized the written Chinese language. More than any other man, he has mastered the learning both of his own and of the occidental nations. Ch'en Tu-hsiu, the literary leader of the Communists and a thorough radical, is a scholar whose opinions carry weight.

All this seems far from the state cult of Confucius, and yet it is very relevant to it. That cult began under the Han and continued under succeeding dynasties, as the religious side of a state institution, the creation and employment of the scholar class by the government. It was the recognition in religion of the preëminence of the Confucian doctrines, embodied in the canon which was the basis of education. Confucius was first the patron saint of scholars, and then, through the examination system, of the administration of the empire carried out largely by those scholars. The teachings of Confucius were found to be sympathetic toward the institutions of the empire with the emperor himself as their head, and the scholar class became an invaluable aid to the rulers. Consequently, the cult of Confucius was fostered by the emperors and developed until it rivaled the most sacred rites of the state religion, the sacrifices to Heaven and Earth.

Under the republic the scene was changed. The examination system was abolished, the classics were no longer the basis of all education, the empire was succeeded by a democracy, at least to the extent that the emperor himself and his officials disappeared. The emphasis in education and in scholarship shifted to science, and even the classical language ceased to be the vehicle of literary expression. It is obvious that such changes must affect the cult.

The men who came into power in Peking with Yüan Shih-k'ai were as conservative as they felt they could wisely be, and many of them were scholars educated under the empire. Naturally they endeavored to carry on the old activities as far as possible. In the first year of the republic, in an article in the temporary government gazette,[4] the Ministry of Education of the new government called attention to the fact that it would soon be time for the sacrifices to Confucius. In view of the fact that the official dress of the republic had not been fixed, it was recommended that the spring sacrifice should be postponed. The importance of the sacrifices was emphasized, as well as the necessity for preparation and reverence.

On August 18, 1912, the government gazette announced the various arrangements and ritual for official ceremonies.[5] The ceremonies were divided into five classes—celebrations, rites (of sacrifices), marriages, funerals, and official visits. It was declared that reverence should be shown by removing the hat, which appears to be a clear case of deliberately borrowing a foreign custom, and by three bows. The kowtow was not mentioned, but later it came back into occasional use, although the bow was sufficient.

In the issue of the gazette for February 21, 1913, the correct ceremonial dress was defined.[6] The beautiful embroideries and rich colors of the empire vanished, and in their place was plain black silk without the numerous insignia of rank.

The issue for February 8, 1914,[7] contained a presidential decree concerning the sacrifices to Confucius. A rebellion by the partisans of Sun Yat-sen had been suppressed, Nanking had been sacked, and Yüan Shih-k'ai, stronger than ever, was maturing his plans for seizing the throne. A conference on political affairs [8] had recently been held, and made a report. Among other matters discussed at the conference were the rites paid to Confucius, and an unanimous resolution had been passed that as the sacrifice to the sage was a traditional rite, the old times of sacrifice should still be used. The rites should be the *Ta ssu,* and the ceremony, clothes, and vessels should be similar to those of the sacrifice to Heaven. The president should sacrifice in the Confucian temple at the capital, and the ranking official of the district should sacrifice in the provincial temples. If any of these men could not be present, they should send representatives. On the opening day of school and on Confucius' birthday, people might sacrifice if they desired, but there was no need of definite regulations. This last sentence referred to the customs in schools, and the activities of the organizations of Confucian literati, such as the *K'ung chiao hui.*

In the decree, Yüan Shih-k'ai quoted the report of the *Cheng chih hui* and added, "The doctrines of Confucius and the classic literature are without equal among mankind. The offering of incense and of sacrifice is historic, and it is appropriate for the republic to follow the old customs. The resolution of the *Cheng chih hui* (the conference) should be accepted."

The same issue of the gazette contained a presidential decree regulating the worship of Heaven, which was considered as a public sacrifice for the nation as a whole. Yüan Shih-k'ai assumed that the worship of Heaven, because of its antiquity, could not be abolished. "The people of the five races" [9] had been allowed to worship Heaven freely in the past, and therefore the sacrifice might be made.[10]

Behind these decrees lay the struggle between the old ideas and the new. The radicals of the revolution had cast every tradition to the winds. Temples were stripped of their images so that superstition might no longer exist. Kant, Huxley, Spencer, and Haeckel were referred to more often than Chu Hsi and Wang Shou-jen, while a little later young China became enthusiastic over Bertrand Russell and John Dewey, but ignored Tagore.

Against these ideas the older scholars and leaders set their face, and for a while it seemed as if they might succeed. Yüan Shih-k'ai was placed between the efforts of K'ang Yu-wei, who wished China to adopt Confucianism formally as a state religion, and the radicals, who had no use for religion at all. Christians and Buddhists joined against the adoption of Confucianism, while the radicals argued that Confucianism was a political device of the emperors and that Confucius himself was a monarchist who taught the duty of subjects toward their ruler. An issue of the government gazette contained the following edict.

"Religious liberty of belief is allowed in all nations. The Republic of China is organized by the five races. Their history, customs, and religious beliefs differ, and therefore it is not proper to establish a state religion [11] against the will of the people. The yearly sacrifices to the *Hsien sheng* [Confucius] and the *Hsien hsien* [his disciples] are recorded in the rites of the Manchu dynasty. They have nothing to do with the religious question.[12] They contain nothing contradictory to the principles of republican government, and therefore we should continue the tradition of making these sacrifices, which should become a fixed custom, in order that the people of the four directions [*i.e.*, every one] may know it. But fearing that men far and near might suspect that the reverential rites paid to Confucius are only the first step toward a state religion, we now make clear the idea behind them. The worship of Confucius [a number of details are specified] is based on the respect of the majority. It will preserve rites which have not lapsed for thousands of years. Religious belief is left entirely in the hands of the people [that is, they may have a religious faith in Confucius or not, as they choose]. In order to avoid misunderstanding, I make this public announcement."

This clever pronouncement pleased every one. The conservatives had at least the satisfaction of seeing the sacrifices continued, while the radicals and the missionaries rejoiced that there was to be no state religion. What the decree meant was that Yüan Shih-k'ai intended to continue the religious practices of the state, but was not going to call them religious.

The government gazette for August 27, 1914,[13] contained a decree saying that the Department of Rites [14] of the presidential office had submitted a form of ritual for the sacrifices to Confucius, with an explanation. The president approved, and asked the department to put its plan into practice.

Two days later [15] the Department of Rites replied in the form of a petition, asking the endorsement of the president. One of the names signed to this petition was that of Hsü Shih-ch'ang, an old scholar of the Manchu period, who later became president of the republic. The petition asked that the ritual should be the same as that of the sacrifices to Heaven, and that the celebrant in the capital should be the president himself. Other ceremonies offered Confucius should be voluntary. Since the Han period, Confucius had been honored with sacrifices, and under Hsüan Tsung [the last Manchu emperor] the sacrifice was of the grade of *Ta ssu*. The petition did not apparently wish the sacrifice to Confucius to correspond exactly to the worship of Heaven, though the language was vague. The petition said that from the time of Ming Yung Lo the temple had been called the *Wen miao,* or "Temple of the Civil Administration," [16] but that the term *civil* was too narrow for Confucius. (In ancient times) Duke Ai of Lu established a Confucian temple,[17] or *K'ung tzu miao,* at Ch'üeh-li,[18] and therefore that term should be used. The titles of the tablets should not be changed, freedom of religious belief should be allowed, and the worship should not be considered religious.

It is difficult to take seriously a statement which first said that the ritual of the Confucian sacrifices should correspond to the sacrifices to Heaven, and immediately afterward claimed that such a sacrifice should not be considered religious. It seems obvious that Yüan Shih-k'ai was simply paving the way toward his assumption of imperial dignity.

There were two other edicts of Yüan Shih-k'ai which dealt with Confucius. In one [19] he stated that the teachings of Confucius were appropriate to the changed conditions under the republic. While it was true that Confucius taught the duty of a subject to his ruler, a doctrine emphasized and exaggerated by the emperors, he also taught the principle of universal brotherhood, and this wider doctrine should be emphasized by the republic. The second [20] eulogized Confucius, and renewed the privileges of the descendants of the sage, and of the four chief disciples.

This ends the available documents concerning the cult. Yüan Shih-k'ai failed, but the power remained in the hands of the northern leaders. Under the presidency of Hsü Shih-ch'ang (1918–1922), a member of the old literati, four new names were added to the temple roll. The sacrifices to Confucius and to Kuan Ti were continued, and the dates were the only religious events which appeared on the official calendar.

The cult was dead, however. The old reasons for its existence had vanished with the founding of the republic, the abolition of the examination system, the new schools, and the newly adopted written language. The temples fell into decay, and were used as workshops by laborers throughout most of the year. The government paid for the sacrifices, but when repairs were necessary, private subscriptions had to be taken. In the provinces the musical instruments fell into such decay that they could no longer be used, and the ritual was a shadow of the days of imperial splendor.

Then came the triumph of the Nationalists, a more radical movement than any that had preceded it. It is difficult to secure a statement of the present policy of the Chinese government. Some leaders have advocated the restoration of the cult. On the other hand, newspapers have reported instances when the picture of Confucius was stoned by students. A correspondent in China has written that the Nationalists will permit sacrifices to the sage himself, but not to his disciples.[21]

The truth seems to be that at present the Chinese are not interested in the sage, or at least not in his cult. A new patron saint of scholars has arisen. In the schools, the pupils bow, not before the tablet of Confucius, but before the picture of Sun Yat-sen.

NOTES

[1] The details of the process of educational reform are taken from Dr. Kuo, pp. 64-98. The remaining portion of his book is concerned with outlines of the modern system of education under the republic.

For a general account of the period, with bibliographies, see E. T. Williams, *Short History of China*, pp. 459-624. Among the reliable books dealing with special phases of the period are Backhouse and Bland, *China under the Empress Dowager;* Duyvendak, *Diary of His Excellency Ching-Shan;* Steiger, *China and the Occident;* Mac Nair, *Modern Chinese History;* Holcombe, *The Chinese Revolution;* Sun Yat-sen, *Three Principles of the People,* translated by Frank Price. K'ang Yu-wei, 孔子改制考, which may be rendered "Confucius as a Reformer," has not been translated. His thesis has been much disputed. Rawlinson, *Revolution and Religion in Modern China,* gives some interesting material.

In the romanization of the proper names occurring in this chapter, the form familiar in news dispatches is used. For instance, Sun Yat-sen and Chiang K'ai-shek are Cantonese, not Mandarin forms.

The birthday of the republic is considered to be October 10, 1911, but the Manchu emperor did not abdicate until 1912.

[2] The author lost everything he possessed in 1927 through looting, and in 1925, after the incident of May 30, he was in some personal danger on a number of occasions. Yet he is convinced that under similar circumstances the American people would have behaved more violently than the Chinese did.

[3] Some of the situations caused by the power of the students were almost incredible. In a government school in the city of Anking, where the author was living, it was necessary for the teachers, in order to leave and enter the school grounds, to secure passes from the head of the student organization. On one occasion, some of the author's students refused to take an examination and were promptly expelled. They set up offices in the building of the Student Union, which took up their case, and for several weeks conducted a virulent campaign against the school, which included picketing, intimidation of students, libelous posters, and articles in the press. Even the police and the parents of the boys were unable to do anything about it. In 1925, one of the author's boys was riding in a *riksha*. The *riksha* man was stopped and reprimanded by a policeman for nearly running down a child, whereupon the boy slapped the policeman in the face. The officer came to the school to complain, and a teacher was asked to look into the case. When the teacher returned some time later, he said that everything had been settled. "How?" "The policeman apologized," he replied. As soon as the power of the students became apparent, politicians and merchants began to corrupt the leaders of the boys with bribes and to use them for their own ends. The student movement began with high ideals and fine accomplishments, but has become a handicap to those who are trying to reconstruct the nation.

[4] *Ling shih kung pao* 臨時公報, March 22, 1912. The republic adopted the European calendar.

[5] *Cheng fu kung pao* 政府公報, *Government Gazette*, No. 110, August 18, 1912.

[6] *Government Gazette*, No. 279, February 21, 1913.

[7] *Government Gazette*, No. 631, February 8, 1914.

[8] *Cheng chih hui yi*, 政治會議, a conference on political affairs.

[9] The Chinese republic (1911-1927) was considered to be a union of five peoples, Chinese, Manchus, Mongolians, Tibetans, and Moslems. They were symbolized by the five colors—red, yellow, blue, white, and black, of the original republican flag. The Nationalists have adopted a new flag.

[10] The statement often made by westerners, that under the empire only the ruler was allowed to worship and appeal to Heaven, is not correct. The *Odes* contain many appeals to Heaven made by subjects, and so does Chinese history since the ancient period. The bride and groom invoke Heaven and Earth at the marriage ceremony. It was the custom in recent times—the author has observed it—for devout Chinese to burn incense to Heaven every day. It was only in certain state rituals, particularly the *ti* sacrifice at the beginning of a reign which corresponded to the western coronation, when the emperor represented the people, that only the emperor could sacrifice. Naturally, for any one but the emperor to perform these state rites was equivalent to open rebellion.

[11] *Kuo chiao* 國教. The term *chiao* is translated "religion" here, because the context shows that it is used in the sense of the occidental idea of a state religion.

[12] *Tsung chiao wen t'i* 宗教問題.

[13] *Government Gazette*, No. 830, August 27, 1914.

[14] *Li chih kuan* 禮制館.

[15] *Government Gazette*, No. 831, August 29, 1914.

[16] 文廟. *Wen* is translated "civil administration," because since the Ming period the Confucian temples have been balanced by the *Wu miao* 武廟

or temples of the military administration, in which the chief figure was Kuan Ti, the god of War. The military temples also had their list of lesser tablets, and were halls of fame for the loyal and able generals of Chinese history since the Three Kingdoms period. Whether this division of the administration, each with its corresponding patron saint, existed as early as the T'ang period, the author does not know, although Kuan Yü was honored by the T'ang. It did exist under the Sung, was abolished by the Mongols, and was revived by the Ming.

[17] *K'ung Tzu miao* 孔子廟, literally, "Temple of the Master K'ung."

[18] This passage shows that the story of the temple to Confucius said to have been erected by Duke Ai of Lu, a contemporary of the sage, was accepted even by late Manchu scholars. This story has no historical basis. It rests upon some commentator's interpolation in the text of Ssu-ma Ch'ien.

[19] *Government Gazette,* June 23, 1914.

[20] *Government Gazette,* November 27, 1914.

[21] In 1929, the remnant of the old Han-lin Academy and a group of conservative scholars, educated under the Manchus, published the official history of the Manchu dynasty, the *Ch'ing shih kao* 清史稿. It was at once suppressed by the Nationalist government, but there are now four copies in this country. As its accuracy is disputed in China, it has not been used as an authority. Chaps. 88-107 contain material on the Manchu state cults and music. Under Book III, on Rites, there is a section on the Confucian temple (Vol. XXV, pp. 5-9). This was the most recent literary effort of the conservatives.

CHAPTER XV

CONCLUSION

Religion is difficult to define in a way that satisfies every one, but this much is safe to say. It is always a part of the general culture of the people who hold it, and at the same time it is an interpretation of that culture. This is unusually clear in the case of the state cult of Confucius. The cult cannot be understood except in terms of the civilization of which it was a part and which it interpreted. It was not for nothing that Confucius was called an uncrowned king, for few men have had so great an influence upon so many people. More than any other, he molded the culture and established the sanctions of the longest-lived and most populous nation in human history, and his preponderating influence was reflected in the worship which was paid him by the state.

The cult of Confucius is particularly interesting to the student of religion for a number of reasons.

Confucius was a religious man, but he was not a religious leader. He did not feel it his duty to reform older beliefs and practices, nor did he emphasize religious duty in his teaching. When he mentioned religion, it was only incidentally; and while he assumed a belief in Heaven and in the ancestors, he said little about either. He was religious in the sense that Washington or Gladstone or Lincoln was religious, but his mission, like their missions, was chiefly in the realm of politics. Defeated in his attempts at political reform, he became a teacher and made contributions both to philosophy proper and to ethics. He could not have expected, nor would he have approved, the worship which was later paid him. It is therefore interesting to see how he came to be worshiped. The reasons for his cult are to be sought in the culture and general ideas of the Chinese, and in the environment which made the development of the cult inevitable. Political conditions caused the prominence of Confucius, after his doctrines had been officially adopted by the state. The religious ideas of the Chinese made it natural that any one who had achieved such prominence should be worshiped.

The cult is also interesting because of its limitations. In spite of the enormous influence of Confucius, it is doubtful whether he has ever received worship from large numbers of people at any time. He was the patron of scholars, and came to receive worship from the state because the state was interested in the creation and maintenance of the scholar class and because it used that class almost exclusively in its administrative system. The scholar class became more important in China than it has been in any other country. The close association of an educational system directed and fostered by the state with the actual administration of the government was the real cause of the growth of the cult. Confucius was the patron, not of the Chinese as a whole, but of a sharply marked class in Chinese society. The position occupied by that class is unique in human history, and therefore the cult of Confucius shows features not to be found elsewhere.

Moreover, the scholar class was naturally the section of the Chinese nation most able to embalm itself in permanent records. Both the continuity of Chinese culture and the fact that Chinese literature was largely the creation of Confucians have given us a mass of material whose digestion would require the work of a college of scholars. Over this vast literature this study has merely skimmed, nor will the sources be exhausted for a long time to come. As one great Sinologist has expressed it, Chinese civilization may be compared to the Pacific ocean, and what we know about it to San Francisco Bay. The cult therefore offers to the student indefinitely great opportunities for investigation. Until quite recently, it was possible to observe the cult at first hand as well as through literature.

As the cult of Confucius was inseparable from schools and scholars, it followed that the two rose and fell together. As schools require both orderly conditions and wealth, it was natural for the cult to be strong under able rulers and weak in times of disorder. In this the cult differed from Buddhism and Taoism, which frequently flourished when the state was decadent.

The difference between Confucianism and its two rival doctrines was accentuated by the fact that the former never developed a professional priesthood, whereas the strength of the latter depended upon communities of monks and nuns. The Confucian sacrifices were performed by scholars and scholar-officials, who owed their place in the cult to their lay, not to their religious, occupations.

The charge has been made that religions are like glow-worms; in

order for them to shine, it must be dark. Confucianism—if it is to be
regarded as a religion—is the best possible refutation of this clever
remark, for no man could be a Confucian unless he were well educated. In fact, it might be said that Confucius could not be worshiped by a man until he had entered the graduate school of Chinese
education.

In spite of, or perhaps because of, this intellectual quality, the
cult never developed anything approaching a creed, and allowed
the greatest liberty of individual belief. From the twelfth century
onward, it may be said that an orthodox Confucian was expected to
believe in the moral nature of the universe as expressed in the term
Heaven, and to believe that the nature of man was good, being derived from Heaven. Within these limits, a man might take any attitude toward Confucius that he wished, provided that he was willing
to perform the customary rites offered to the sage. It is doubtful
whether any Chinese ever felt it necessary to refuse participation in
those rites on religious grounds, unless he had been so instructed
by foreigners. Confucius could be regarded either as a god, or
merely as a great man, and Heaven might be interpreted as a person, or as impersonal law. Even the statement that the nature of man
is good cannot be made an absolute criterion, for recognized Confucians, like Tung Chung-shu, did not accept it. Confucians were
bound together by a unity of culture and education, by the acceptance of Confucius himself as the model for their class, and by the
observances of the cult, not by a uniform acceptance of a formula. A
man was a Confucian because of what he did and what he was,
rather than because of what he believed. The state examinations
never questioned a man as to whether he believed in Confucius.
They merely tested whether a man knew the things Confucius had
said he should know, and did the things Confucius had said he
should do.

Because of the intellectual quality of Confucianism, its religious
side as expressed in the cult of the sage and its literature are free
from many faults common to religions. The cult was entirely free
from the obscene, the licentious, and from any emphasis on sex, and
Confucian literature as a whole is remarkably clean in this respect.
While Taoism and Buddhism are marked by gross superstitions, the
use of amulets and charms, magic of all kinds, relic worship, divination, the belief in ghosts and devils, and hopelessly unhistorical traditions and myths, Confucianism has remained singularly rational. If

it is true, as has been said by foreign observers, that Confucianism does not meet some needs of the human heart, a Confucian might reply that there are some human desires that should be unsatisfied and outgrown.

It is human to desire knowledge of the life after death. Confucianism does not satisfy that. It is human to worship with our senses and to desire visible objects of worship which can be identified, at least by the vulgar, with the deity. Confucianism is defective in this respect. It is human to relinquish the sense of personal responsibility and to lay the burden of our salvation or our damnation upon savior or devil. Confucianism does not do this.

Confucianism is not a missionary religion, if it is a religion at all. It is certainly an interpretaton of life and a view of the universe, which would make it a religion if the term is defined broadly. A good Confucian is a man who realizes in his life the intention of Heaven, and if he does that, Confucianism is content to let him believe what he will. No religious persecutions comparable to those which have sometimes defaced the history of Christianity can be laid at the door of the Confucians. Temples have been occasionally destroyed, monastic establishments broken up, endowments appropriated by the state, and monks and nuns forced back into secular life, but the Confucians have made few martyrs.

The philosophic ideals of Confucianism may be, and have been, questioned. They are rational rather than mystic, and by their nature are peculiarly conservative. Moreover, Confucianism was connected with scientific notions which have now been given up, such as the theory of the five elements. It was influenced by external stimuli. Most serious of all, Confucianism was unquestionably used as a political tool by the emperors. Nevertheless, Confucianism is one of the major achievements of the human mind, and its noble code of ethics makes it worthy of the deepest respect.

From the time of Confucius himself, about 500 B. C., until 140 B. C., Confucianism was merely one of a number of competing schools of thought, which differed among themselves in their theories of philosophy, ethics, and politics. Religion did not enter strongly into their debates. While the Confucian canon contained the evidence of the old Chinese religion, Confucianism had in it a marked element of skepticism, especially toward the older nature worship, and it did not stand for the ancient faith as fully as did Meh Ti. In politics the chief struggle was between the Confucians, standing for the feudal system, and the Legalists, who advocated an absolute central authority. There was no question of the worship of Confucius during that period, and the statement that there was such worship is unhistorical, except in the sense that every Chinese is worshiped by his descendants.

While the' Confucian movement continued to grow in the older feudal states of central north China, the Legalists controlled the state of Ch'in on the northwest frontier. When Ch'in absorbed the rest of the country, Ch'in Shih Huang attempted to conciliate the Confucians, but failing in this, he was forced into an attempt to destroy the literature of his opponents. The attempt failed, and actually stimulated Confucianism under the Han emperors by creating an interest in the burned classics. The Ch'in empire fell, but the early Han rulers continued the Ch'in policies in most matters. Meanwhile the Confucians increased in numbers and influence until, in 140 B. C., Han Wu Ti officially adopted Confucian principles as the policy of the state. The eventual form of government combined features of both the Legalist and the Confucian systems; but while Confucius and his followers received glory and credit, Ch'in Shih Huang and the Legalists were abused and discredited. The chief Confucian features which were adopted by the government were the importance of education, the recovered canon as the basis of education, and the participation of the wise and learned in the administration of the government.

The result of this change in state policy was the development of a remarkable system of schools under the Han emperors who followed Wu Ti. The graduates of these schools were examined by the state and appointed to official positions, while the scholars were subsidized by the government. This ensured the continued existence of a scholar class, and as the Confucian canon was the subject-matter of education, Confucius was regarded as the model of scholars. The scholar class proved useful to the emperors in their difficulties with the feudal lords, and provided the state with a group of trained administrators who were loyal to the emperor because they owed everything to him.

The ancient religion of the Chinese contained two main features, the worship of nature deities, of which the chief was Heaven or Shang Ti, and the worship of ancestors. The gods were vague and but slightly personified until the third century B. C., when the poems of Ch'ü Yüan, which deal with divinities localized in the Yangtse valley, exhibit gods with definite individuality. Even earlier than this, the worship of the nature gods and of men had been combined in the cult of the gods of the Land and Grain, which began as folk cults, but developed into cults of tutelary political gods of the feudal states, the rulers appointing the spirits of deceased men to these spiritual offices.

Considerable changes came over the religious and scientific thought of the Chinese during the third and second centuries B. C. The religion of Ch'in had been somewhat different from that of the older feudal states of China proper, and as the first Han emperors continued the state religion of Ch'in, these newer religious features were grafted on to the older state cults. The philosophic development of the Chou period had resulted in considerable cosmological and scientific speculation, which was stimulated by Taoist thought and which may be illustrated by the theory of the five elements and the practical researches for the drug of immortality. After the changes made by Han Wu Ti, all these were combined into an intellectual system which was called Confucianism, but which was really quite different from the original teaching of Confucius and his immediate disciples. Among the religious developments resulting from this fusion was the offering of sacrifices to great men of the past, who were practically deified. At first such men were mythological characters regarded as culture heroes, or the founders of dynasties, but more recent historical characters were later included in such cults.

It was an ancient custom for the Chinese rulers to sacrifice to all spirits. In Ch'in such spirits were localized in shrines, with cults, temples, and priests. Ch'in Shih Huang extended or at least recognized officially the extension of this custom to the entire empire. Han Kao Tsu followed his example, and as he was allied to the Confucians politically, he visited the grave of Confucius and sacrificed there; but his example, while it gave great prestige to Confucius, does not appear to have resulted in a distinct cult, although Ssu-ma Ch'ien says that it became the custom for officials of the district to announce their appointment to Confucius, as the patron of the district, by visiting his grave.

Han Wu Ti still further enhanced the position of the sage, and shortly before the beginning of the Christian era, one of the emperors, at the request of Mei Fu, ennobled the descendants of the sage. A little later, the emperor P'ing erected, or repaired, the temple to Confucius in Ch'ü-fu. The petition of Mei Fu and the action of Han Kuang-wu about a quarter of a century later show that what cult there was connected with Confucius was carried on entirely by his descendants, and was therefore similar to the ordinary ancestral worship, except that the prominence of Confucius led to the priest-descendants' being ennobled by the emperor and officially commanded to offer sacrifices. Between Mei Fu and Han Kuang-wu came the period dominated by Wang Mang, to which the actions of P'ing Ti belong. While definite evidence is lacking beyond the erection of the Confucian temple at Ch'ü-fu and general laudatory statements, it is probable that Wang Mang contributed to the prominence of Confucius, and so indirectly to the formation of the cult. He unquestionably emphasized education and built dormitories for large numbers of students. It is the opinion of some modern scholars that important works, attributed to an earlier period, were really created during the time of Wang Mang. Of these the most important is the *Chou li,* or "Regulations of Chou," which exerted a great influence upon subsequent ideas of education. That Wang Mang has received no credit has been due to the general detestation in which he has been held because he usurped the throne. Han Kuang-wu ennobled two branches of the family, one of which sacrificed to T'ang, from whom Confucius was considered to have been descended, and the other to Confucius himself.

The first mention of a regular cult of Confucius, carried on by men who were not descended from the sage, is the decree of Han Ming Ti in A. D. 59, which ordered that sacrifices should be paid to the sage in the government schools. This is the real beginning of the cult of Confucius as the patron of scholars and education, and it is a different thing from the occasional visits of emperors or their representatives to Ch'ü-fu. From the time of Ming Ti it was the custom to have regular worship of Confucius in the schools; but while there were shrines, there cannot be said to have been Confucian temples, and the ritual and objects of worship are unknown.

During the medieval period, the religious situation in China was further complicated by the development of Chinese Buddhism and by the growth of a school of thought which endeavored to harmonize the doctrines of Confucianism, Taoism, and Buddhism. Neither the schools nor the cult of Confucius flourished during that time of general disorder. The cult existed, and Yen Hui was grouped with the sage in the sacrifices as the *P'ei,* or correlate. The association of a correlate with the sage was due to the Chinese predilection for

pairs. The period was marked by the development of a new aristocracy, which secured control of the schools. This caused a reform
to be made by the first emperor of the Sui dynasty, who reduced
the number of students.

The T'ang dynasty perfected the examination system, developed
the schools even beyond the Han standard, created the Han-lin Academy, and honored both Confucius and the representative of his family. The sage now became the patron of the officials, who were drawn
from the scholar class, and as such, a prominent figure in the state
religion. Temples to Confucius were erected in all cities of the empire. These temples became national halls of fame where not only
the sage himself, but his disciples and the great Confucians of later
ages received honor and sacrifice. The T'ang emperors after T'ai
Tsung cannot be called Confucians. They arranged the various spirits
connected with the state religion in a hierarchy whose members
received titles and were promoted at the will of the emperor. Confucius was treated exactly like the other divinities of the state cults,
while his temples, filled with images and pictures, resembled those
of Buddhist and Taoist gods and showed influences from other
cults. The excesses of the Buddhists and Taoists, under imperial
patronage, caused a reaction led by Han T'ui-chih.

Most of the Sung emperors were genuinely Confucian. Under this
dynasty there was a great revival of interest in the indigenous Chinese canon, which is called by western scholars the Neo-Confucian
movement. The problem of the Neo-Confucians was to reconstruct
Confucian thought in such a way as to present an adequate cos-
mology which would answer the questions raised by the development of philosophy since the Han period, in particular by Buddhism,
and yet remain true to the canonical ideal. In doing this they were
influenced by non-Confucian thought, but they sincerely tried to base
their conclusions on the canon. While their systems were different
from Chou philosophy, they were certainly more critical and historical than the Confucians of the Han period, as well as closer to the
position of Confucius himself. There were several distinct schools
of Sung thought, but the movement as a whole may be said to have
culminated in the philosophy of Chu Hsi. The cult of Confucius was
further elaborated without striking changes, but the attempt of a
Taoist emperor to give Confucius the title of *ti*, "god-emperor," was
defeated.

The Mongols adopted Chinese culture and patronized the cult of

Confucius so well that the sacrifices reached their greatest height of splendor, but made no fundamental changes.

Under the Ming, the full force of the Neo-Confucian movement, with its rationalistic and historical tendencies and its opposition to Buddhism and Taoism, began to be felt. Until 1500, Chu Hsi dominated Chinese thought; but after that date, the influence of Wang Shou-jen combated, though it did not overcome, that of the Sung philosopher. Throughout the period, attempts were made to separate the cult of Confucius from the nature cults, and even to eliminate these from the state religion. Hung Wu took away the official titles given by the state to all gods but Confucius. A little later, an attempt was made to revise the titles of Confucius and his disciples. Finally, in 1530, the cult was thoroughly reformed, and among the other changes made at that time were the elimination of images, pictures, and the titles of nobility given to Confucius and his followers. It is seldom that such sweeping changes have been made within a cult without disrupting it, but the cult of Confucius survived—a tribute to the genius for compromise and the acceptance of an established fact which is a characteristic of the Chinese.

Under the Manchus, intellectual interest shifted from metaphysics to historical criticism. An enormous amount of material valuable for the study of the cult was assembled. The Manchu emperors patronized the Confucians and secured their support, being especially liberal in adding tablets to the Confucian temple. There were no serious changes in the cult, the Manchus continuing the Ming policy, but just at the end of the dynasty the sacrifices to Confucius were placed on an equality with those to Heaven and Earth. If this step were intended to placate an increasingly hostile public opinion, it was unsuccessful, as the dynasty collapsed shortly after.

The contact between China and the modern European nations began during the Ming period and continued throughout the Manchu period. During the nineteenth century the conflict between European-American and Chinese ideas, particularly in the field of education, became acute. The Chinese literati, naturally conservative, opposed changes in the classical education. The weak emperors were indifferent, or were unable to overcome this opposition. It finally became evident to the more liberal and intelligent Chinese that fundamental changes would have to be made. In the end this was accomplishd by expelling the Manchus and setting up the republic.

The republic brought on the modernization of China with a rush.

Among the first of the old institutions to go were the old schools, the canonical studies which had formed the basis of the curricula, the examination system, and the close connection between the schools and the civil service. These changes cut at the roots of the state cult of Confucius by destroying the chief reasons for its existence. A new generation of scholars pointed out that the state cult had been used by emperors, particularly the Manchus, for political ends, which were opposed to republican principles, and that Confucius himself had emphasized the duty of a subject to his ruler, which had no place in a democratic state. Even more important than these factors was the shifting of interest away from the indigenous civilization to modern culture and science.

For a number of years most of China was under the control of a northern group of politicians who were as conservative as they dared be. A serious attempt was made to carry on the cult of Confucius in the old fashion, but with the assumption of power by the Nationalists this came to an end. At present the situation is not clear, but it seems evident that the state is no longer vitally interested in the cult of Confucius, even if it permits private sacrifices to him. In the schools, the cult of Sun Yat-sen as the ideal of the republic has at least temporarily supplanted the cult of Confucius.

It would be presumptuous to prophesy the future of the cult. There have been many instances of cults continuing to exist for hundreds of years after all reasons for their existence, except habit and momentum, had vanished. It may be that Confucianism will be adapted to meet changed conditions in the way suggested by Yüan Shih-k'ai. Instead of emphasizing the relation of subject to ruler, the state may stress the wider Confucian doctrine of the universal brotherhood of mankind. It is still true, as Confucius said, that the only way to understand the present is to understand the past, and no one can understand either the present or the past in China without a knowledge of the canon, any more than one can understand European civilization without some knowledge of the Bible. The canon will continue to be studied by Chinese scholars, more so in the future, probably, than they are being studied just now; for there is sure to be a reaction against the influence of foreign thought, just as there is already a reaction against foreign political influence. With the canon Confucius is inseparably connected, and it is possible that he will again be the human symbol of the Chinese people.

The position of Confucius depends largely on the political future of China. Will the republic prove to be permanent? How long will the present disorder continue? Some of the changes in Chinese civilization are sure to be permanent, but it would be most regrettable if a lack of interest in Confucius were one of them. Whatever the revised position of the sage and his cult may be, it is safe to assume that Confucius will never again approach the status of a deity. It is to be hoped that the students of China may continue to reverence one who is so worthy of the highest honor and reverence, but that the tendency to transform him into a nature god or a political tutelary divinity has disappeared.

The history of Confucianism illustrates the price which must be paid by a man whose doctrines are adopted by the state. A simple and unassuming man, Confucius became the center of an elaborate cult which would have been repugnant to him. He protested against the assumption of royal titles by his duke, and yet he was given the same titles himself. Profoundly skeptical of all nature worship and believing only in the supremacy of Heaven, which to him was a monotheistic deity, he was worshiped with rites which he would have regarded as superstitions, and ranked as a member of a polytheistic pantheon. Though he was fearless in his denunciation of political unrighteousness, his name was used to bolster corrupt government. Though he was a great thinker, his doctrines were used to suppress thought, and theories which would have been foreign and abhorrent to him were grafted upon his intellectual system.

Yet he has been a model and an inspiration to the scholars and thinkers of his nation for 2,400 years. He represents fundamental positions in philosophy and ethics. His own character was such that one cannot read the story of his life and of his conversations with his disciples without coming to love him. Confucius richly deserves the words which often appear above his altar, "The teacher of ten thousand generations."

APPENDICES

APPENDIX I

I. THE MAIN HALL

A. THE CENTRAL OR NORTH ALTAR

A single tablet, bearing the inscription *Chih sheng hsien shih* K'ung Tzu 至聖先師孔子, "Confucius, the perfectly holy teacher of antiquity."[2]

B. THE P'EI 配 OR CORRELATE ALTARS

1. *Eastern* P'ei

1. *Fu sheng* Yen Tzu 復聖顏子, *i.e.,* Yen Hui.
He received sacrifices[3] in A.D. 72. During the Wei 魏 and Chin 晉 dynasties, his tablet was placed on the *P'ei* altar. In 628 the tablet was ranked next to that of Confucius.

Yen's *Ming* (name) was Hui 回 and his *Tzu* (title) was Tzu 子.[4]

2. *Hsu sheng,* Tzu Ssu Tzu 述聖子思子.
He received sacrifices in 1108. In 1236, the tablet was placed on the *Cheh* altar; and in 1267, on the *P'ei* altar.

Tzu Ssu was the grandson of Confucius, and his surname was therefore K'ung. *M.,* Chieh 伋.

2. *Western* P'ei

1. *Tsung sheng,* Hseng Tzu 宗聖曾子.
He received sacrifices in 720. In 1267, the tablet was placed on the *P'ei* altar.

M., Sen 參 *T.,* Tzu 子, and Tzu-yü 子輿. He was descended from Tseng Kuo 曾國 and was a native of Nan Wu 南武 in the state of Lu 魯.

2. *Ya shen*, Meng Tzu 亞聖孟子, *i.e.,* Mencius.

He received sacrifices on the *P'ei* altar in 1084. The Temple Record says nothing as to when his tablet was first placed in the temple, but from other sources it appears to have been in 1084. It would seem that Mencius was not in the temple at all until he was made a correlate.

M., *K'o* 軻; *T.,* Tzu-yü 子輿, and Tzu-ch'ei 子車. He was descended from Lu Kung Tseh 魯公族 and Meng Sen 孟孫 and was a native of Tsou 鄒.[5]

c. The Cheh 哲 Altars

1. *Eastern* Cheh [6]

1. Ming Tzu 閔子.

He received sacrifices in 720.

M., Sen 損; *T.,* Tzu-ch'ien 子騫. He was a native of Lu, and a personal disciple of Confucius, under whom he studied ethics.

2. Jen Tzu 冉子.

He received sacrifices in 720.

M., Ken 耕; *T.,* Po-niu 伯牛. He belonged to the family of Chung Kung 仲弓 and was a native of Yün 郓 in Lu. He was a personal disciple of Confucius, under whom he studied ethics.

3. Tuan Mu-tzu 端木子.

He received sacrifices in 720.

M., Tsu 賜; *T.,* Tzu-kung 子貢. He was a native of Wei 衞 and a personal disciple. Noted for his mastery of the rules of behavior, for his ability as a speaker, and as an economist.

4. Chung Tzu 仲子.

He received sacrifices in 720.

M., Yu 由; *T.,* Tzu-lu 子路, and Chi-lu 季路. He was a native of Pien 卞, but his family originally came from Pien 弁 A personal disciple, noted for his bravery and impetuosity. He was killed when he refused to desert his lord.

5. P'u Tzu 卜子.

He received sacrifices in 647. In 720 his tablet was placed on the *Cheh* altar.

M., Shang 商; *T.,* Tzu-hsia 子夏. A native of Wei and a personal disciple, noted for his erudition and as the founder of a school of his own.

6. Yu Tzu 有子.

He received sacrifices in 720. His tablet was placed on the *Cheh* altar in 1738.

M., Ju, 若; *T.*, Tzu-yu 子有. A native of Lu, and a personal disciple who is said to have resembled Confucius.

2. *Western* Cheh

1. Jen Tzu 冉子.
He received sacrifices in 720.

M., Yung 雍; *T.*, Chung-kung 仲弓. He was a native of Lu and descended from Po Niu 伯牛. A personal disciple and a student of ethics.

2. Tsai Tzu 宰子.
He received sacrifices in 720.

M., Yü 予; *T.*, Tzu-wo 子我. A native of Lu, and a personal disciple, noted as an orator.

3. Jen Tzu 冉子.
He received sacrifices in 720.

M., Ch'iu 求; *T.*, Tzu-yu 子有. He came of the family of Chung-kung 仲弓. He was a personal disciple and a student of politics.

4. Yen Tzu 言子.
He received sacrifices in 720.

M., Yen 偃; *T.*, Tzu-yu 子游. He was a native of Wu 吳 but his family originally came from Lu. A personal disciple, and later known as a teacher of music and of ritual.

5. Chuan-sun Tzu 顓孫子.
He received sacrifices in 720. His tablet was placed on the *Cheh* altar in 1267.

M., Shih 師; *T.*, Tzu-chang 子張. He was a native of Ch'eng 陳, and a personal disciple, noted for the dignity of his appearance and manner.

6. Chu Tzu 朱子 (1130-1201).[7]
He received sacrifices in 1241. His tablet was placed on the *Cheh* altar in 1712.

M., Hsi 熹 ; *T.,* Yüan-hui 元晦, and Chung-hui 仲晦. The great Sung philosopher and interpreter of the classics.

II. THE *WU* 廡 OR CLOISTERS

A. HSIEN HSIEN [8]

1. *Eastern* Wu

1. Kung-sun Ch'iao 公孫僑.
He received sacrifices in 1857.[9] His tablet was first placed on the western side, then changed to its present position.

T., Tzu Ch'an 子產. He was a minister of his native state of Ch'eng 鄭 for forty years. An older contemporary of Confucius, but not a disciple of the sage.[10]

2. Lin Fang 林放.
He received sacrifices in 739. The position of the tablet was changed in 1530, but it was replaced in 1724.

T., Tzu-li 子立. He was a native of Lu. A personal disciple who questioned Confucius about the rites.[11]

3. Yüan Hsien 原憲.
He received sacrifices in 739.

M., Chung-hsien 仲憲; *T.,* Tzu-ssu 子思. A native of Sung and a personal disciple, who endeavored to retire from the world, but failed.

4. Nan-kung Kuo 南宮适.
He received sacrifices in 739.

M., T'ao 絛; *T.,* Tzu-yung 子容. He was the son of Meng Hsi-tzu 孟僖子 of Lu, but lived in Nan-kung, from which he took his name, and he is sometimes called Ching-hsueh 敬叔 of Nan-kung. A personal disciple, who specialized on the *Odes.* He married the niece of Confucius.

5. Shang Chü 商瞿.
He received sacrifices in 739.

T., Tzu-mu 子木. A personal disciple, who made a special study of the *Book of Changes.*

6. Ch'i-tiao K'ai 漆雕開.
He received sacrifices in 739.

T., Tzu-jo 子馬. He was a native of Tsai 蔡. A personal disciple, who refused official employment and devoted himself to the study of the *Book of History.*

7. Ssu-ma Keng 司若耕.

He received sacrifices in 739.

He was also called Ssu-ma Li-keng 司馬黎耕. *T.,* Tzu-niu 子牛. A personal disciple.

8. Liang Tsan 梁鱣.

He received sacrifices in 739.

T., Shou-yü 叔魚. A native of Ch'i 齊 and a personal disciple, twenty-nine years younger than Confucius.

9. Jen Ju 冉孺.

He received sacrifices in 739.

T., Tzu-lu 子魯. A native of Lu and a personal disciple, fifty-one years younger than Confucius.

10. Po Chien 伯虔.

He received sacrifices in 739.

T., Tzu-hsi 子皙 and Tzu-hsi 子析. A personal disciple, fifty years younger than Confucius.

11. Jen Chi 冉季.

He received sacrifices in 739.

T., Tzu-ch'an 子產. A personal disciple who was diligent in spreading the doctrine of Confucius. A native of Lu.

12. Ch'i-tiao T'u-fu 漆雕徒父.

He received sacrifices in 739.

He was also called Ch'i-tiao Tsung 漆雕從. *T.,* Tzu-wen 子文. A personal disciple.

13. Ch'i-tiao Cha 漆雕哆.

He received sacrifices in 739.

T., Tzu-lien 子斂. A native of Lu and a personal disciple.

He received sacrifices in 739.

14. Kung-hsi Ch'ih 公西赤.

T., Tzu-hua 子華. A native of Lu and a personal disciple, forty-two years younger than Confucius, with whom he discussed the significance of the ancestral temples.

15. Jen Pu-ch'i 任不齊.

He received sacrifices in 739.

T., Tzu-hsien 子選. A native of Ch'u 楚 and a personal disciple.

16.   Kung-liang Ju 公良儒.
He received sacrifices in 739.

T., Tzu-cheng 子正, and Tzu-yu 子幼. A native of Ch'eng and a personal disciple. When the Duke of P'u attempted to stop Confucius, the sage was protected by this disciple.

17.   Kung Mei-ting 公肩定.
He received sacrifices in 739.

Another *M.* was Chien-ting 堅定; *T.*, Tzu-chung 子仲. A native of Lu, or Chin 晉, and a personal disciple.

18.   Chiao Tan 鄡單.
He received sacrifices in 739.

T., Tzu-chia 子家. A personal disciple.

19.   Han-fu Hei 罕父黑.
He received sacrifices in 739.

T., Tzu-hei 子黑. In the *Family Sayings* he is called Tsai Fu-hei 宰父黑. A personal disciple.

20.   Yung Ch'i 榮旂.
He received sacrifices in 739.

T., Tzu-ch'i 子旂 and Tzu-lin 子麟. A personal disciple, and a student of economics.

21.   Tso Jen-ch'eng 左人郢.
He received sacrifices in 739.

Another *M.* was Ch'eng 郢; *T.*, Tzu-han 子行. A personal disciple, and a native of Lu.

22.   Cheng Kuo 鄭國.
He received sacrifices in 739.

T., Tzu-t'u 孔子. He is said to have constructed a dike 300 *li* long in the state of Han, for which the rules of the neighboring state of Ch'in wished to kill him, but he convinced the ruler that the dike was good for both states.

23.   Yüan K'ang 原亢.
He received sacrifices in 739.

T., Tzu-chi 子籍. He was also called Yüan K'ang-chi. A personal disciple.

24.   Lien Chieh 廉潔.

He received sacrifices in 739.

T., Tzu-yung 子庸. A personal disciple.

25. Shou Chung-hui 叔仲會.

He received sacrifices in 739.

T., Tzu-ch'i 子期. A native of Lu, and a personal disciple, fifty years younger than Confucius. He acted as the attendant of the sage.

26. Kung-hsi Yü-ju 公西輿如.

He received sacrifices in 739.

T., Tzu-shang 子上. A personal disciple.

27. Kuei Hsüan 邽巽.

He received sacrifices in 739.

T., Tzu-lien 子斂. A native of Lu, and a personal disciple.

28. Ch'en K'ang 陳亢.

He received sacrifices in 739.

T., Tzu-k'ang 子亢, and he was also called Tzu-ch'in 子禽. A native of Ch'en 陳, and a personal disciple, forty years younger than Confucius. He was interested in extraordinary events, and asked the question about Confucius' instruction of his son.

29. Ch'in Chang 琴張.

He received sacrifices in 739.

M., Lao 牢; *T.,* Tzu-chang 子張. A native of Wei and a personal disciple.

30. Pu Shou-ch'eng 步叔乘.

He received sacrifices in 739.

T., Tzu-ch'ü 子車. A native of Ch'i and a personal disciple.

31. Ch'in Fei 秦非.

He received sacrifices in 739.

T., Tzu-chih 子之. A native of Lu and a personal disciple.

32. Yen K'uai 顏噲.

He received sacrifices in 739.

T., Tzu Sheng 子聲. A native of Lu and a personal disciple.

33. Yen Ho 顏何.

He received sacrifices in 739. His tablet was removed in 1530, but replaced in 1724.

T., Tzu-jen 子冉. A personal disciple.

34. Hsien Tan 縣亶.
He received sacrifices in 1724.

T., Tzu-hsiang 子象. A native of Lu. There is some dispute concerning the existence of this disciple. He is not mentioned in Ssu-ma Ch'ien, but appears in the *Family Sayings*.

35. Mu P'i 牧皮.
He received sacrifices in 1724. The tablet was originally in the western cloister, but was moved to its present position later.

Mu P'i was a contemporary of Confucius, but not a disciple. He was a learned eccentric who occasionally visited the sage.

36. Yo Cheng-k'a 樂正克.
He received sacrifices in 1724.

T., Chen-tzu 正子. A native of Ch'i, and a disciple of Mencius.

37. Wan Chang 萬章.
He received sacrifices in 1724. A disciple of Mencius.

38. Chou Tun-yi 周敦頤 (1017-1074).
He received sacrifices in 1241.

T., Mao-shou 茂叔. A native of Ying-tao 營道. The earliest of the great Sung philosophers.

39. Ch'eng Hao 程顥 (1032-1086).
He received sacrifices in 1241.

M., Hsiang-tzu 珦子; *T.*, Po-shun 伯淳. Ch'eng Ming-tao 程明道, as he was called after his death, was a pupil of Chou Tun-yi and brother of Ch'eng Yi-hsüan, an opponent of Wang An-shih, and one of the six great Sung thinkers.

40. Shao Yung 邵雍 (1011-1078).
He received sacrifices in 1167.

T., Yao-fu 堯夫. He studied the *Book of Changes* under Li Chih-tsai 李之才. He is also called Shao An-lo 邵安樂. He represents the influence of philosophic Taoism among the Confucians.

2. *Western* Wu

1. Chü Yüan 蘧瑗.
He received sacrifices in 739. In 1530, this tablet was removed, but it was replaced in 1724. The tablet was first placed in the eastern cloister and later changed to the western cloister.

M., Po-yü 伯玉. He was a minister of his native state of Wei in the time of Confucius.

2.   T'an-t'ai Mieh-ming 澹臺滅明.

He received sacrifices in 739. The tablet was originally in the eastern cloister.

T., Tzu-yü 子羽. A native of Lu and a personal disciple. The following story is told of him. He was crossing a river with a valuable piece of jade when he was attacked by two dragons who desired the jewel. After defeating them, he threw the jade into the water, but it refused to sink, and in the end he broke it.

3.   Mi Pu-chi 宓不齊.[12]
He received sacrifices in 739.

T., Tzu-chien 子賤. A native of Lu, and a personal disciple. As a magistrate he was able to govern the people merely by playing music, for which Confucius called him a superior man.

4.   Kung-yeh Ch'ang 公冶長.
He received sacrifices in 739.

T., Tzu-ch'ang 子長. He was also called Tzu-chih 子芝. He was a native of Lu, but his family originally came from Ch'i. A personal disciple, who married the daughter of Confucius. He is said to have understood the language of birds, and to have been put in prison because of a trick played on him by a bird.

5.   Kung-hsi Ai 公皙哀.
He received sacrifices in 739.

T., Chi-shen 季沈. He was also called Chi-tsu. A native of Ch'i and a personal disciple. He received no official appointment, which led Confucius to say that the government was inefficient.

6.   Kao Ch'ai 高柴.
He received sacrifices in 739.

T., Tzu-kao 子羔. A native of Ch'i or Wei and a personal disciple. He was filial and benevolent, and would never step on another's shadow.

7.   Fan Hsü 樊須.
He received sacrifices in 739.

T., Tzu-ch'ih 子遲. A native of Lu and a personal disciple.

8.   Shang Tseh 商澤.
He received sacrifices in 739.

T., Tzu-hsiu 子秀. A native of Lu, and a personal disciple who was known as a classical scholar.

9. Wu-ma Shih 巫馬施.
He received sacrifices in 739.

T., Tzu-ch'i 子旗. He was a personal disciple. He succeeded Mi Pu-ch'i as magistrate, and once asked the latter how he had governed the district well merely by playing music. Mi said that it was because he had known how to use the abilities of others, and had not depended entirely upon himself. Wu-ma admitted his own inferiority.

10. Yen Hsin 顏辛.
He received sacrifices in 739.

T., Tzu-liu 子柳. A native of Lu and a personal disciple.

11. Tsao Hsiu 曹邺.
He received sacrifices in 739.

T., Tzu-hsün 子循. A native of Tsai and a personal disciple. There are different opinions as to what his name was, and nothing is known of his life.

12. Kung-sun Lung 公孫龍.
He received sacrifices in 739.

T., Tzu-shih 子石. A native of Ch'u and a personal disciple, fifty-three years younger than Confucius. He is not to be confused with the famous sophist of the same name.

13. Ch'in Shang 秦商.
He received sacrifices in 739.

T., P'i-tzu 不茲. A native of Lu or Ch'u, and a personal disciple.

14. Yen Kao 顏高.
He received sacrifices in 739.

M., Ch'an 產; *T.,* Tzu-ch'iao 子驕, and K'o 刻. A native of Lu and a personal disciple, known as a warrior and a charioteer.

15. Jan-ssu Ch'ih 壤駟赤.
He received sacrifices in 739.

T., Tzu-tsung 子從; also called Tzu-t'u 子徒. A personal disciple, who studied the *Book of Poetry* and the *Book of History*.

16. Shih Tso-shu 石作蜀.
He received sacrifices in 739.

T., Tzu-ming 子明; also called Shih Tzu-shu 石子蜀. A personal disciple.

17. Kung-hsia Shou 公夏首.
He received sacrifices in 739.

T., Tzu-ch'eng 子乘. A personal disciple.

18. Hou Ch'u 后處.
He received sacrifices in 739.

T., Tzu-li 子里, and Li-chih 里之. A native of Ch'i, and a personal disciple.

19. Hsi Yung-tien 奚容葳.
He received sacrifices in 739.

T., Tzu-hsi 子皙. He was a native of Wei and a personal disciple, ambitious and a good scholar.

20. Yen Tsu 顏祖.
He received sacrifices in 739.

T., Hsiang 襄; also called Yen Hsiang 顏相. A native of Lu, and a personal disciple.

21. Chü Ching-chiang 句井疆.
He received sacrifices in 739.

T., Tzu-chiang 子疆. A native of Wei and a personal disciple.

22. Ch'in Tsu 秦祖.
He received sacrifices in 739.

T., Tzu-nan 子南. A personal disciple.

23. Hsien Ch'eng 縣成.
He received sacrifices in 739.

T., Tzu-ch'i 子祺 and Tzu-huang 子橫. A native of Lu and a personal disciple.

24. Kung-tsou Chü-tzu 公祖句茲.
He received sacrifices in 739.

T., Tzu-chuh 子之. A personal disciple.

25. Yen chi 燕伋.
He received sacrifices in 739.

T., Ssu 思. A personal disciple.

26. Lo K'ai 樂欬.[13]
He received sacrifices in 739.

T., Tzu-sheng 子聲. A native of Lu, and a personal disciple.

27. Ti Hei 狄黑.
He received sacrifices in 739.

T., Hsi 皙. He was a personal disciple.

28.   K'ung Chung 孔蔑.
He received sacrifices in 739.

T., Tzu-mieh 子蔑. A nephew of Confucius.

29.   Kung-hsi Tien 公西蔑.
He received sacrifices in 739.

T., Tzu-su 子索, and Tzu-shang 子上. A personal disciple.

30.   Yen Chih-p'u 顏之僕.
He received sacrifices in 739.

T., Tzu-shou 子叔. A native of Lu and a personal disciple.

31.   Shih Chih-ch'ang 施之常.
He received sacrifices in 739.

T., Tzu Heng 子恆, and Tzu Ch'ang 子常. A personal disciple.

32.   Shen Chang 申棖.
He received sacrifices in 739.

T., Chou 周. Ssu-ma Ch'ien calls him Shen T'ang 申棠; the
Family Sayings, Shen So 申續. A native of Lu, and a personal
disciple.

33.   Tso-ch'iu Ming 左邱明.
He received sacrifices in 647.

He was descended from a family of Ch'u and was a minister of
his native state of Lu. Until recently he was generally considered
as the author of the famous commentary on the *Spring and Autumn
Annals* which bears his name. The present view is that an historical
work by a Tso Ch'iu, of about 400 B.C., was made over into a commentary on the *Annals.*

34.   Ch'in Jan 秦冉.
He received sacrifices in 647. The tablet was removed in 1530,
but replaced in 1724.

T., K'ai 開. A personal disciple.

35.   Kung-ming Yi 公明儀.
He received sacrifices in 1853, first in the eastern, later in the
western Wu. A disciple of Tzu Chang, and later of Tseng Tzu.

36.   Kung-tu Tzu 公都子.
He received sacrifices in 1724.
A disciple of Mencius.

37.   Kung-sun Ch'ou 公孫丑.
He received sacrifices in 1724.
A disciple of Mencius.

38.   Chang Tsai 張載 (1020-1077).
He received sacrifices in 1241.

T., Tzu-hou 子厚. One of the six great Sung philosophers.

39.   Ch'eng Yi 程頤 (1033-1108).
He received sacrifices in 1241.

T., Cheng-shou 正叔; he is also called Yi-ch'uan 伊川. One of
the six great Sung philosophers. With his brother he studied under
Chou Teng-yi.[14]

B. HSIEN Jü

1. *Eastern* Wu

1.   Kung-yang Kao 公羊高.
He received sacrifices in 647.

A native of Ch'i, a disciple of Tzu Hsia, and the author of a
commentary on the *Spring and Autumn Annals*.

2.   Fu Sheng 伏勝.
He received sacrifices in 647.

T., Tzu Chien 子賤. He was a native of Chi Nan 濟南.
He played a prominent part in the recovery of the text of the
Book of History in the second century B.C.

3.   Mao Heng 毛亨.
He received sacrifices in 1863.

He flourished in the last quarter of the third century B.C. and
lived on into the Han period. A poet, said to have been a pupil
of Hsün Tzu, and to have handed down a version of the text of
the *Odes*.

4.   K'ung An-kuo 孔安國.
He received sacrifices in 647.

Called Wu-tzu 武子. A descendant of Confucius in the eleventh
generation, who flourished about the middle of the second century
B.C. He discovered texts of the classics hidden in the wall of a
house of the H'ung family.

5.   Hou Tsang 后蒼.
He received sacrifices in 1530.

A native of Yen 郯, of Tung Hai 東海. Flourished about the
middle of the first century B.C. He studied under Meng Ch'ing
孟卿 and Hsia-hou Shih-ch'ang 夏矦始昌, and himself had a

number of famous pupils, including K'uang Heng 匡衡, and the two Tai 二載.[15]

6. Hsü Shen 許慎.
He received sacrifices in 1875.

T., Shou-chung 叔重. He was a native of Chao-ling 召陵 in Ju-nan 汝南. Flourished in the first century A.D., and is said to have lived until 120 A.D. Author of the *Shuo Wen,* the dictionary which stabilized the Chinese written language.[16]

7. Cheng K'ang-ch'eng 鄭康成 (A.D. 127-196).
He received sacrifices in 647. His tablet was removed in 1530 and replaced in 1724. It was originally in the western cloister.

M., Yuen 元. He was a native of Kao-mi 高密 in Po Hai 北海. A student of Ma Jung 馬融, and the greatest of the Han commentators on the classics.

8. Fan Ning 范甯 (339-401).
He received sacrifices in 647. His tablet was removed in 1530 and replaced in 1724. It was originally in the western cloister.

T., Wu-tzu 武子. His home was in Tan-yang 丹陽 in the present province of Anhui. He wrote a commentary on the *Spring and Autumn Annals,* and reformed the system of education.

9. Lu Cheh 陸贄 (754-805).
He received sacrifices in 1826.

T., Ching-yü 敬輿. He was a native of Chia-hsing 嘉興 in Su-chou 蘇州 (Soochow). A member of the Han-lin, and a minister of state from 780 to 805.

10. Fan Chung-yen 范仲淹 (989-1052).
He received sacrifices in 1715.

T., Hsi-wen 希文. He came from Shao-chou 邵州, but moved to a district of Su-chou. A scholar, statesman, and general of the reign of Sung Jen Tsung. He died in exile, having been sent away because he desired to reform the government. His petitions to the emperor have been published.

11. Ou-yang Hsiu 歐陽修 (1007-1072).
He received sacrifices in 1530.

T., Yung-shou 永叔. A contemporary of Fan Chung-yen and the friend and supporter of the earlier Neo-Confucians, exiled because of his opposition to Wang An-shih. A scholar, poet, essayist and statesman, known also for his love of birds.

12. Ssu-ma Kuang 司馬光 (1017-1086).

He received sacrifices in 1267, originally in the western cloister.

T., Chün-shih 君實. He was a native of Hsia-hsien 夏縣 in the present province of Shensi. A Sung statesman noted as the leading opponent of Wang An-shih, and the author of a great historical work, the *Tsu chih t'ung chien* 資治通鑑, which the school of Chu Hsi expanded into the *T'ung chien kan mu.*

13. Hsieh Liang-tso 謝良佐 (eleventh century).
He received sacrifices in 1850.

A native of Shang-tsai 上蔡. He is known to have received the degree of Chin-shih in 1085. One of four famous scholars of the two Ch'eng, the others being Yang Shih, Lü Ta-lin, and Lo Tsung-yen. He was imprisoned and degraded. An essayist.

14. Lü Ta-lin 呂大臨 (eleventh century).
He received sacrifices in 1895.

T., Yü-shou 與叔. He was a native of Lan-t'ien 藍田. Studied under Chang Tsai and the two Ch'eng. A scholar but not an official, and the author of a ten-volume work on antiques.

15. Lo Tsung-yen 羅從彥 (1072-1135).
He received sacrifices in 1614.

T., Chung-su 仲素. A pupil of Ch'eng Yi. He retired to private life, teaching and writing commentaries on the *Doctrine of the Mean* and the *Spring and Autumn Annals,* as well as some essays.

16. Li Kang 李綱 (1083-1140).[18]
He received sacrifices in 1851.

T., Po-chi 伯紀. He was a native of Chao-wu 邵武. A general as well as an author, and a member of the war party during the reign of Sung Kao Tsung.

17. Chang Ch'ih 張栻 (1133-1180).
He received sacrifices in 1261, originally in the western cloister.

T., Ching-fu 敬夫. He was a native of Mien-chueh 緜竹 in Han-chou 漢州. He studied under Hu Hung, and wrote commentaries on the *Analects* and Mencius, as well as essays.

18. Lu Chiu-yüan 陸九淵 (1139-1192).
He received sacrifices in 1530, originally in the western cloister.

T., Tzu-ching 子靜. He was a native of Hsiang-shan 象山

in T'ai Chou 台州, whence he is usually called Lu Hsiang-shan. He opposed his friend Chu Hsi, emphasizing virtue and the nature, rather than inductive knowledge and education.

19. Ch'eng Shun 陳淳 (1153-1217).

He received sacrifices in 1724.

T., an Hsiang-ch'ing 安卿. He was a native of Lung-ch'i 龍溪. A disciple of Chu Hsi.

20. Chen Teh-hsiu 眞德秀 (1178-1235).

He received sacrifices in 1437, originally in the western cloister.

T., Ching-yüan 景元, later changed to Hsi-yüan 希元. He lived in P'u-ch'eng 甫城. A member of the Han-lin, of great influence in making the school of Chu Hsi the predominating force in Chinese thought at the close of the Sung period.

21. Ho Chi 何基 (1188-1268).

He received sacrifices in 1724, originally in the western cloister.

T., Tzu-kung 子恭. In his interpretation he followed Huang Han 黃幹. His works are published in thirty volumes, among them treatises on the *Great Learning* and the *Doctrine of the Mean*.

22. Wen T'ien-hsiang 文天祥 (1236-1282).

He received sacrifices in 1843, originally in the western cloister.

T., Sung-jui 宋瑞, and Lu-shan 履善. A native of Chih-shui 吉水. A minister of the last Sung emperors. Taken captive by the Mongols, he preferred death to a change of allegiance, thereby winning the praise of his captors. Author of several essays.

23. Chao Fu 趙復 (latter half of the thirteenth century).

He received sacrifices in 1724.

T., Jen-p'u 仁甫. He was a native of Teh-an 德安 in Hupeh. The leading scholar of the Mongol period, who taught the doctrines of the two Ch'eng and Chu Hsi in the north.

24. Chin Lu-hsiang 金履祥 (1232-1303).

He received sacrifices in 1724, originally in the western cloister.

T., Chih-fu 吉父. He was a native of Nan-ch'i 蘭谿 in Wu-chih 婺之. In his interpretation he followed Ho Chi. He would not become an official under the Mongols, but retired to private life, teaching and writing.

25. Ch'eng Hao 陳澔 (1261-1341).

He received sacrifices in 1724, originally in the western cloister.

T., K'o Ta 可大. He was a native of Tu-ch'ang 都昌. Also called Yün-chuang 雲莊. A scholar who refused an official career under the Mongols, and wrote on the *Rites*. The line of teachers connecting him with Chu Hsi is: Chu Hsi, Huang Kan, Jao Lu, Ch'eng Ta-yu, Ch'eng Hao. He is not to be confused with the Sung Confucian whose name is romanized in the same way.

26.   Fang Hsiao-jü 方孝孺 (1357-1402).
He received sacrifices in 1863.

T., Hsi-chih 希直, also called Hsi-ku 希古. A native of Ning-hai 甯海. He specialized on the five *Ti*. The tutor of Ming Hui Ti, he refused allegiance to Ch'eng Tsu (Yung Lo) and was tortured to death. A few of his essays are preserved.

27.   Hsieh Hsüan 薛瑄 (1389-1464).
He received sacrifices in 1571, originally in the western cloister.

T., Teh-wen 德温. He followed Mencius and the Sung Confucians in teaching that the nature is good. His doctrines were similar to those of the Yüan scholars Hsü Huai-yü 徐懷玉, Wei Hsi-wen 魏希文, and Wang Su-heng 王素亨. A Ming official and an essayist.

28.   Hu Chü-jen 胡居仁 (1434-1484).
He received sacrifices in 1584.

T., Shou-hsin 叔心. He was a native of Yü-kan 餘干. He was not an official. In his teaching he emphasized the Confucian virtues and quietude.

29.   Lo Ch'in-shun 羅欽順 (1465-1547).
He received sacrifices in 1724.

T., Yün-sheng 允升. He was a native of T'ai-ho 泰和 in Kiangsi. He followed the Ch'eng in interpreting Confucius, and was the author of essays. His official career was checkered, and eventually he retired.

30.   Lü Tsai 呂柟 (1479-1542).
He received sacrifices in 1863, originally in the western cloister.

T., Chung-mu 仲木. He was a native of Kao-ling 高陵 in Shensi. He studied under Shui Ching-chih, belonged to the school of the Ch'eng and Chu Hsi, and wrote on the *Book of Changes*, the poetry of Mao, and other classics. Although a graduate, he was too outspoken for an official, and after teaching thirty years, he died poor. This was not unusual at that and later periods.

31. Liu Tsung-chou 劉宗周 (1578-1645).

He received sacrifices in 1822, originally in the western cloister.

T., Ch'i-tung 起東. He was a native of Shan-yin 山陰. He studied under Hsü Fu-yüan 許孚遠, and taught in the Tung-lin College. As an official near the close of the Ming dynasty, he opposed capital punishment and heavy taxes. A prolific writer on the *Book of Changes* and other classics, he also wrote a number of biographies.

32. Sun Ch'i-fung 孫奇逢 (1584-1675).

He received sacrifices in 1828, originally in the western cloister.

T., Ch'i-t'ai 啟泰. He was a native of Yung-ch'eng 容城 in Chili. He followed the Sung scholar, Su Lao-ch'ien 蘇老泉 in his interpretation of the classics.

33. Chang Lu-hsiang 張履祥 (died 1674).

He received sacrifices in 1871.

T., K'ao-fu 考夫. He was a native of T'ung-ch'eng 桐城. He studied under Liu Tsung-chou, and followed the Ch'eng and Chu Hsi. He was not an official, but wrote essays and was interested in agriculture.

34. Lu Lung-ch'i 陸隴其 (1630-1692).

He received sacrifices in 1724, originally in the western cloister.

T., Chia-shu 稼書. He was a native of Chekiang. He followed Chu Hsi and opposed Wang Yang-ming. An official and author.

35. Chang Po-hang 張伯行 (flourished about 1700).

He received sacrifices in 1878.

T., Hsio-hsien 孝先. He followed Chu Hsi, and was a noted teacher.

2. *Western* Wu

1. Ku-liang Ch'ih 穀梁赤 (fourth century B.C.).

He received sacrifices in 647.

T., Yüan-shih 元始. He was a native of Lu. A disciple of Tzu Hsia, who wrote a commentary on the *Spring and Autumn Annals.*

2. Kao-t'ang Sheng 高堂生.

He received sacrifices in 647.

A native of Lu, he flourished in the last half of the third century B.C., during the Ch'in and early Han periods. A commentary on the *I li* is ascribed to him, and a part of the *Book of Rites*. He is said to have preserved some of the classical texts in his memory.

3. Tung Chung-shu 董仲舒 (second century B. C.).
He received sacrifices in 1330, originally in the eastern cloister.
The adviser of Han Wu Ti and the leading Confucian of the Western Han period, known for his work on the *Spring and Autumn Annals*.

4. Liu Teh 劉德.
He received sacrifices in 647.
A scholar and member of the ruling family of the Han dynasty, Prince of Ho-chien 河間. He flourished about the middle of the second century B. C. A patron of literature, he aided in the fixing of the classic texts.

5. Mao Ch'ang 毛萇.
He received sacrifices in 647.
A poet and scholar, the protégé of Liu Teh, who is said to have established the text of the *Odes*. He is called the lesser Mao, with reference to the older poet of the same surname.

6. Tu Tzu-ch'un 杜子春.
He received sacrifices in 647, originally in the eastern cloister.
A scholar of the closing decades of the first century B. C., who lived into the reign of Han Ming Ti in the middle of the first century A. D. He studied under Liu Hsin and became an authority on the *Regulations of Chou,* which he is said to have edited.

7. Chu-k'o Liang 諸葛亮 (A. D. 181-234).
He received sacrifices in 1724, originally in the eastern cloister.
T., K'ung-ming 孔明. He was a native of Lang-ya 瑯琊 in Yang-tu 陽都. The friend and counselor of Liu Pei during the Three Kingdoms period, famous for his wisdom and loyalty.

8. Wang T'ung 王通 (584-618).[19]
He received sacrifices in 1530, originally in the eastern cloister.
As a young man he offered twelve suggestions for pacifying the country. When these were rejected, he retired to Lung-men 龍門, where he taught, among his scholars being Fang Hsüan-lin 房玄齡, Li Ching 李靖, and Wei Cheng 魏徵 of the T'ang period. He wrote commentaries on the *Analects* and other classics.

9. Han Yü 韓愈 (768-823).
He received sacrifices in 1084.

T., T'ui-chih 退之. He is commonly called by his posthumous title Wen-kung 文公. A native of Teng-chou in Nan-yang 南陽. The leading Confucian of the T'ang period and an opponent of Buddhism and Taoism.

10.   Hu Yüan 胡瑗 (993-1059).
He received sacrifices in 1530.

T., Yi-chih 翼之. He was a native of T'ai-chou in Hai-lin 海陵. He studied with Sen Fu 孫復 on Mt. T'ai. A great scholar, and the adviser of Fan Chung-yen. He wrote on the *Book of Changes,* and became head of the *T'ai Hsioh,* or imperial academy.

11.   Han Ch'i 韓琦 (1008-1075).
He received sacrifices in 1852, originally in the eastern cloister.

T., Tzu-kuei 稚圭. He was a native of Hsiang-chou 相州 in An-yang 安陽. A contemporary of Fan Chung-yen and a minister under several emperors, much loved by the people. Author of essays.

12.   Yang Shih 楊時 (1053-1135).
He received sacrifices in 1495, originally in the eastern cloister.

T., Chung-li 中立. He was a native of Chiang-lo 將樂 in Nan-chien 南劍. He studied under Ch'eng Yi and took a degree, but refused an official position in exchange for the life of a teacher and author.

13.   Yu Tso 游酢 (twelfth century).
He received sacrifices in 1892.

T., Ting fu, 定夫. He was a native of Chien-yang 建陽. He studied under Ch'eng Yi with Yang Shih, took a degree, and taught in the imperial academy. Author of commentaries on the *Book of Changes* and the *Four Books.*

14.   Yin Tuan 尹焞 (1071-1142).
He received sacrifices in 1724.

T., Yen-ming 彦明, and Teh-ch'ung 德充. He was a native of Lo-yang 洛陽. A pupil of Ch'eng Yi, author of a commentary on the *Analects,* and a member of the war party under Sung Kao Tsung.

15.   Hu An-kuo 胡安國 (1074-1138).
He received sacrifices in 1437.

T., K'ang-hou 康侯. He was a native of Tsung-an 崇安

in Chien-ning 建寧. He studied under Hsieh Liang-tso, and followed the interpretation of the Ch'eng. After taking a degree, he taught in the imperial academy and wrote essays, a supplement to Ssu-ma Kuang, and a treatise on the *Spring and Autumn Annals*.

16. Li T'ung 李侗 (1093-1163).

He received sacrifices in 1614, originally in the eastern cloister.

. *T.*, Yüan-chung 愿仲. He studied under Lo Tsung-sun, and later retired in order to teach and write essays. The teacher of Chu Hsi.

17. Lü Tsu-chien 呂祖謙 (1137-1181).

He received sacrifices in 1261, originally in the eastern cloister.

T., Po-kung 伯恭; *H.*, Tung-lai 東萊. He studied under Lin Chih-ch'i 林之奇, Wang Ying-shen 汪應辰, and Hu Hsien-yu 胡憲游. A scholar and debater, and a friend of Chu Hsi. He wrote on the *Book of Changes* and other classics, and also wrote treatises on the methods of administration of different dynasties. essays.

18. Yüan Hsieh 袁爕 (twelfth century).

He received sacrifices in 1868.

T., Shou-ho 叔和. He was a native of Ch'ing-yüan fu 慶元府. Head of the imperial academy, and the author of essays.

19. Huang Kan 黃幹 (1152-1221).

He received sacrifices in 1724.

T., Chih-ch'ing 直卿. *H.*, Mien-chai 勉齋. He was a native of Min 閩 in Kuangsi. A pupil of Chu Hsi, a successful teacher, and writer on the canon.

20. P'u Kuang 輔廣 (twelfth century).

He received sacrifices in 1879.

T., Han-ch'ing 漢卿. Pupil of Chu Hsi, successful teacher, and writer on the canon and history.

21. Tsai Shen 蔡沈 (1167-1230).

He received sacrifices in 1437, originally in the eastern cloister.

T., Chung-meh 仲默. He was a native of Chien-yang 建陽. A follower of Chu Hsi, who wrote a commentary on the *Book of History* at Chu Hsi's request. He would not accept official position.

22. Wei Liao-weng 魏了翁 (1178-1245).

He received sacrifices in 1724, originally in the eastern cloister.

T., Hua-fu 華父. He was a native of P'u-chiang 浦江. He studied under P'u Kuang and Li Fan. On his father's death he retired and taught, but later resumed his official career and petitioned against bad government, though not connecting himself with any party. He wrote on the canon.

23. Jen Po 壬柏 (1197-1274).

He received sacrifices in 1724, originally in the eastern cloister.

T., Hui Chih 會之. He studied under Ho Chi 何基. Author of commentaries on the canon.

24. Lu Hsiu-fu 陸秀夫 (1236-1279).

He received sacrifices in 1859.

T., Chün-shih 君實. He was a native of Yen-ch'eng 鹽城 in Ch'u-chou 楚州. A minister of the last Sung emperor, with whom he fled to Kuangtung. Seeing that all was lost, he took the boy emperor on his back and leaped into the sea.

25. Hsü Heng 許衡 (1209-1281).

He received sacrifices in 1313.

T., P'ing-chung 平仲. He was a native of Ho-nei 河內. He studied under Yao Ch'u 姚樞, together with Tu Meh 竇默. A follower of Chu Hsi, a scholar and essayist, an authority on history, tactics and astronomy, and a high official under Kubilai.

26. Wu Ch'eng 吳澄 (1247-1331).[20]

He received sacrifices in 1443. His tablet was removed in 1530, but replaced in 1737. Originally it was in the eastern cloister.

T., Yu-ch'ing 幼清. He was a native of Tsung-jen 崇仁 in Kiangsi. An official and member of the Han-lin under Kubilai, he retired and devoted himself to teaching. Author of books on the canon, and of commentaries on the *Tao teh ching* and *Chuang Tzu*.

27. Hsü Ch'ien 許謙 (1271-1337).[21]

He received sacrifices in 1724, originally in the eastern cloister.

T., Yeh Chih 益之. He was a native of Chin-hua 金華 He held no office, but studied at home for forty years, wrote essays, and taught.

28. Tsao Tuan 曹端 (1376-1434).

He received sacrifices in 1860, originally in the eastern cloister.

T., Cheng-fu 正夫. He was a native of Mien-ch'i 澠池 in

Honan. As a local commissioner of education he improved the schools, and wrote works on the canon, the *Four Books,* and the *T'ai Chi Tu,* or *Plan of the Great Ultimate.*

29. Ch'en Hsien-chang 陳獻章 (1428-1500).
He received sacrifices in 1584.

T., Kung P'u 公甫. He was a native of Hsin-hui 新會 He studied under Wu Yü-pi 吳與弼. An author, painter, and calligrapher.

30. Tsai Ch'ing 蔡清 (1453-1508).
He received sacrifices in 1724.

T., Chieh-fu 介夫. He was a native of Fukien. He studied under Ho Ch'iao-hsin 何喬新, of the school of Chu Hsi. An official, and author of works on the *Book of Changes* and the *Four Books.* He emphasized inaction and emptiness.

31. Wang Shou-jen 王守仁 (1472-1528).
He received sacrifices in 1574, originally in the eastern cloister.

T., Po-an 伯安. He was a native of Yü-t'ao 餘姚. Usually called Wang Yang-ming 王陽明, from the place where he lived. He studied under Lou Liang 婁諒. A scholar, administrator, and general, and the leading philosopher of the Ming period. He followed Lu Hsiang Shan, and opposed some of the positions of Chu Hsi. Known for his doctrines that knowledge should be sought by introspection and that knowledge and action are inseparable.

32. Lü K'un, 呂坤 (1536-1618).
He received sacrifices in 1826.

T., Shou-chien 叔簡. An educator and official, he recommended scholars to the government. He retired and wrote on the rites, emphasizing *Tao.*

33. Huang Tao-chou 黃道周 (1585-1646).
He received sacrifices in 1825, originally in the eastern cloister.

T., Yu-ping 幼平. He was a native of Chang-p'u 漳浦. As an official he ignored precedent and red tape. A scholar, and a writer on the *Book of Changes* and other canonical books, as well as on painting and calligraphy.

34. Lu Shih-yi 陸世儀 (seventeenth century).
He received sacrifices in 1875.

T., Tao-wei 道威. He was a native of Ch'ang-chou 倉州 in

Kiangsu. He studied under Liu Tsung-chou 劉宗周. He retired, taught, and wrote on the *Book of History* and the *Odes*.

35. T'ang Pin 湯斌 (1627-1687).

He received sacrifices in 1823, originally in the eastern cloister.

T., K'ung-po 孔伯. He was a native of Huai-chou 睢州 in Honan. He studied under Sun Ch'i-feng 孫奇逢. A member of the Han-lin, he emphasized practice, and wrote on the Lo-yang school.

This ends the list of tablets as given in the record, which brings the arrangement practically to the end of the Manchu period. Some time ago, Professor Duyvendak, of the University of Leiden, said that he believed four more tablets had been added under the republic during the presidency of Hsü Shih-ch'ang 徐世昌 (1918-1922). A search through the copies of the Government Gazette, now in the Library of Congress, failed to reveal any edicts canonizing these men. The author then wrote to Mr. Leonard Tomkinson of Anking, who, after considerable difficulty, secured the following four names, which his informants, Chinese scholars, thought had been added to the temple roll.

Ku Yen-wu 顧炎武 (1613-1682).

T., T'ing-lin 亭林. He was a native of K'un-shan 崑山. The author of essays, called *Ji chi lu* 日知錄.

Huang Tsung-hsi 黃宗羲 (1610-1696).

T., Li-chou 黎州. He was a native of Chekiang. Author of a commentary on the *Book of Changes*, and of a study of the Ming scholars, *Ming jü hsioh an* 明儒學案.

Wang Fu-chih 王夫之 (seventeenth century).

T., Ch'uan-shan 船山. He was a native of Hunan. Author of *Tu t'ung chien lun* 讀通鑑論.

Li Erh-ch'ueh 李二曲 (seventeenth century).

His *Tzu* is not given. A native of Tsou-chih 盩厔 in Shensi. His writings were collected and published by his pupils in twenty-two volumes. He was appointed an official lecturer in 1671.

METHOD OF ARRANGING THE TABLETS

The following note appended to the record indicates the methods used in fixing the order of the tablets.

"The editors,[22] in accordance with a decree issued in the eighteenth year of the reign of Ch'ien Lung, determined the order of the tablets. Among the *Hsien hsien,* the first position was given to Chü **Yüan** and Lin Fang. In the plan called the *Wen-weng t'u* 文翁圖, these two are placed with the seventy-two disciples of Confucius. As Chü Yüan was older than Confucius, he was placed at the head of the seventy-two. The other tablets, from Yen-t'ai Mieh-ming to Mu P'i, are arranged according to the ancient order. No change was made, because the age and order of the disciples given by Ssu-ma Ch'ien differ from that in the *Family Sayings,* and the question as to which is correct cannot be determined. The disciples of Mencius were ranked next to those of Confucius. Then come the tablets of Chou, Chang, the two Ch'eng, and Shao (the Sung philosophers). Shao was older than the others, but their doctrine [23] was more important. Chang was ranked above the two Cheng because their father was the younger cousin of Chang.[24]

"The *Hsien jü* were arranged according to their age and generation. In the reign of Ch'ien Lung, scholars collected the records of famous men in the *Hui tien t'ung li,*[25] which was used as the standard in arranging the order.

"Kung-sun Ch'iao and Kung-ming Yi were added to the *Hsien hsien.* The former was older than Chü Yüan, therefore his tablet should be ranked higher, but in order to avoid comparison they were placed in different cloisters. Lin Fang should be on an equality with Chü Yüan, but as a compromise he was placed second to Kung-sun Ch'iao.

"Mu P'i was a disciple of Confucius, and Kung-ming Yi a disciple of Tseng Tzu, therefore Mu P'i was ranked No. 35 in the eastern cloister, and Kung-ming Yi was ranked No. 35 in the western. The order of the remaining tablets was not changed.

"Fifteen tablets were added to the *Hsien jü,* arranged according to their dates.

"The book was presented to the emperor for approval.

"Printed according to imperial decree by Li Kuan-t'ao 李觀濤 of Hsiao-kan hsien 孝感縣 in Hupeh. The text corrected by Tu Tsung-yü 杜宗預, an official of Hsiao-kan hsien."

NOTES

¹ The list of tablets and the dates, the various names, and the homes of the men commemorated are taken from one of the plans or records of the Confucian temple which have appeared from time to time, the 續枲文廟祀位. A list of such records is given in the Chinese bibliography. Each name has also been looked up in the *Chung kuo jen ming ta tsu tien* 中國人名大辭典 and any further biographical items of interest added, but no attempt has been made to give full accounts of the men, even in outline, and where the man is well known, in such cases as Mencius and Chu Hsi, all supplementary details have been omitted. The record used is later than the ones consulted by Watters and Doré. The arrangement is that used at the close of the Manchu period, which is different in many instances from that found in earlier editions, as may be seen by a comparison of the order of names with that found in Doré, as well as in the added names. The tablets are called *shen wei* 神位, or *p'ai wei* 牌位. The accounts have been compared with those given in the thirteenth volume of Doré, and in many instances, with those in Giles' *Chinese Biographical Dictionary,* and differences noted. The romanization is in the modern Mandarin, which is not earlier than the Mongol period, and so does not represent the way in which the names of the earlier men were pronounced. In the case of the personal disciples of Confucius it has not seemed worth while to give the references in such books as the *Analects* in which they are mentioned. Confucius has a title before his surname, which is followed by the words *fu tzu* 夫子 in some temples, although not in this record. The four correlates also have titles before the surname, which is followed by the word *tzu* 子 ("master"). In ancient China, this was the equivalent of the fourth grade of nobility, and was used for distinguished scholars. The word is also used as a suffixed title to the names on the *Cheh* altars, which have no prefixed title. ⁻

² In some temples, the title on the tablet is followed by the three words *chih shen wei* 之神位 ("the seat of the spirit of").

³ *Tsung ssu* 從祀, literally "added sacrifices," a term invented in the T'ang period, when the first names of disciples were added to the temple. It means that on this date the tablet was placed in the temple.

⁴ One of the difficulties in such a study is the number of names used by a single man. As many as possible are given here. The surname does not change, but the remaining names may vary considerably. The chief names

APPENDIX

are the *ming* 名, and the *tzu*字, or literary name, chosen by the man himself, sometimes translated as "style." There are also the *hao*號, or familiar name, posthumous titles like Wen-kung 文公, ("Duke of Literature,") and nicknames like (Wang) Yang-ming. In the case of the tablets in the cloisters, the *ming* is given with the surname. *Ming* is abbreviated as *M.*, *tzu* as *T.*, and *hao* as *H.*, following Giles' usage.

[5] Before the Sung period, the tablets of the correlates, the *Cheh,* and the *Hsien Hsien* were all called *chio*爵. The present titles were given in 1530. In 1329, the four correlates were given the following titles:

Yen Hui: Yen kuo fu sheng kung 兗國復聖公

Tseng Tzu: Ch'eng kuo tsung sheng kung 成國宗聖公

Tzu Ssu: Ch'i kuo hsü sheng kung 沂國述聖公

Mencius: Tsou kuo ya sheng kung 鄒國亞聖公

These titles, which end with the words meaning "Holy Duke"聖公, were taken away in 1530.

The fundamental principle in arranging the tablets is that of age, the older men receiving the place of honor, and men of the Han period being honored before those of the T'ang. There are numerous exceptions to this rule, however, in the case of men who were especially important. These exceptions include the four correlates, two of whom were not immediate disciples; the *Cheh,* all of whom are prominent in the *Analects;* and the Sung philosophers, who have been ranked ahead of the Han and T'ang Confucians. The date at which a man's tablet was put in the temple had nothing to do with his ranking. For instance, Tzu Ch'an, a famous character of the Spring and Autumn period, was not a disciple of Confucius, and his tablet was not placed in the temple until 1857. Yet he was at once placed at the head of the *Hsien Hsien,* because he was older than Confucius himself.

[6] The title *Hsien hsien* 先賢 ("The illustrious of antiquity") was given in 1530 to all those honored in the temple who belonged to the Chou period and to six Sung Confucians. Fuller accounts of these men may be found in Doré (Vol. XIII). Unfortunately, Doré does not usually give his authorities. Some of these men are listed in Giles, *Chin. Biog. Dict.*

[7] No dates are given for the older disciples, since Maspero has shown that exact dates mean nothing for the ancient period. Confucius and his disciples may be considered to have flourished about 500 B.C. For the later Confucians, the dates of birth and death are given when known. The dates are given in western chronology; for instance A.D. 739, instead of "the twenty-seventh year of the reign T'ang K'ai-yüan."

[8] The *Hsien hsien* are grouped at the northern ends of the two cloisters, the north being the place of honor. Number one is at the end next the main hall. At the southern ends are the *Hsien jü* 先儒 ("scholars of antiquity"). Most of the *Hsien hsien* were personal disciples of Confucius, and of many of them little is known beyond the name.

[9] As the tablet of Tzu Ch'an was placed in the temple in 1857, and the record used by Doré was published in 1826, he does not appear on Doré's list. This is true of a number of other names.

[10] Tzu Ch'an, although not a disciple of the sage, was probably included because he was praised by Confucius. He was an older contemporary of the sage. For an account of his contribution to Chinese thought, see Forke, *Chin. Phil.*, pp. 92-98. It is probable that still earlier worthies praised by Con-

fucius were not included because custom would require them to be ranked higher than the sage himself.

[11] For references to these men in the *Analects,* etc., see Doré, Vol. XIII.

[12] Giles (p. 238) has *Fu* instead of *Mi,* a mistake.

[13] The character for this surname may be pronounced either *Lo* 樂 ("happiness"), or *Yo* ("music"). As a surname *Lo* is used.

[14] The five Sung Confucians were made *Hsien hsien* in 1642, but ranked below the others having this title, all of whom belonged to the Chou period.

[15] In some instances it is hard to understand why the men were honored by having their tablets placed in the temple. It will usually be found, where men have neither held official position nor written great books, that they have been teachers who numbered among their pupils men who later became famous.

[16] No attempt has been made to give a list of works by the various Confucians whose tablets are in the temple. Such a bibliography may be found in Doré, Vol. XIII, pp. 257-261.

[17] Doré (Vol. XIII, p. 245) says the tablet was placed in the temple in 1619. The author has followed the Record in dating the event in 1614 (the forty-second year of the reign Ming Wan Li).

[18] The *Chung kuo jen ming ta tsu tien* contains accounts of several men of this name.

[19] There are accounts of three men named Wang T'ung in the *Chung kuo jen ming ta tsu tien.*

[20] The Record is inconsistent in giving the age of the man and the date of his death. I have followed Giles (p. 878) in placing his death in 1331, which agrees with his age as given in the Record.

[21] The *Chung kuo jen ming ta tsu tien* gives accounts of three men of this name.

[22] The Chinese term is *ch'en teng* 臣等

[23] *Tao teh* 道德, the title of the work of Lao Tzu, here "doctrine."

[24] *Piao ti* 表弟. The Ch'eng belonged to a later generation.

[25] *Hui tien t'ung li.*

APPENDIX II

TABLE 1

ARRANGED BY THE PERIODS IN WHICH THE MEN LIVED

The contemporaries of Confucius are omitted from the table. Although the standard number of Confucius' immediate disciples is still seventy-two, the full list of seventy-seven given by Ssu-ma Ch'ien and the *Family Sayings* have tablets in the temples.

Chou Period

Disciples of Tseng Tzu:...................Kung-ming Yi
                                         Tzu Ssu
Disciples of Tzu Hsia:....................Ku-liang Ch'ih
                                         Kung-yang Kao
˙Disciple of Tzu Ssu:.....................Mencius
Disciples of Mencius:....................Cheng K'eh
                                         Wan Chang
                                         Kung-tu Tzu
                                         Kung-sun Ch'ou

Han Period

Cheng K'ang-ch'eng	K'ung An-kuo
Fu Sheng	Liu Teh
Hou Tsang	Mao Ch'ang
Hsü Shen	Mao Heng
Kao Ch'ang-sen	Tu Tzu-ch'un

Tung Chung-shu

Three Kingdoms and Medieval Period

Chu-k'o Liang	Wang T'ung

Fan Ning

T'ang Period

Han T'ui-chih	Lu Cheh

Sung Period

Chang Ch'ih
Chang Tsai
Cheng Teh-hsiu
Ch'eng Hao
Ch'eng Kao
Ch'eng Yi
Chou Tun-yi
Chu Hsi
Fan Chung-yen
Han Ch'i
Ho Chi
Hsieh Liang-tso
Hu An-kuo
Hu Yüan
Huang Kan
Jen Po
Li Kang

Li T'ung
Lo Tsung-yen
Lu Chiu-yüan
Lu Hsiu-fu
Lü Ta-lin
Lü Tsu-chien
Ou-yang Hsiu
P'u Kuang
Shao Yung
Ssu-ma Kuang
Tsai Shen
Wei Liao-weng
Wen T'ien-hsiang
Yang Shih
Yin Tuan
Yu Tso
Yüan Hsieh

Yuen Period

Chao Fu
Ch'eng Hao
Ching Nu-ch'ang

Hsü Heng
Hsü Ch'ien
Wu Ch'eng

Ming Period

Ch'eng Hsien-chang
Fan Hsiao-jü
Hsieh Hsüan
Hu Chü-jen
Huang Tao-chou
Liu Tsung-chou

Lo Ch'ing-shun
Lü K'un
Lü Tsai
Sun Ch'i-feng
Tsai Ch'ing
Tsao Shui

Wang Shou-jen

Ch'ing Period

Chang Lu-hsiang
Chang Po-hang
Huang Tsung-yi
Ku Yen-wu

Li Ji-chiu
Lu Lung-ch'i
Lu Shih-yi
T'ang Pin

Wang Fu-chih

TABLE 2

Dates When Tablets Were Placed in the Temple

This analysis includes only those tablets which are still in the temple, not those which were placed there and later removed. Before the T'ang period, the only disciple to receive sacrifices in the temple was Yen Hui.

T'ang Period

(88 tablets)

Cheng Kuan .... 21st year, 647; 13 tablets
K'ai Yuen .... 8th year, 720; 11 tablets
                                27th year, 739; 64 tablets

Sung Period
(12 tablets)

Yuen Feng .... 7th year, 1084; 2 tablets
Ta Kuan .... 2d year, 1108; 1 tablet
Ch'ien Tao .... 3d year, 1167; 1 tablet
Kao Yiu .... 1st year, 1241; 5 tablets
Ching Ting .... 2d year, 1261; 2 tablets
Hsien Kao .... 3d year, 1267; 1 tablet

Yuen Period
(2 tablets)

Huang Ching .... 2d year, 1313; 1 tablet
Chih Shun .... 1st year, 1330; 1 tablet

Ming Period
(16 tablets)

Cheng T'ung .... 2d year, 1437; 3 tablets
                                8th year, 1443; 1 tablet
Hung Chih .... 8th year, 1495; 1 tablet
Chia Ching .... 9th year, 1530; 5 tablets
Lung Ch'ing .... 5th year, 1571; 1 tablet
Wan Li ....12th year, 1584; 3 tablets
                                42d year, 1614; 2 tablets

Ch'ing Period
(44 tablets)

K'ang Hsi .... 54th year, 1715; 1 tablet
Yung Cheng .... 2d year, 1724; 20 tablets

Tao Kuang	....	2d year, 1822;	1 tablet
		3d year, 1823;	1 tablet
		5th year, 1825;	1 tablet
		6th year, 1826;	2 tablets
		8th year, 1828;	1 tablet
		23d year, 1843;	1 tablet
Hsien Feng	....	1st year, 1851;	1 tablet
		2d year, 1852;	1 tablet
		3d year, 1853;	1 tablet
		7th year, 1857;	1 tablet
		10th year, 1860;	1 tablet
T'ung Chih	....	2d year, 1863;	3 tablets
		7th year, 1868;	1 tablet
		10th year, 1871;	1 tablet
Kuang Hsü	....	1st year, 1875;	2 tablets
		4th year, 1878;	1 tablet
		5th year, 1879;	1 tablet
		18th year, 1892;	1 tablet
		21st year, 1895;	1 tablet

The Republic

Presidency of Hsü Shih-ch'ang, 1918-1922; 4 tablets

APPENDIX III

TABLETS IN THE TSUNG SHENG TSU

To the north of the main hall of a Confucian temple is a separate building, also a temple, but on a smaller scale. It is called the *Tsung Sheng Tsu* 崇聖祠, and is dedicated to the ancestors of Confucius in the direct line for five generations. They are first mentioned in the Sung period. In 1530, in the reign of Ming Chia Ching, the hall was called *Ch'i Sheng Tsu* 啓聖祠, but in 1723 the present name was given, and the present titles were given to the men honored. Before 1530, the tablets were called *cho*. Beginning on the east, there are the following five tablets on the main altar.

1. Ch'ang Sheng Wang Po Hsia Kung 昌聖王伯夏公
2. Yu Sheng Wang Ch'i Fu Kung 裕聖王祈父公
3. Chao Sheng Wang Mu Chin Fu Kung 肇聖公木金父公
4. Yi Sheng Wang Fan Shou Kung 詒聖王防叔公
5. Ch'i Sheng Wang Shou Liang Kung 啟聖王叔梁公

The place of honor is in the center, No. 3. K'ung Fu-chia, the direct ancestor of Confucius in the sixth generation, was an official of the state of Sung. He was killed by another official, in consequence of which his son migrated to Lu and became the founder of the Lu branch of the family. It is this son who holds the place of honor on the altar. No. 5 is the father of Confucius; no. 1, his grandfather; no. 4, his great-grandfather; and no. 2, his great-great-grandfather.

I. *P'EI* ALTARS

A. EASTERN P'EI

1. K'ung Shih Meng P'i 孔氏孟皮·
He received sacrifices in 1857. The half-brother of Confucius.
2. Yen Shih 顏氏·
He received sacrifices in 739, and was placed on the *P'ei* altar in 1530. *M.*, Wu-yao 無繇. The father of Yen Hui.
3. K'ung Shih 孔氏·

269

He received sacrifices in 1267, and was placed on the *P'ei* in 1530. *M., Li* 鯉. The son of Confucius, and father of Tzu Ssu.

B. WESTERN P'EI

1. Tseng Shih 曾氏.
He received sacrifices in 739, and was placed on the *P'ei* in 1530. *M.,* Hsi 皙. The father Tseng Tzu.

2. Meng-sen Shih 孟孫氏.
He received sacrifices in 1530. *M.,* Cheh 激. The father of Mencius.

These men have the title *Hsien hsien*. K'ung Li is honored as the father of Tzu Ssu, not as the son of Confucius.

II. THE *WU* OR CLOISTERS

A. EASTERN WU

1. Chou Shih 周氏.
He received sacrifices in 1595. *M.,* P'u-ch'eng. The father of Chou Teng Yi.

2. Ch'eng Shih 程氏.
He received sacrifices in 1530. *M.,* Hsiang 珦. The father of Ch'eng Yi and Ch'eng Hao.

3. Tsai Shih 蔡氏.
He received sacrifices in 1530. *M.,* Yüan-ting 元定. The father of Tsai Shen, and the friend of Chu Hsi.

B. WESTERN WU

1. Chang Shih 張氏.
He received sacrifices in 1724. *M.,* Ti 迪. The father of Chang Tsai.

2. Chu Shih 朱氏.
He received sacrifices in 1530. *M.,* Sung 松. The father of Chu Hsi.

These men have the title *Hsien jü*.

Although the Record says that two of the men honored in the temple as *P'ei,* the fathers of Yen Hui and Tseng Tzu, received sacrifices in the T'ang period, no verification of this has been found in the T'ang history, nor any mention of this temple as early as the T'ang period.

APPENDIX IV

THE BEGINNINGS OF THE CULT OF CONFUCIUS

The statement, found in the Temple Plans and in many books on Confucius, that the sage received sacrifices from others than his own family in a regular cult during the pre-Christian era, ultimately rests on a paragraph in Ssu-ma Ch'ien's life of Confucius. The following is the Chinese text of this passage:

魯世世相傳以歲時奉祠孔子家而諸儒亦講禮鄉飲
大射於孔子家孔子家大一頃故所居堂弟子內後世
因廟藏孔子衣冠琴車書至于漢二百餘年不絕高皇
帝過魯以太牢祠焉諸矦卿相至常先謁然後從政

Against the evidence of this passage, there is the complete lack of verification by any other source and the positive statement in the petition of Mei Fu, in 8 B.C. My own opinion is that either Ssu-ma Ch'ien was mistaken, or else the paragraph is a later addition to his history. The Chinese text of Mei Fu is as follows:

今仲尼之廟不出闕里孔氏子孫不免編戶以聖人而
歆匹夫之祀非皇天之意也

Translations of these passages will be found in chapter VII.

BIBLIOGRAPHY

French, German and English Bibliography.
Chinese Bibliography.
Japanese Bibliography.

I

CHINESE BIBLIOGRAPHY

Only those books are listed here which have not been translated, or only partially translated. The list is wider than that actually used in the preparation of the text.

LITERATURE OF THE CHOU PERIOD

Title

國語
呂氏春秋
離騷
戰國策
百子全書

DYNASTIC HISTORIES

欽定二十四史　　光緒壬寅春月上海文瀾書局石印
清史稿

MISCELLANEOUS

Title	*Author*
七緯	
神仙傳	
玉海	
文獻通考	馬端臨
通志	
冊府元龜	
春明夢餘錄	
明會典	
大清會典	

欽定大淸會典圖
欽定大淸會典則例
欽定大淸會典事例
欽定禮部則例
皇朝通志
皇朝文獻通考
欽定續文獻通考
闕里文獻考
欽定光祿寺則例
大淸通例
欽定國子監志
闕里志
闕里廣志
直省釋奠禮樂記
禮樂彝器圖譜
中祀合編
皇朝祭器樂舞錄　　　　郭柏蔭
續棻文廟祀位
日知錄
史記探源　　　　崔適
新學僞經考　　　　康有爲
孔子改制考　　　　康有爲
先秦政治思想史　　　　梁啓超
淸代通史　　　　蕭一山
白話本國史　　　　呂思勉
中國哲學史大綱　　　　胡適
中國哲學史　　　　謝无量
東西文化及其哲學　　　　梁漱溟
最近之五十年
辭源

中國人名大辭典
山東通志
袞州府志
曲阜縣志
懷甯縣誌
大清世宗憲皇帝聖訓
大清高宗純皇帝聖訓
大清宣宗成皇帝聖訓
大清睿宗睿皇帝聖訓
大清穆宗毅皇帝聖訓
臨時公報
政府公報
政治公報
聖賢像贊
聖績圖

文廟總圖 found in 古今圖書集成， 經濟彙編，
禮儀典， 文廟祀典部彙考，
欽定大清會典圖， 欽定國子監志，
曲阜縣志， 山東通志， 闕里圖部，
闕里志．

文廟祭祀圖 found in 古今圖書集成， 經濟彙編，
禮儀典， 文廟祀典部彙考，
皇朝祭器樂舞錄．

文廟正壇陳設圖 found in the same books as the preceding
subject.

JAPANESE BIBLIOGRAPHY

Only the first three books listed here are referred to in the text, but the other works are listed for the convenience of any one who may care to investigate the subject more fully.

Title	Author	Publisher	Date
中國文化史	高桑駒吉 (Takakuwa)	商務印書館	
中國倫理學史	三浦藤 (Miura)	商務印書舘	
支那哲學史	遠藤隆吉 (Ryukichi Endo)		
孔子傳	遠藤隆吉	丙午出版社	
孔子研究	蟹江義丸	金港堂	
孔子號〔孔子略傳〕	服部宇之吉	東亞學術研究會	
孔子及孔教	服部宇之吉		
孔子祭典會演講			
孔子事蹟圖解	瑞陽口授	嵩山房	
孔子四學說	松材正一	育成會	
論語鑑			
孔子	吉田藤吉	博文舘	
孔子	白河次郎	東亞書房	
萬世之師孔子	東池濃	玄黃社	
孔子一代記	北尾紅翠齋畫	嵩山房	
孔子家語諺解	高田識		
孔子家語國字解	高田彪周卿合註		
孔子行狀圖解	小林新兵		

BIBLIOGRAPHY 279

JAPANESE BIBLIOGRAPHY ROMANIZED

Title	Author	Publisher	Date
Koshi Kenkyu	Kanie Yoshimaru	Kinkodo	Meiji 37
Koshigo	Hattori Unokichi	Toagaku kenkyukai	Meiji 44
Koshi saiten kai koen	——	——	Meiji 41
Koshi jiseki zukai	Zuiyo	Kozanbo	Bunka 2
Koshi Seiskizu	——	——	Kanei
Koshiden	Endo Ryukichi	Heigo shuppansha	Taisho 10
Koshi no gakusetsu	Matsumura Shoichi	Ikuseikai	Meiji 35
Rongo kan	——	——	——
Koshi	Yoshida Tokichi	Hakubunkan	Meiji 35
Koshi	Shirakawa Jiro	Toa shobo	Meiji 43
Bansei no shi Koshi	Akaike	Geno sha	Showa 3
Koshi ichidaiki	Kitao Kosui	Kozanbo	Tenpo 9
Koshi oyobi Koshikyo	Hattori Unokichi	——	Taisho 6
Koshi kaisei ko	Kiyoyasu Yui	——	——
Koshi kago	Dazai Shundai	Kozanbo	Kanpo 2
Koshi kago	Ki Oshuku	Kozanbo	Kanei 15
Koshi kago	Takata Shikigenkai	Kozanbo	Kansei 6
Koshi kago kokujikai	Takata Hyoshukyo	Kozanbo	Kansei 5
Koshi gyojo zukai	Kogayashi Shinbei	Kozanbo	Kansei 5

The author wishes to acknowledge his indebtedness to Mr. E. S. Shinozaki for this Japanese bibliography.

III

FRENCH, GERMAN, AND ENGLISH BIBLIOGRAPHY

(Only those titles are given which are mentioned in the text or notes.)

AMIOT, *De la musique des Chinois; Mémoires concernant . . . les Chinois*, Vol. VI (Paris, Nyon, 1780).
——————, *Vie de Koung-tsée; Mémoires concernant . . . les Chinois*, Vol. XII (Paris, Nyon, 1786).
ADDISON, J. T., *Ancestor Worship in China* (Shanghai, National Christian Council, 1924).

BACKHOUSE, E., and BLAND, J. O. P., *China under the Empress Dowager* (Philadelphia, Lippincott, 1910).
BEAL, S., *Life of Hiuen Tsiang* (London, Trübner, 1911).
——————, *Travels of Buddhist Pilgrims* (London, Trübner, 1869).
BIOT, E. C., *Essai sur l'histoire de l'instruction publique en Chine.* (Paris, Duprat, 1845).
——————, *Le Tcheou-li* (Paris, Duprat, 1851). 2 vols.
BIALLAS, F. X., *Konfuzius und sein Kult* (Peking, Pekinger Verlag, 1928).
BLODGETT, H., "The Worship of Heaven and Earth by the Emperor of China," *Journal of the American Oriental Society*, Vol. XX, pp. 58–68.
BREDON, J., *Peking* (Shanghai, Kelly & Walsh, 1922).
BRETSCHNEIDER, E., *Medieval Researches from Eastern Asiatic Sources* (London, 1888). 2 vols.
BREWITT-TAYLOR, C. H., *Romance of the Three Kingdoms* (Shanghai, Kelly & Walsh, 1926). 2 vols.
BRUCE, J. P. *Chu Hsi and His Masters* (London, Probsthain, 1923).
——————, *The Philosophy of Human Nature* (London, Probsthain, 1922).

BUSHELL, S. W., "The Stone Drums of the Chou Dynasty," *Journal of the North China Branch of the Royal Asiatic Society,* Vol. VIII, pp. 133 f.

CARTER, T. F., *The Invention of Printing in China* (New York, Columbia University Press, 1925).

CHAVANNES, E., *Inscriptions et pièces de chancellerie chinoises de l'epoque mongole. T'oung Pao,* 2d series, Vol. IX, pp. 297–428.

——————, *Le T'ai Chan. Annales du Musée Guimet* (Paris, Leroux, 1910).

——————, *Mémoires historiques de Se-ma Ts'ien* (Paris, Leroux, 1895–1905). 5 vols.

——————, *T'oung Pao* (1905), p. 546; (1907), p. 185.

CHI LI, *The Formation of the Chinese People* (Cambridge, Harvard University Press, 1928).

CLENNELL, W. J., *The Historical Development of Religion in China* (London, Unwin, 1917).

CONRADY, A., "China," *Ulsteins Weltgeschichte* (1910).

CORDIER, H., *Histoire générale de la Chine* (Paris, Geuthner, 1920). 4 vols.

COURANT, M., "Essai historique sur la musique classique des Chinois," *Enc. de la musique et Dict. du Conservatoire* (Paris, 1912), pp. 77–241.

COUVREUR, S., *Li ki* (Ho Kien Fou, Imprimerie de la Mission Catholique, 1898).

CRANMER-BYNG, L., *Introduction to Yang Chu's Garden of Pleasure.* Wisdom of the East Series. (London, Murray, 1912.)

DE GROOT, J. J. M., *Les Fêtes annuelles à Emoui. Annales du Musée Guimet,* Vols. XI–XII (Paris, 1886).

——————, *Sectarianism and Religious Persecution in China* (Amsterdam, Müller, 1904). 2 vols.

——————, *The Religious System of China* (Leyden, Brill, 1892). 6 vols.

——————, "Two Gods of Literature and a God of Barbers," *China Review,* Vol. IX, pp. 188 f.

DEFRÉMERY ET SANGUINETTI, *Voyages . . . Ibn Batuta* (Paris, 1858). 4 vols.

DE HARLEZ, C., *Babylonian and Oriental Record,* Vols. VI–VII (1893–1894).

——————————, *L'Ecole philosophique moderne de la Chine* (Bruxelles, Hayez, 1890).

——————————, *Textes taoistes. Annales du Musée Guimet*, Vol. XX (Paris, Leroux, 1891).

DELAMARRE, L. C., *Histoire de la Dynastie des Ming* (Paris, Duprat, 1865).

DE MAILLA, J. A. M. de M., *Histoire générale de la Chine* (Paris, Pierres & Clousier, 1777). 13 vols.

DE VISSER, M. W., *The Dragon in China and Japan* (Amsterdam, Müller, 1913).

DORÉ, H., *Recherches sur les Superstitions en Chine* (Chang-hai, Imprimerie de la Mission Catholique, 1918). 14 vols.

DUBS, H. H. *Hsüntze, the Moulder of Ancient Confucianism* (London, Probsthain, 1927).

——————————, *The Works of Hsüntze* (London, Probsthain, 1928).

DU HALDE, J. B., *Description . . . de l'Empire de la Chine* (London, Cave, 1788). 2 vols. Anonymous English translation.

DUYVENDAK, J. J. L., *The Book of Lord Shang* (London, Probsthain, 1928).

——————————, *The Diary of His Excellency Ching-Shan* (Leyden, Brill, 1924).

EDKINS, J., "The City of Confucius," *Journal of the North China Branch of the Royal Asiatic Society*, Vol. VIII, pp. 79 f.

EITEL, E. J., *Handbook of Chinese Buddhism* (Tokyo, Sanshusha, 1904).

Encyclopedia Sinica, S. Couling, editor (Shanghai, Kelly & Walsh, 1917). 2 vols.

FERGUSON, J. C., *Chinese Mythology, Mythology of All Races Series*, Vol. VIII (Boston, Marshall Jones, 1928).

FORKE, A., *Geschichte der alten chinesischen Philosophie* (Hamburg, Friederichsen, 1927).

——————————, *Lun-Hêng. Mitteilungen des Seminars für Orientalische Sprachen*, Vols. IX–XI (1906–1908).

——————————, *Mê Ti, des Sozialethikers und seiner Schüler philosophische Werke* (Berlin, 1922).

——————————, *World Conception of the Chinese* (London, Probsthian, 1925).

FORSYTH, A. C., *Shantung, the Sacred Province of China* (Shanghai, Christian Literature Society, 1912).

FRANKE, O., *Beiträge zum konfuzianischen Dogma.*

——————, *Studien zu Geschichte des konfuzianischen Dogmas und der chinesischen Staatsreligion* (Hamburg, Friederichsen, 1920).

GAUBIL, A., *Abrégé de l'histoire chinoise de la grande dynastie Tang. Mémoires concernant les Chinois,* Vols. XV–XVI (Paris, Nyon, 1791).

GETTY, A., *The Gods of Northern Buddhism,* 2d ed. (Oxford, Clarendon Press, 1928).

GILES, H. A., *An Introduction to the History of Chinese Pictorial Art* (Shanghai, Kelly & Walsh, 1918).

——————, *Chinese Biographical Dictionary* (Shanghai, Kelly & Walsh, 1898).

GILES, L., *Taoist Teachings. Wisdom of the East Series* (London, Murray, 1912).

GRANET, M., *Danses et légendes de la Chine ancienne* (Paris, Alcan, 1926).

——————, *Chinese Civilization* (New York, Knopf, 1930).

GRUBE, W., *Religion und Kultus der Chinesen* (Leipzig, Haupt, 1910).

HENKE, F., *The Philosophy of Wang Yang Ming* (Chicago, Open Court, 1916).

HIRTH, F., *Ancient History of China* (New York, Columbia University Press, 1911).

——————, *China and the Roman Orient* (Leipzig, 1885).

HODOUS, L., *Folkways in China* (London, Probsthain, 1929).

HOLCOMBE, A. N., *The Chinese Revolution* (Cambridge, Harvard University Press, 1930).

HOWARTH, H., *History of the Mongols* (London, 1888).

HU SHIH, *The Development of the Logical Method in Ancient China* Shanghai, Oriental Book Co., 1922).

——————, "Wang Mang," *Journal of the North China Branch of the Royal Asiatic Society,* Vol. LIX, pp. 218 f.

HUANG, P., *Mélanges sur l'administration, Variétés Sinologiques,* Vol. XXI (Chang-hai, Imprimerie de la Mission Catholique, 1902).

HUANG, K. Y., and SHRYOCK, J. K., "A Collection of Chinese Prayers," *Journal of the American Oriental Society*, Vol. XLIX, No. 2.

HUMMELL, A., Report of the Library of Congress, Division of Chinese Literature (1928–29; 1929–30), Appendix Z.

HUTCHINSON, A. B., "The Family Sayings of Confucius." *Chinese Recorder*, Vols. IX–X.

JOHNSTON, R. F., *Buddhist China* (London, Murray, 1913).

KUO, P. W., *The Chinese System of Public Education* (New York, Columbia University Press, 1915).

LALOY, L., *La Musique Chinoise* (Paris, 1910).

LATOURETTE, K. S., *A History of Christian Missions in China* (New York, Macmillan, 1929).

LAUFER, B., *Jade* (Chicago, Field Museum, 1911).

—————, *Confucius and His Portraits* (Chicago, Open Court, 1912).

—————, *Sino-Iranica* (Chicago, Field Museum, 1919).

—————, *Chinese Pottery of the Han Dynasty* (Leyden, 1909).

LE GALL, S., *Le Philosophe Tchou Hi, sa doctrine, son influence. Variétés sinologiques*, Vol. VI (Chang-hai, Imprimerie de la Mission Catholique, 1894).

LEGGE, J., *Chinese Classics.*

    Vol. I. *Analects, Great Learning, Doctrine of the Mean* (Oxford, Clarendon Press, 1893).

    Vol. II. *Mencius* (Oxford, Clarendon Press, 1895).

    Vol. III. *Book of History* (London, Trübner, 1865).

    Vol. IV. *Book of Poetry* (London, Trübner, 1871).

    Vols. V–VI. *Spring and Autumn Annals, and the Tso Chuan* (Oxford, Clarendon Press, 1872).

—————, *Sacred Books of the East* (Oxford, Clarendon Press).

    Vol. XVI. *Yi King (Book of Changes)* (1882).

    Vols. XXVII–XXVIII. *Li Ki (Book of Rites)* (1895).

    Vols. XXXIX–XL. *Texts of Taoism (Tao Teh Ching, Chuang Tzu.)* (1891.)

    Travels of Fa-hien (Oxford Clarendon Press, 1886).

MacNair, H. F., *Modern Chinese History* (Shanghai, Commercial Press, 1927).

McClatchie, T., *Confucian Cosmogony* (Shanghai, Presbyterian Mission Press, 1874).

Margoulies, G., *Le Kou-Wen Chinois* (Paris, Geuthner, 1926).

Maspero, H., "Le Songe de l'ambassade de l'empereur Ming," *Bull.· de l'Ecole fr.,* Vol. X, pp. 95 f.

——————, "Origins of the Chinese Civilization," trans. by C. W. Bishop, *Smithsonian Report,* 1927, pp. 433–452.

——————, *La Chine antique* (Paris, Boccard, 1927).

Mayers, W. F., *Chinese Reader's Manual* (Shanghai, Presbyterian Mission Press, 1924).

Mei, Y. P., *The Works of Motse* (London, Probsthain, 1929).

Montgomery, J. A., *The History of Yaballaha III* (New York, Columbia University Press, 1927).

Pao Chao Hsieh, *The Government of China (1644–1911)* (Baltimore, 1925).

Parker, E. H., *Studies in Chinese Religion* (London, Chapman & Hall, 1910).

Pelliot, P., "Meou-tseu, ou les doutes levés." *T'oung Pao,* 2d series, Vol. XIX, pp. 255–433.

——————, "Notes sur quelques artistes des six dynastie et des T'ang." *T'oung Pao,* Vol. XXII, pp. 215 f.

Pfizmaier, *Sitzungsberichte der phil.-hist. Klasse der Kaiserl. Akademie der Wissenschaften zu Wien,* Vol. XXXIX, pp. 345 f.

Phelps, D. L., "The Place of Music in the Platonic and Confucian Systems of Moral Education," *Journal of the North China Branch of the Royal Asiatic Society,* Vol. LIX, pp. 128 f.

Rawlinson, F., *Revolution and Religion in Modern China* (Shanghai, Presbyterian Mission Press, 1929).

Reichelt, K. L., *Truth and Tradition in Chinese Buddhism,* trans. by K. van W. Bugge (Shanghai, Commercial Press, 1927).

Schlegel, G., "On the Invention and Use of Firearms." *T'oung Pao,* 2d series, Vol. III, pp. 1 f.

Segalen, V., "Le Tombeau du fils du roi de Wu. Bulletin de l'Ecole Française de l'extrême-Orient," Vol. XXII.

Segalen, V., de Voisins, G., Lartigue, J., *Mission archéologique en Chine* (Paris, 1923, 1924). 2 vols.

Seufert, W., "Urkunden zur staatlichen Neuordnung unter der Han-Dynastie," *Mitteilungen des Seminars für Orientalische Sprachen,* 1922, pp. 3 f.

Shryock, J. K., "Suggestions of Occidental Thought in Ancient Chinese Philosophy," *Open Court,* June, 1929, pp. 341-359.

————, *The Temples of Anking and Their Cults* (Paris, Geuthner, 1931).

Sirén, O., *La sculpture Chinoise du Ve au XIVe siècle* (Paris, Van Oest, 1926). 4 vols.

Soothill, W. E., *The Analects of Confucius* (Yokohama, 1910).

Steele, J., *The I Li* (London, Probsthain, 1917). 2 vols.

Steiger, G. N., *China and the Occident* (New Haven, Yale University Press, 1927).

Sun Yat Sen, *The Three Principles of the People,* trans. by F. Price (Shanghai, Commercial Press, 1928).

Tchang, M., *Tombeau des Liang. Variétés sinologiques.* Vol. XXXIII (Chang-hai, T'usewei Press, 1912).

Tomkinson, L., "Early Legalist School" *Open Court* June-Dec. (Chicago, 1931).

————, *Social Teachings of Meh Tse, Transactions of the Asiatic Society of Japan,* 2d series, Vol. IV (Yokohama, Kelly & Walsh, 1927).

Tschepe, A., *Historie du Royaume de Ts'in* (Chang-hai, T'usewei Press, 1909).

Van Aalst, J. A., *Chinese Music* (Shanghai, Kelly & Walsh, 1884).

Watters, T., *A Guide to the Tablets in a Temple of Confucius* (Shanghai, Presbyterian Mission Press, 1879).

Wieger, L., *Histoire des croyances religeuses et des opinions philosophiques en Chine* (Chang-hai, T'usewei Press, 1922).

————, *Textes historiques* (Chang-hai, Imprimerie de Hien-hien, 1922).

Wilhelm, R., *History of Chinese Civilization* (London, Harrap, 1929).

Williams, E. T., *A Short History of China* (New York, Harper, 1928).

WINTERNITZ, M., *Geschichte der Indischen Literatur* (Leipzig, 1908).

WU KUO CHENG, *Ancient Chinese Political Theories* (Shanghai, Commercial Press, 1928).

WYLIE, A., *Notes on Chinese Literature* (Shanghai, Presbyterian Mission Press, 1922).

YULE, H., *Book of Ser Marco Polo,* edited by H. Cordier (London, Murray, 1915).

ZUCKER, A. E., *The Chinese Theatre* (New York, Little, Brown, 1925).

INDEX

Ai, duke of Lu, 93, 94, 95, 105, 218
America, 199, 212
Amiot, 93
Amoghavajra, Indian Buddhist in China, 132, 138
An Lu-shan, rebel of the T'ang period, 140, 147
Analects, 9, 11, 56, 72, 123, 132
Anfu Club, 211
Anhui, province of, 197, 205, 211
Aquinas, 199
Arabs, 130
Archery Bout, 95

Bayan, a Mongol commander, 157
Bible, 232
Biot, 69, 98, 103
Board (Ministry) of Civil Offices, 137
Board (Ministry) of Rites, 136, 137, 155, 156, 186, 187, 189, 217
Bodhidharma, Buddhist patriarch, 115, 120, 139
Book of Changes, 4, 11, 29, 34, 72, 103, 132, 150, 151
Book of Filial Piety, 11, 40, 57, 72, 118, 134, 138
Book of History, 4, 5, 6, 11, 12, 13, 17, 23, 28, 29, 30, 34, 40, 41, 43, 50, 56, 65, 66, 67, 72, 80, 103
Book of Music, 34, 67
Book of Odes, 4, 6, 11, 12, 13, 17, 23, 28, 34, 37, 40, 43, 50, 53, 56, 57, 66, 67, 139
Book of Rites, 11, 14, 30, 43, 65, 66, 67, 80, 82, 84, 87, 94, 99, 101, 103, 138, 150, 176
Boxers, 206, 209
Buddha, 116, 118, 132, 141, 153
Buddha, bone of, 132, 140, 141, 142
Buddha, image of, 115, 202
Buddhism, 33, 115, 116, 117, 118, 120, 122, 131, 132, 133, 139, 140, 141, 148, 149, 151, 152, 183, 184, 201, 203, 214, 224, 225, 229, 230

Buddhist temples, 139, 198
Buddhists, 26, 116, 117, 118, 132, 138, 140, 147, 150, 166, 217, 230
Burning of the Books, 22, 23, 37
Burying of the Scholars, 22, 23

Champa, 148
Chang Ch'ien, ambassador of Han Wu Ti to the Yueh Chi, 33
Chang Chih-t'ung, viceroy under the Manchus, 209
Chang Liang, adviser of Han Kao Tsu, 27, 99
Chang T'ai-yen, scholar of the period of the Republic, 214
Chang Tao-lin, founder of the Taoist society, 114, 153
Chang Tsang, Han scholar, 14
Chang Tseh, Sung official, 155
Chang Tso-lin, war-lord of Manchuria under the Republic, 211
Chang Tsung, adviser of Ming Chia Ching, 187, 188, 189
Chang Yung, philosopher of the medieval period, 117, 118
Ch'ang-an, capital of the T'ang empire, 73, 167
Ch'ang Ch'ün, Taoist adviser of Genghiz Khan, 166
Chao, duke of Ch'in, 17
Chao Chia, marquis of, Han period, 99
Chao Fu, scholar of Mongol period, 167
Chao Kuan, official of Han Wu Ti, 42
Chao Tzu-lieh, Sung official, 156
Charlemagne, 131, 147
Chavannes, 21, 24, 33, 86, 93, 95
Cheh, title used for a group of Confucian scholars, 138, 139, 153, 154, 155, 172, 174, 190, 202
Ch'en P'ing, minister of Han Kao Tsu, 27
Ch'en Sheh, rebel of the Ch'in period, 25